Praise for *Trauma Treatment Toolbox*

"A marvelous concise yet comprehensive collection of tools for the trauma therapist. Dr. Sweeton describes the techniques in just the right level of detail to enable the reader to both deliver the intervention and provide a cogent, motivating rationale for its use. There's something in here to help every patient! I'll be consulting this creative volume for years to come."

—**Alex Jordan, PhD,**
Harvard Medical School and McLean Hospital

"This book is a tremendous resource for mental health providers and their clients. It is jam-packed with worksheets that lead readers through brain-based tools including focused breathing, awareness of body, movement, meditations and cognitive techniques. The meat consists of an extensive set of tools based on bottom up (using the body to change the brain) and top-down (using the reflective capabilities of the brain) approaches to brain change designed to help trauma survivors. An amazing book! Every therapist will want to use the tools in this book whether they specialize in trauma or not."

—**Debra Burdick, LCSW, BCN,**
author of numerous books on mindfulness and ADHD,
including *Mindfulness Skills Workbook for Clinicians and Clients*

"I love this book! With information and research for clinicians followed by protocols and scripts for each trauma tool, these top down (cognitive) approaches are very different than the usual thought challenging methods of CBT. I definitely will be adding this book to my current library and urge everyone working with these clients to do the same."

—**Kate Cohen-Posey, MS, LMHC, LMFT** ,
author of the *Brief Therapy Client Handouts* books and
creator of the *Handy Brain Model*

Trauma Treatment Toolbox

165 Brain-Changing Tips,
Tools & Handouts to
Move Therapy Forward

Jennifer Sweeton, PsyD

Published by
PESI Publishing & Media
PESI, Inc.
3839 White Ave
Eau Claire, WI 54703

Cover Design: Amy Rubenzer
Editing: Donald Altman
Layout: Bookmasters & Amy Rubenzer

Proudly printed in the United States of America

ISBN: 9781683731795

PESI
Publishing
& Media
pesipublishing.com

About the Author

Dr. Jennifer Sweeton is a licensed clinical psychologist and internationally-recognized expert on anxiety and trauma, women's issues, and the neuroscience of mental health. She completed her doctoral training at the Stanford University School of Medicine, the Pacific Graduate School of Psychology, and the National Center for PTSD. Additionally, she holds a master's degree in affective neuroscience from Stanford University, and studied behavioral genetics at Harvard University.

Dr. Sweeton resides in the greater Kansas City area, where she owns a group private practice, Kansas City Mental Health Associates. She formerly served as the President of the Oklahoma Psychological Association, and holds adjunct faculty appointments at the University of Kansas School of Medicine and the University of Oklahoma Health Sciences Center. She is the current President-Elect of the Greater Kansas City Psychological Association. Dr. Sweeton offers psychological services to clients in Oklahoma, Kansas, and is a sought-after trauma and neuroscience expert who has trained thousands of mental health professionals in her workshops.

This book is dedicated to my daughter, Annaliese.
May you always enjoy a strong, integrated, resilient brain!

Table of Contents

PART II | Bottom-Up Tools

PART III | Top-Down Tools

Acknowledgements

Several individuals supported the creation and publication of this book. Many thanks go to my husband Tim, my parents, Linda Jackson at PESI, the entire PESI team, and the fellow mental health therapists who read and helped edit the manuscript. This wouldn't be possible without all of you!

How to Use This Workbook

Trauma Treatment Toolbox was created for mental health clinicians who want to take a brain-based approach to their trauma treatment. While there are many books and workbooks on trauma treatment, this is the first workbook that emphasizes a brain-based approach by presenting tools and techniques that are believed to change the brain in specific ways. Due to recent advancements in neuroscience and psychotherapy research, clinicians are now able to choose therapeutic techniques that change the brain in specific ways that facilitate post-trauma recovery.

This toolbox provides a bridge between brain science and application, sharing with clinicians the most recent and relevant information about the five key brain areas impacted by trauma. Most importantly, it shows how to effectively help traumatized clients heal their brains using straightforward, easy-to-implement techniques.

ROADMAP TO USING THIS WORKBOOK

Though the human brain weighs only three pounds, its components are extraordinarily interconnected and complex. To better help you, as a clinician, make sense of the brain and how therapy can help recovery from trauma, this workbook intentionally presents information in a specific order. This order reflects my recommendation that trauma treatment begin with psychoeducation regarding the neuroscience of trauma, and then progress to various approaches described below.

My years of practice have helped me recognize that it is best to begin with psychoeducation, as it allows clients to gain an understanding of what is happening in the brain, why they feel the way they do, and what it means for recovery. When clients discover that their trauma symptoms do not reflect weakness or a moral deficit, but rather brain changes that can be altered with therapy, it can instill hope and reduce stigma.

Part I, **Brain Basics for Trauma Recovery,** lays the foundation for trauma work by describing key brain areas, ways to change the brain, and a general roadmap for trauma treatment. It is here that you will learn about the most important brain areas impacted by psychological trauma. Part II, **Bottom-Up Tools,** gives you a variety of what are known as "bottom-up" techniques that use the body in order to change the brain. As described in Chapters 4-6, you will learn how to use tools that engage the body, breathing, and movement. Part III, **Top-Down Tools**, focuses on techniques and methods for engaging the reflective capabilities of the brain for trauma treatment. These top-down approaches have been shown to be very effective, and Chapters 7-8 will introduce you to a variety of tools to use with clients, from meditations to cognitive reappraisal techniques.

This workbook is designed for clinicians to be able to open it to any page and begin using that tool right away, with no previous information required.

While there is a rationale for the format of this workbook, it is not required that clinicians read it from cover to cover in order to understand how to use the techniques presented each part of the workbook. Each chapter and each tool stands alone and can be used without reference to earlier sections of the workbook.

USING THE TOOLS AND HANDOUTS

Each tool in this workbook includes a short list of the post-trauma symptoms it treats, relevant research findings, a written description of the tool, and tips for clinicians regarding how the tool is best used. Keep in mind that while most of the handouts included in the workbook were designed for client use, they can be helpful for clinicians to reference as well.

Clinicians are encouraged to copy, download or print these handouts as needed, and to provide them to clients to illustrate teaching points and to encourage at-home practice of the tools. To make the handouts easy to use, each technique presented in this workbook (breathing, meditations, cognitive tools, etc.) is accompanied by a concisely written description and visual depiction of the brain areas it changes, as well as how this is beneficial for treating post-trauma symptoms.

The wide-ranging materials in these pages—from the handouts, worksheets and psychoeducational materials to the detailed visual depictions of different brain regions and instructions for how to complete each tool— will provide you with inspiring new strategies and many useful approaches for healing trauma and changing lives. It is my hope that *Trauma Treatment Toolbox* will help you feel confident in your ability to help clients heal after traumatic events using evidence-informed approaches.

PART I

Brain Basics for Trauma Recovery

1

The Neuroscience of Trauma

Neuroscience research is helping us peer inside the brain to understand how psychological trauma is associated with multiple types of brain change, including alterations in brain activation, volume of structures, connectivity among key brain regions, brain waves, and neurochemicals. Additionally, brain change can be inferred using psychophysiological approaches, which can inform researchers about various indices of stress and, indirectly, some types of brain activity. When treating trauma, it is possible to reference research examining brain change from several different perspectives.

What's really happening in the brain when someone experiences trauma? This workbook focuses primarily on brain activations associated with psychological trauma, drawing from both neuroimaging and psychophysiological research. Five key brain areas involved in trauma are emphasized, and techniques that have been shown to alter the activation of these brain areas are presented in the *Trauma Treatment Toolbox*.

YOUR BRAIN ON TRAUMA

As you explore the five main brain areas implicated in trauma that are described briefly below, keep in mind that none of these areas is isolated or works alone. There is connectivity between all of these areas, and trauma recovery helps to increase connectivity and create a more integrated brain.

1. **Fear Center (Amygdala):** The main objective of the amygdala is to determine whether a particular situation, context, person, etc. presents a threat or danger. It's an area that has been called the "smoke alarm" by trauma expert Dr. Bessel van der Kolk and colleagues (van der Kolk, McFarlane, & Weisaeth, 1996). One goal of trauma treatment is to reduce activation of this area of the brain. De-activation of this area can reduce reactivity to trauma triggers and the arousal and reactivity symptoms of PTSD (such as hypervigilance, feeling on guard, etc.).

2. **Interoception Center (Insula):** The insula is the main site of interoception and proprioception. Proprioception involves one's sense of balance and awareness of where the body is located in space. For example, the ability to walk and know where your legs and body are positioned—even with your eyes closed—is possible because of proprioception. Without this ability, one might just fall down. Interoception is one's ability feel into internal experience and connect with internal sensations. For instance, feeling hungry, warm, or jittery are all examples of interoception. In trauma, the insula is often dysregulated, which makes it difficult to identify and manage emotions and distressing physical sensations. When the insula is strong, individuals are better able to feel into their own bodies, identify the emotions they are experiencing, and regulate them.

3. **Memory Center (Hippocampus):** The hippocampus is known as the memory center of the brain. It is also sometimes called the "timekeeper" (van der Kolk, 2014), since it is responsible for putting a time stamp on our memories. This allows us to experience past events as happening in the past, not the present. In individuals who experience post-trauma symptoms, it is often the case that this area

of the brain is less active, and smaller, than those of individuals who have not experienced trauma or an anxiety disorder. This results in memory and stress regulation difficulties. Increased activation of this area of the brain helps individuals feel safe in the present moment, and can help reduce fear when trauma triggers occur.

4. **Thinking Center (Prefrontal Cortex)**: The prefrontal cortex (PFC) is comprised of several smaller structures, which together are considered the thinking center of the brain. The PFC is involved in functions such as concentration, decision-making, self-awareness, and awareness of others. In traumatized brains, however, it is common for this area of the brain to be underactive, making it difficult for individuals to concentrate, make decisions, connect with others, and be self-aware. Increased activation of the PFC leads to clearer thinking, improved concentration, a sense of connectedness to others, and better self-awareness.

5. **Self-Regulation Center (Cingulate Cortex):** The cingulate cortex, and more specifically, the anterior cingulate cortex (ACC) or dorsal anterior cingulate cortex (dACC), is involved in conflict monitoring, error detection, and self-regulation, including regulation of emotion and thoughts. This area of the brain is often underactive in individuals experiencing post-trauma sequelae, which can result in difficulties with emotion regulation, thought regulation, and decision-making. Increased activation of this area can be immensely helpful, as it improves individuals' abilities to regulate unhelpful or painful emotions and manage distressing thoughts.

Additionally, connectivity between these key brain areas can impact an individual's symptoms and functioning in a positive way. Below, some basic information regarding neural connectivity is provided:

- **Cortical-Subcortical Connectivity:** Connections between the self-regulation/thinking areas of the brain (prefrontal cortex and cingulate cortex) and the fear brain (amygdala) can allow for down-regulation of the amygdala, thereby reducing fear responses and negative emotions. This can be thought of as turning off or quieting the alarm on the brain's smoke detector.

- **Insular Connectivity:** When bidirectional connections between the amygdala and insula are strong, it leads to exaggerated fear responses. This is because the insula detects aversive bodily sensations and then communicates this to the amygdala (fear center), which may then catastrophize those sensations.

THE BRAIN ON TRAUMA

The five key areas of the brain include the amygdala (fear center), insula (interoception center), hippocampus (memory center), prefrontal cortex (thinking center), and cingulate cortex (self–regulation center). Each of these areas, and the key connections among them, are shown on the next page.

The Brain On Trauma

UNDERACTIVE
Self-Regulation Center (Cingulate)

DYSREGULATED
Interoception Center (Insula)

UNDERACTIVE
Memory Center (Hippocampus)

OVERACTIVE
Fear Center (Amygdala)

UNDERACTIVE
Thinking Center (Prefrontal Cortex)

Understanding the Amygdala

This subcortical area of the brain, where the amygdala resides, is one of the first structures to process sensory information. The main objective of the amygdala is to determine, very quickly, whether a certain situation, context, person, etc. presents a threat or danger. It's always on, always receiving input from all your senses—even the orienting muscles in the neck as you turn your head to survey your surroundings for safety or danger.

Everything the amygdala evaluates is viewed through the lens of potential danger or threat. For example, when your cat walks into your living room, the amygdala receives sensory information about your cat (through vision, and perhaps sound or touch) and immediately evaluates whether or not it is dangerous. The amygdala asks, "Is this a lion? A tiger? A cat? Is it a safe cat?" Its main objective is to determine whether a situation, person, animal, etc. is threatening. No wonder this area has been called the smoke alarm by trauma experts van der Kolk, McFarlane, and Weisaeth (1996), as the main job of the amygdala is to detect danger. When this fear center interprets a situation as threatening, it activates, much like a smoke alarm when it senses smoke.

The stronger the threat is perceived to be, the higher the activation of the amygdala. When this activation occurs, the amygdala begins to suppress the functioning of the higher thinking areas of the brain needed for rational thought and emotion regulation, and activates the stress pathway through communication with the hypothalamus. In turn, the activation of the stress pathway (the hypothalamic-pituitary-adrenal axis) activates the stress response in the body (the sympathetic nervous system), which mobilizes an individual's resources and helps them to manage the threat through fleeing, fighting, or freezing.

The amygdala is often hyper-activated in those suffering from post-trauma symptoms, as well as those suffering from anxiety disorders (and some other disorders as well). One goal of trauma treatment is to reduce activation of this area of the brain. De-activation of this area can reduce the stress response, reactivity to trauma triggers, and the arousal and reactivity symptoms of PTSD (such as hypervigilance, feeling on guard, etc.).

KEY RESEARCH FINDINGS

- Increased activation of the amygdala in PTSD (Shin, Rauch, & Pitman, 2006)
- Hyper-reactivity of the amygdala in PTSD (Ledoux, 2000)
- Exaggerated responses to non-trauma-related emotional stimuli in PTSD (Rauch et al., 2000; Shin et al., 2005)
- The stronger the amygdala activation, the more severe the PTSD symptoms (Protopescu et al., 2005)

Amygdala: The Fear Center

About The Fear Center

This subcortical area is located very deep in the brain. Being a subcortical structure, it is outside of conscious control and conscious awareness, but can be very powerful. The main objective of the amygdala is to determine, very quickly, whether a situation, context, person, etc. presents a threat or danger. This area has been called the smoke alarm by trauma experts because the main job of the amygdala is to "smell," or detect, danger. When this fear center interprets a situation to be threatening, it activates.

The stronger the threat is perceived to be, the higher the activation of the amygdala. When this activation occurs, the amygdala begins to shut down the functioning of the higher thinking areas of the brain needed for rational thought and emotion regulation, and it activates the stress pathway (the hypothalamic pituitary-adrenal axis) and the stress response in the body (the sympathetic nervous system). In dangerous situations, this is helpful; the amygdala helps the body and brain prepare to take action to stay safe! The result is that we can flee, fight, or freeze.

The Fear Center in the Traumatized Brain

The amygdala is often hyper-activated in those suffering from post-trauma symptoms, as well as those suffering from anxiety disorders (and some other disorders as well). When this happens, it becomes difficult to think clearly, focus, stay self-aware, and use healthy coping strategies. It may also lead some individuals to respond to non-threatening situations, people, or other stimuli as though they are dangerous. For example, if someone was attacked by a dog as a child and develops post-trauma symptoms after this event, they may come to fear all dogs after that, even friendly ones. This is because the amygdala begins to interpret *all* dogs as dangerous. One goal of trauma treatment is to reduce activation of this area of the brain. De-activation of this area can reduce the stress response, reactivity to trauma triggers, and the arousal and reactivity symptoms of PTSD (such as hypervigilance, feeling on guard, etc.).

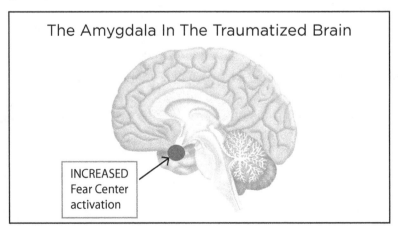

The Amygdala In The Traumatized Brain

INCREASED Fear Center activation

Understanding the Hippocampus

Right now, let's try an experiment. Take a moment to recall a favorite memory, and as you do, see if you can also remember when this occurred. Your ability to access where and when this past event occurred is due to the hippocampus, which is known as the memory center of the brain. It is also sometimes called the timekeeper (van der Kolk, 2014), since it is responsible for putting a time stamp on our memories. This allows us to experience past events as happening in the past, not the present.

While several areas of the brain are involved in memory, broadly, the hippocampus is considered the main structure involved in explicit, declarative, and autobiographical memories. In other words, this is the area of the brain that stores memories that people can consciously access. Examples of hippocampal memories may include significant birthday occasions, holidays, or distressing events.

The reason this area of the brain is so important in trauma is that during times of intense stress or trauma it becomes under-activated and, over time, may even shrink, causing memory-related difficulties. This is one reason why eye witness testimony is so controversial; memories stored while under stress can be distorted, or not even stored at all, and this is partially due to under-activation of the hippocampus. In individuals who experience post-trauma symptoms, it is often the case that this area of the brain is less active, and smaller, than in those individuals who have not experienced trauma or an anxiety disorder. The main issue in trauma with regard to the hippocampus is that it is small and under-active, which leads to memory difficulties.

In the context of PTSD, the hippocampus often provides inaccurate information to the amygdala. When the amygdala processes sensory information, it asks the question, "Is this dangerous?" To determine whether it is dangerous, it often consults with the hippocampus, asking it the question, "Has this situation/context/person/stimulus ever been dangerous before?" If the hippocampus is not functioning properly, it may respond to the amygdala inaccurately, informing it that a benign situation or stimulus is in fact dangerous.

For instance, the sound of a car backfiring may be misinterpreted as a gun being fired. In these cases, it is often the hippocampus that provides the misinformation to the amygdala regarding the dangerousness of different situations. Increased activation of this memory center, on the other hand, can remind individuals that they are safe in the present moment, and can help individuals extinguish fear responses when trauma triggers arise.

KEY RESEARCH FINDINGS

- Reduced hippocampal activation (Bremnar et al., 1999; Liberzon & Sripada, 2007)
- Reduced hippocampal volume, neuronal integrity, and functional integrity in PTSD (Shin, Rauch, & Pitman, 2006)
- Hippocampal cell loss in PTSD (Bremner et al., 2003)

Hippocampus: The Memory Center

About the Memory Center

The hippocampus is known as the memory center of the brain. It is also sometimes called the timekeeper by trauma experts. The hippocampus is the main brain structure that stores memories that you can consciously access. Right now, if you take a moment to access a pleasant memory, the fact that you can recall when and where it occurred is due to the hippocampus.

However, during times of intense stress or trauma, the memory center of the brain becomes under-activated, and can even shrink, causing memory-related difficulties. This is one reason why eye witness testimony is so controversial; memories stored while under stress can be distorted, or not even be stored at all, and this is partially due to under-activation of the hippocampus.

The Memory Center in the Traumatized Brain

The main issue in trauma with regard to the hippocampus is that it is small and under-active, which leads to memory difficulties and other issues.

For instance, when the hippocampus becomes under-activated, it can provide inaccurate information to the amygdala. To determine whether a situation is dangerous the amygdala asks the hippocampus the question, "Has this situation ever been dangerous before?" If the hippocampus is not functioning properly, it may respond to the amygdala inaccurately, informing it that a harmless situation or stimulus is dangerous. This causes the person to feel afraid or triggered even when no danger is present. These individuals may also experience past memories as happening in the present, since an under-activated hippocampus may forget to put the "time stamp" on the memory! Increased activation of this memory center, on the other hand, can remind individuals that they are safe in the present moment, and can help individuals extinguish fear responses when trauma triggers arise.

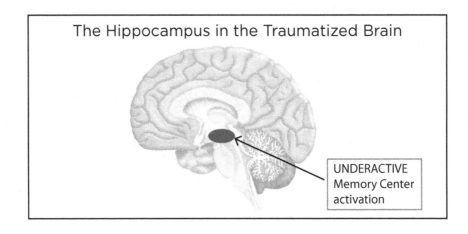

The Hippocampus in the Traumatized Brain

UNDERACTIVE Memory Center activation

Understanding the Insula

The insula, or the interoception center, is the main site of interoception and proprioception. Proprioception involves one's sense of balance and awareness of where the body is located in space. Interoception is one's ability to feel into internal experience and connect with internal sensations. For instance, when you experience feeling hungry, warm, or jittery, these are all examples of interoception.

This too-often overlooked area of the brain is extremely important because without a strong and regulated insula, emotion identification and regulation become very difficult. Imagine, for example, a client who suffers from panic disorder. If they cannot feel into the body and be aware of the physical sensations that are part of their panic, it would be extremely difficult to treat their panic disorder! This is because the experience of emotion is not simply cognitive; emotion is always experienced in the body.

When an individual is able to feel into the body and connect with internal sensations, those sensations provide critical information about the emotion the individual is experiencing. The ability to do this is often called "felt sense" by trauma expert Peter Levine (1997). In trauma, however, the insula is often dysregulated. This condition disrupts and limits individuals' abilities to feel into the body and work with physical sensations. For instance, in traumatized brains, the insula may be under-activated, hyper-activated, or hyper-reactive (overly sensitive) to shifts in internal sensations. When the insula is over-activated, there can be emotional reactivity and outbursts (emotion under-modulation); when it is under-activated, there may be dissociation and numbing. Both of these extremes are common in PTSD.

One goal of trauma treatment—and the goal of the bottom-up tools found in Part II—is to build a strong but regulated insula. With a more regulated insula, individuals improve interoception, and they experience fewer emotional outbursts and dissociative symptoms (including numbing). Additionally, with a strong insula, individuals are better able to feel into their own bodies, identify the emotions they are experiencing, and skillfully regulate them.

KEY RESEARCH FINDINGS

- Less activation in the right anterior insula in PTSD than in healthy controls during "affective set-shifting," indicating cognitive rigidity (Simmons et al., 2009)
- Hyperactivity of the insula during processing of emotional information in those suffering from PTSD (Etkin & Wager, 2007)
- Post-traumatic stress symptoms were associated with lower insula volumes in combat veterans with PTSD (Herringa et al., 2012)
- Re-experiencing symptoms of PTSD is associated with right anterior insula hyperactivation (Hopper et al., 2007)
- In PTSD, the insula is hyper-reactive or "hyper-responsive" (Hughes & Shin, 2011)

Insula: The Interoception Center

About the Interoception Center

The insula, or the interoception center, allows you to be aware of, and connect with, all of your internal sensations and experiences. Examples of interoception are when you feel hungry, warm, or jittery. This too-often overlooked area of the brain is extremely important. That's because without a strong and regulated insula, it is very difficult to identify not only physical sensations, but also emotions. This is because emotions are always experienced in the body as well as the mind!

When you are able to feel into the body and connect with internal sensations, those sensations provide critical information about the emotion you are experiencing. These feelings are very different depending on the situation. For example, you may notice that when you experience love for a child, it feels different in the body than when you experience anger about an injustice.

The Interoception Center in the Traumatized Brain

In trauma, the insula is often dysregulated, which disrupts individuals' abilities to feel into the body and work with physical sensations. For instance, in traumatized brains, the insula may be under-activated, hyper-activated, or hyper-reactive (overly sensitive) to shifts in internal sensations. When the insula is over-activated there can be emotional reactivity and outbursts (emotion under-modulation); when it is under-activated, there may be dissociation and numbing. Both of these extremes are common in PTSD.

One goal of trauma treatment is to build a strong but regulated insula. With a more regulated insula, individuals improve interoception and, as a result, experience fewer emotional outbursts and dissociative symptoms (including numbing). Additionally, with a strong insula, individuals are better able to feel into their own bodies, identify the emotions they are experiencing, and regulate them.

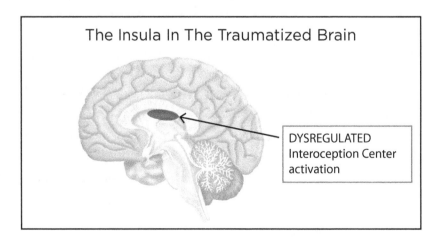

The Insula In The Traumatized Brain

DYSREGULATED Interoception Center activation

Understanding the Prefrontal Cortex

The prefrontal cortex (PFC), or thinking center, is comprised of several smaller structures, which together are considered the thinking center of the brain. The outer, more lateral areas of the prefrontal cortex (sometimes referred to as the dorsolateral PFC) are involved in decision-making, concentration, awareness of others, empathy, social intelligence, and other executive functions. The center areas of the PFC (sometimes referred to as the medial PFC or ventromedial PFC) are involved in self-awareness, self-regulation, and personality. While survival is possible without these areas of the brain, they are necessary for functioning well in the world and forming relationships with others.

In traumatized brains, it is common for the PFC, generally, to become underactive, making it difficult for individuals to concentrate, make decisions, connect with others, and to be self-aware. Increased activation of the PFC leads to clearer thinking, improved attention and concentration, a sense of connectedness to others, and better self-awareness.

KEY RESEARCH FINDINGS

- Under-activation of the medial PFC in PTSD (Kasai et al., 2008; Matsuo et al., 2003)
- Smaller volume and less responsiveness of the medial PFC in PTSD (Shin, Rauch, & Pitman, 2006)
- Under-activation in the ventromedial PFC and dorsolateral PFC in PTSD (Huang et al., 2014)
- Post-traumatic growth broadly, and "related to others" specifically, is associated with increased dorsolateral PFC activation and grey matter (Nakagawa et al., 2016)

Prefrontal Cortex: The Thinking Center

About the Thinking Center

The prefrontal cortex (PFC) is the part of the brain associated with some of our most uniquely human qualities. This region of the brain is quite large and is comprised of several smaller structures. Together, these structures are referred to as the thinking center.

The outer, more lateral areas of the PFC (sometimes referred to as the dorsolateral PFC) are involved in decision-making, concentration, awareness of others, empathy, social intelligence, and other executive functions. The center areas of the PFC (sometimes referred to as the ventromedial PFC) are involved in self-awareness, self-regulation, and personality. While we can survive without these areas of the brain, they are necessary for us to function well and to have close, healthy relationships with others!

The Thinking Center in the Traumatized Brain

In traumatized brains, it is common for the PFC to become underactive. When this occurs, it can be difficult for individuals to concentrate, make decisions, connect with others, and to be self-aware. When you can't access the PFC, it can be hard to "reason through" triggering or stressful situations; functioning at work or in relationships can be difficult. However, if you activate the PFC, you'll gain clearer thinking, improved attention and concentration, a sense of connectedness to others, and better self-awareness—all important ingredients for a sense of well-being in daily life.

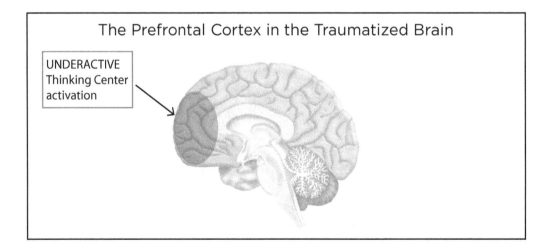

The Prefrontal Cortex in the Traumatized Brain

UNDERACTIVE Thinking Center activation

Understanding the Cingulate

The cingulate cortex, referred to as the self-regulation center, is involved in self-regulation, including regulation of emotion and thoughts. It is also activated when we are trying to work out conflicting thoughts or emotions (known as conflict monitoring), and when we catch the mind wandering away during a mindfulness practice or other focused awareness practice.

The cingulate cortex is often underactive in individuals experiencing post-trauma sequelae or trauma triggers, which can result in difficulties with emotion regulation, thought regulation, good decision-making, and judgment. Increased activation of this area can be immensely helpful, as it improves individuals' abilities to regulate unhelpful or painful emotions and manage distressing thoughts. With strong activation of the self-regulation center, it may also be possible for individuals to down-regulate activation of the amygdala, leading to less emotional reactivity to trauma triggers.

KEY RESEARCH FINDINGS

- Under-activation of the rostral anterior cingulate cortex in PTSD (Hopper et al., 2007)
- Smaller volume of anterior cingulate cortex in individuals with combat-related PTSD (Woodward et al., 2006) or early life abuse (Kitayama, Quinn, & Bremner, 2006)
- Less activation in the anterior cingulate cortex in PTSD (Garfinkel & Liberzon, 2009)

Cingulate: The Self-Regulation Center

About the Self-Regulation Center

The cingulate cortex, referred to as the self-regulation center, is a high up, cortical area of the brain involved in the regulation of emotion and thoughts. For instance, when you wake up from an upsetting dream and feel angry, you may tell yourself, "That was just a dream, it wasn't real, and so it doesn't make sense to feel angry about it." This attempt to stop feeling angry requires activation of your self-regulation center, and with a strong cingulate cortex, you will be able to reduce the anger you feel (which is coming from the amygdala), even if the emotion regulation does not occur as quickly as you would like it to!

We can think of this area of the brain as a master control center that attempts to quiet the amygdala (Fear Center) from the top-down, and collaborates with the prefrontal cortex (Thinking Center) to enhance decision-making and functioning. For instance, when you practice meditation, the prefrontal cortex and cingulate cortex interact (and are hopefully strongly connected); the prefrontal cortex allows you to focus on your breath, a thought, word, etc., and your cingulate cortex alerts the prefrontal cortex when your mind wanders so it can redirect attention to that stimulus once again.

This area of the brain is also activated when we are trying to work out conflicting thoughts or emotions (known as conflict monitoring), or when we catch the mind wandering during a mindfulness practice. For example, if you feel conflicting emotions about your mother, perhaps both anger and compassion, the self-regulation center will help you work out these emotions. When you sit with your eyes closed and try to just focus on the breath, but soon notice that your mind has wandered over to some thought, that awareness of the mind wandering is the cingulate cortex activating.

The Self-Regulation Center in the Traumatized Brain

The cingulate cortex is often underactive in the traumatized brain. This can result in difficulties with emotion regulation, thought regulation, and decision-making. Increasing activation in this area can be immensely helpful, as it improves individuals' abilities to regulate unhelpful or painful emotions and manage distressing thoughts. With strong activation of the self-regulation center it may also be possible to reduce stress and activation of the fear center of the brain, leading to less emotional reactivity to trauma triggers.

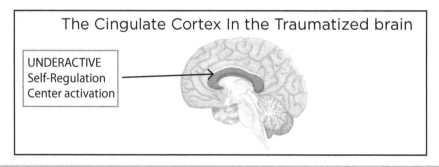

The Cingulate Cortex In the Traumatized brain

UNDERACTIVE Self-Regulation Center activation

Understanding Brain Connectivity

The activity of key brain areas is important to understand because it explains why traumatized individuals experience such strong and distressing symptoms. This understanding can help therapists choose techniques that change the brain in ways that reduce these symptoms. However, the strength of the <u>connections</u> between some of the key areas described in this chapter is also important, because the amount of connectivity between some of these brain components can also impact the symptoms of traumatized clients. Two types of connectivity are especially relevant:

1. **Cortical-Subcortical Connectivity:** Connections running from the self-regulation and thinking centers of the brain (prefrontal cortex and cingulate cortex) down to the amygdala (fear center) can allow for down-regulation of the amygdala, thereby reducing fear responses and negative emotions.

   However, if these connections are underdeveloped (as can be the case in the traumatized brain), it can be difficult for cortical areas to down-regulate the fear center, thereby reducing one's ability to manage trauma triggers or fear. Strengthening these connections can improve the ability to reduce fear and other distressing emotions, and help individuals manage and reduce arousal and the reactivity symptoms of PTSD. The tools presented in this workbook can help strengthen these connections when practiced regularly.

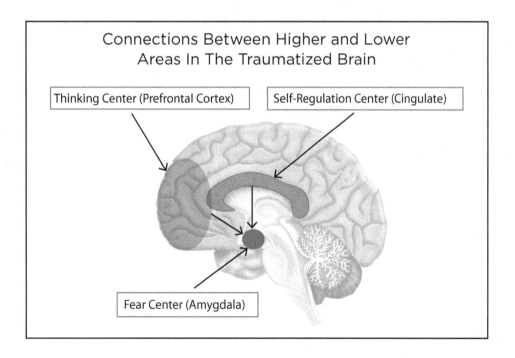

Connections Between Higher and Lower Areas In The Traumatized Brain

Thinking Center (Prefrontal Cortex)

Self-Regulation Center (Cingulate)

Fear Center (Amygdala)

2. **Insular Connectivity:** In traumatized or anxious brains, the connections between the amygdala (fear center) and insula (interoception center) are often very strong. When this happens, it leads to exaggerated fear responses and a hypersensitivity to physical sensations. This is because the insula detects uncomfortable or painful sensations, or unwanted or previously conditioned bodily sensations, and then communicates these to the fear center, which may then over-react to those stimuli, leading to catastrophic interpretations.

When these brain regions are strongly connected *and* hyperactive, it leads to over-reaction in response to small changes in the body, leading the individual to interpret physical sensations as unbearable or dangerous. Weakening this connectivity allows individuals to interpret sensations more accurately and can reduce arousal and the reactivity symptoms of PTSD.

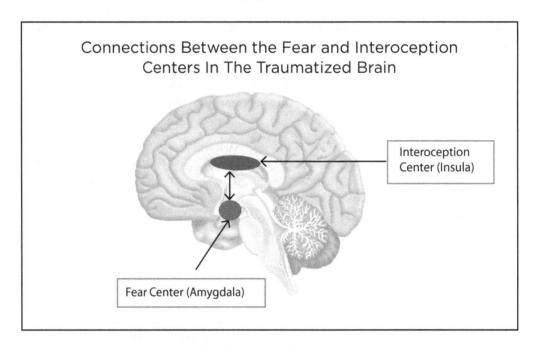

KEY RESEARCH FINDINGS

- In individuals with a history of interpersonal trauma, strong connections were found between the amygdala and insula (Krause-Utz et al., 2014)
- In PTSD, connections from the PFC to the amygdala are weak, which may impair individuals' ability to regulate emotional responses (Thomason et al., 2015)

2

Integrating Brain Change Approaches

Every clinician, at some point or another, has heard clients bemoan the fact that they just can't change. That may be a good time to let them know the findings of cutting edge brain science:

NEUROPLASTICITY IS NOT ONLY POSSIBLE, IT IS INEVITABLE

In fact, every experience, sensation, and interaction with others or the environment changes the brain, even if just to reinforce pre-existing networks. Since the human brain has approximately 86 billion neurons, each connecting to thousands of others, our capacity for brain change is enormous. This is good news, since the purpose of psychotherapy is to help clients intentionally change their brains to become healthier and happier.

Our brains are designed to change throughout life. As mental health clinicians, it is our goal to help clients make neuroplasticity work for them, not against them, by eliciting brain change using three approaches described by several brain scientists (i.e., Taylor et al., 2010; van der Kolk, 2014): bottom-up, top-down, and horizontal.

BOTTOM-UP APPROACHES TO BRAIN CHANGE

Bottom-up techniques work through the body to change the brain, especially the lower, subcortical areas of the brain outside of conscious awareness and conscious control. For instance, bottom-up techniques can be utilized to de-activate the amygdala (fear center) or to strengthen and regulate the insula (site of interoception). While it may be possible to also alter higher, cortical structures (such as the thinking center) of the brain using bottom-up techniques, this is less common. Examples of bottom-up techniques include breathing exercises, body scan, progressive muscle relaxation, autogenic training, yoga, exercise, tai chi, and some meditations.

TOP-DOWN APPROACHES TO BRAIN CHANGE

In top-down techniques, the mind is engaged to change the brain. In other words, the brain, especially the higher cortical areas, can be altered with thoughts. For example, top-down techniques can be used to strengthen the prefrontal cortex (thinking center) or cingulate (emotion regulation center). It is possible to alter lower brain structures (such as the amygdala) using top-down methods, but this is often difficult. This is because during times of stress the amygdala suppresses the functioning of the thinking and emotion regulation centers of the brain, making it difficult for those areas to activate and exert downward influence. Examples of top-down techniques include cognitive reappraisal or restructuring, talk therapy, some acceptance and commitment therapy techniques, trauma-focused interventions that emphasize discussing traumatic events in detail, and some meditations.

HORIZONTAL APPROACHES TO BRAIN CHANGE

Horizontal techniques change the brain though inter-hemispheric or cross-modality processing. A focus on these approaches is beyond the scope of this workbook, but expressive arts therapies are examples of horizontal processing, such as art therapy, dance/movement therapy, and music therapy, as well as eye movement desensitization and reprocessing (EMDR).

INTEGRATING MULTIPLE APPROACHES TO BRAIN CHANGE

As a general rule, techniques and interventions that combine multiple approaches to brain change—for instance, those that contain both bottom-up and top-down elements—tend to be more efficient, and result in faster, more dramatic brain change. The reason is that when multiple approaches to brain change are utilized at the same time, the brain is getting a "workout" from multiple directions at once, the exercises tend to be challenging (which promotes larger brain change), and several brain regions are impacted at once.

While this handbook categorizes techniques as being largely bottom-up or top-down, note that most of the methods taught here contain both bottom-up and top-down elements, and also sometimes horizontal elements.

Bottom-Up Approaches to Brain Change

Bottom-up techniques work through the body to change the brain, especially the lower, subcortical areas of the brain outside of conscious awareness and conscious control. For instance, bottom-up techniques can be utilized to de-activate the amygdala (fear center) or to strengthen and regulate the insula (site of interoception).

When treating trauma, it is recommended to start with bottom-up techniques such as sensory awareness or breathing exercises, as opposed to top-down techniques such as cognitive therapy or trauma-focused techniques. Examples of bottom-up techniques are found in Part II, Chapters 4-6 of this handbook.

They include (but are not limited to):

- Sensory awareness techniques
- Autogenic training
- Breathing techniques
- Poses
- Some meditations
- Movement-based techniques

Change the Brain Bottom-Up

Bottom-up approaches produce brain change by working through the body. The body and the brain are connected by the spinal cord, which transmits information from the body to the brain, and vice versa. It is possible to alter the brain by sending signals through the body for the brain to process. Bottom-up, body-based techniques work best for changing the lower parts of the brain, such as the fear brain, which are outside of conscious awareness and are difficult to control top-down (with your mind).

For example, if you have ever noticed how challenging it is to simply stop feeling anxious by telling yourself, "Stop it!" you know how difficult it can be to down-regulate the fear center of the brain with your thoughts. A more effective way to regulate the lower areas of the brain is to work from the other direction, bottom-up, as opposed to top-down.

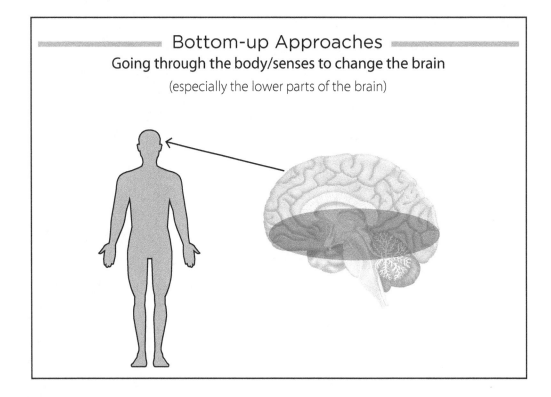

Your Brain on Bottom-Up Techniques

While different techniques change the brain in a variety of ways, bottom-up techniques tend to change the lower regions of the brain, including subcortical structures. When treating trauma, relevant structures that can be altered using bottom-up techniques include the hippocampus (which is not a subcortical structure but is located deep in the brain close to subcortical areas), insula, and amygdala. Specifically, bottom-up techniques may alter these brain areas in the following ways.

1. **Amygdala (Fear Center):** De-activation of this area helps to reduce reactivity when trauma triggers arise. It also reduces the stress response (sympathetic nervous system arousal) and results in a decrease in arousal and reactivity symptoms, such as hypervigilance, feeling on guard, etc.

2. **Insula (Interoception Center):** In PTSD, the insula is often dysregulated. When it is over-activated, there is emotional reactivity and outbursts (emotion under-modulation); when it is under-activated, there is dissociation and numbing. Both extremes are common in PTSD. With a more regulated insula, individuals improve interoception, and they experience fewer emotional outbursts and dissociative symptoms (including numbing).

3. **Hippocampus (Memory Center):** Activation of the hippocampus helps remind the individual that they are safe in the present moment, and is involved in the extinction of fear responses when trauma triggers arise. The increased competence the individual experiences in managing negative memories can reduce the avoidance symptoms of PTSD.

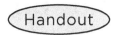

Your Brain on Bottom-Up Techniques

Bottom-up techniques may change the brain in **three** ways:

1. **Less activation in the fear center (amygdala) of the brain:**
   - Reduces how strongly you react to trauma triggers
   - Reduces the stress response and increases the relaxation response
   - Decreases hypervigilance and the feeling of "always being on guard"

2. **More regulated activation of the interoception center (insula) of the brain:**
   - Reduces how strongly you react to trauma triggers
   - Reduces anger and other emotional outbursts
   - Reduces dissociation
   - Reduces numbing

3. **More activation of the memory center (hippocampus) of the brain:**
   - Increases feeling of safety
   - Reduces fear, especially when faced with trauma triggers
   - Increases ability to cope with negative memories
   - Helps individuals experience traumatic events as occurring in the past (in other words, trauma memories become "time stamped")

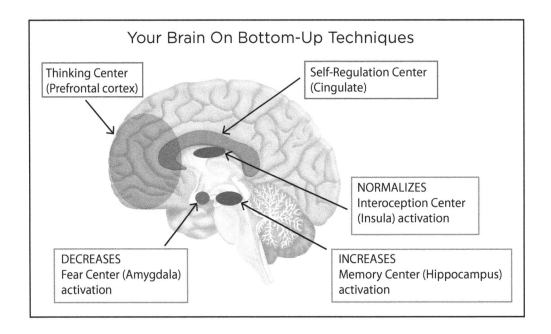

Top-Down Approaches to Brain Change

Top-down techniques use a variety of methods that engage awareness and thinking to change the brain. Research shows that thoughts can be used to alter brain regions, especially high cortical areas such as the prefrontal cortex (thinking center). Top-down approaches are critical to incorporate in trauma treatment, as individuals with post-trauma sequelae show under-activation of the thinking and emotion regulation centers of the brain.

While it is recommended that the first phase of trauma treatment focus on learning bottom-up techniques, treatment is not complete without a subsequent strong emphasis on top-down techniques. Examples of top-down techniques are found in Part III, Chapters 7-8 of this workbook.

Examples of bottom-up techniques are found in Part III, Chapters 7-8 of this handbook. They include (but are not limited to):

- Open awareness meditations
- Closed concentration meditations
- Cognitive restructuring techniques
- Cognitive techniques that work with memories

Change the Brain Top-Down

While the brain is responsible for producing thoughts, thoughts also produce brain change. Techniques that use thoughts, or the mind, to change the brain are referred to as "top-down" approaches. Whenever we try to focus on something, change our thinking, or redirect our thoughts, we are practicing changing our brain from the top down. Therapy techniques that work with thoughts are often utilized to change the upper, cortical parts of the brain, including the thinking and emotion regulation centers of the brain.

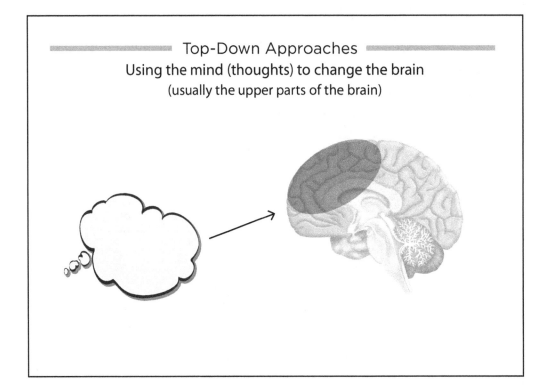

Top-Down Approaches
Using the mind (thoughts) to change the brain
(usually the upper parts of the brain)

Your Brain on Top-Down Techniques

Top-down techniques tend to change the upper regions of the brain, including cortical structures. When treating trauma, relevant structures that can be altered using top-down techniques include the prefrontal cortex and the cingulate. Specifically, top-down techniques may alter these brain areas in the following ways.

1. **Prefrontal Cortex (Thinking Center):** Increased activation of the thinking center. In PTSD, the prefrontal cortex is often under-activated. Activation of this area helps improve focus and concentration, problem-solving, decision-making, self-awareness, emotional intelligence, and connection to others.

2. **Cingulate Cortex (Emotion Regulation Center):** Increased activation of the emotion regulation center. In PTSD, the cingulate is often under-activated. Activation of this area helps improve conflict monitoring, emotion regulation, thought regulation and, more broadly, self-regulation.

Your Brain on Top-Down Techniques

Top-down techniques change the brain in **two** ways:

1. **More activation in the thinking center (prefrontal cortex) of the brain:**

   ◦ Increases your ability to think clearly when stressed

   ◦ Increases self-awareness

   ◦ Increases emotional intelligence ("EQ") and allows you to attune better to others

   ◦ Increases your ability to problem-solve and concentrate

2. **More activation in the self-regulation center (cingulate) of the brain:**

   ◦ Increases your ability to regulate emotions

   ◦ Increases your ability to regulate or change distressing thoughts

   ◦ Increases your ability to process and solve "mixed emotions" or competing thoughts

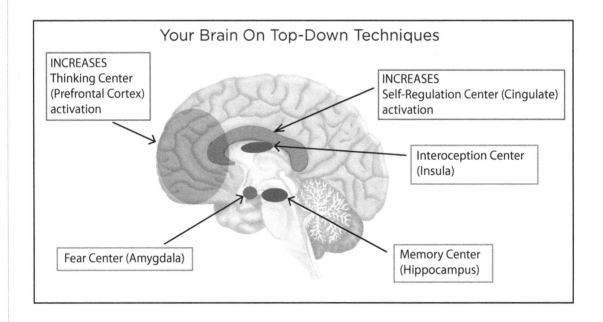

Your Brain On Top-Down Techniques

INCREASES Thinking Center (Prefrontal Cortex) activation

INCREASES Self-Regulation Center (Cingulate) activation

Interoception Center (Insula)

Fear Center (Amygdala)

Memory Center (Hippocampus)

Roadmap for Treating Trauma

Treating trauma can be complex and difficult, and each client's therapy roadmap will be a little different. However, there are some general guidelines for trauma treatment that can help clinicians determine where to begin, and how to progress, with clients. The flowchart shown here provides general recommendations about where to start with traumatized clients, based on their current levels of self-awareness and skill when they begin treatment.

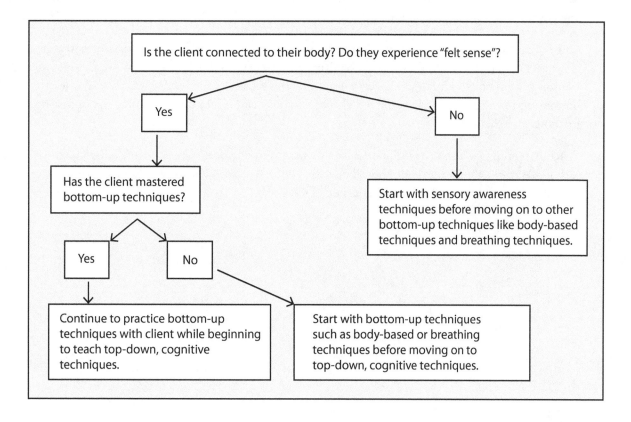

As the flowchart shows, starting with sensory awareness (also called interoceptive exposure) exercises is recommended if the person is not well connected to their body. The reason for this is that clients need to be able to feel into their body, notice sensations, and describe their internal experiences before they can benefit from other bottom-up techniques (such as progressive muscle relaxation) or top-down techniques (such as cognitive restructuring). If, for example, a client with panic disorder had no ability to experience and connect with the physical sensations of panic, it would be nearly impossible to treat their panic attacks, as they would have no way of knowing the early physical indicators of panic and would not be able to learn how to manage them.

It is commonly the case with traumatized clients that there is a difficulty with feeling into the body and noticing internal experiences. This is in large part due to dysregulated insula activity. When the insula is under-activated, for instance, it is difficult to notice internal experiences, and clients feel numb and disconnected from their bodies. In order for therapy to be successful, mental health clinicians need to first help clients re-enter their bodies and become self-aware, and this is best done through the sensory awareness exercises described in Chapter 5.

Once clients report that they are able to notice internal experiences, such as feeling shaky or hot when stressed, the next step is to teach other bottom-up exercises aimed at de-activating the amygdala. Is important that these exercises precede top-down, cognitive techniques, as amygdala activation creates a sense of anxiety and suppresses the activity of cortical areas such as the prefrontal cortex. When this suppression occurs, it becomes very difficult for clients to think clearly and engage in the cognitive tasks that top-down techniques demand. If, for example, a client has a very activated amygdala, their thinking brain may be suppressed so that it is only working at 30% capacity (or 50%, or 70%). This, in turn, makes it very difficult to engage in top-down exercises because the client is only able to access 30% of their thinking brain! The main reason clients often struggle with cognitive techniques is not due to their ineffectiveness. Rather, the reason is that these techniques are often taught too early in therapy, before amygdala activation has been addressed.

Once clients have mastered sensory awareness techniques (if needed) and amygdala de-activating exercises, the next step is to teach top-down, cognitive techniques. While there is no ideal time to make the transition from bottom-up to top-down approaches, it is recommended that clients spend at least a month on bottom-up techniques, practicing on a daily basis for at least 10-20 minutes, before incorporating top-down methods into therapy.

When beginning top-down techniques, it is also recommended to continue emphasizing bottom-up techniques throughout the course of therapy, periodically reviewing these exercises, practicing them in session, and encouraging daily practice outside of therapy.

3

Pendulation and Titration

Somatic experiencing, developed by psychologist and trauma expert Dr. Peter Levine, focuses on helping clients become aware of and release tension trapped in the body after trauma. This tension is largely responsible for the autonomic dysregulation (increased stress response) seen in traumatized clients. Somatic experiencing is a complex and multifaceted approach to trauma treatment and includes several important concepts, two of which are pendulation and titration (Levine, 1997). Pendulation and titration are methods that can be utilized in conjunction with the techniques taught in this book to magnify the brain changing potential of those exercises.

PENDULATION DEFINED

Pendulation, for the purposes of this book, is defined as the intentional shifting between emotional regulation and dysregulation, or amygdala de-activation and activation, to train clients how to re-regulate and stabilize themselves when they become dysregulated. Pendulation can be thought of as a type of brain training in which the clinician facilitates a slight activation of the client's amygdala (fear brain), usually with an emotion induction exercise, and then helps the client de-activate this brain area utilizing bottom-up or top-down techniques. When the amygdala is activated, the client will experience physical manifestations of the stress response, such as faster breathing, increased heart rate, muscle tension, and other sensations.

The clinician helps the client reverse the stress response by utilizing the client's resources, defined as any skills, practices, or thoughts that help the client rebalance their autonomic nervous system and de-activate the amygdala. The result of this training is improved emotion regulation and resilience.

TITRATION DEFINED

The definition of titrate is to "continuously measure and adjust the balance of a physiological function or drug dosage" (Oxford Dictionary). In this context, titration refers to the slow, incremental activation of a client's amygdala and stress response for the purpose of training the client to manage and reduce that activation. It is critical to incorporate titration when pendulating a client's amygdala, since over-activation of the amygdala leads to feelings of overwhelm, a lack of control, and dissociation. This, in turn, often reinforces avoidance behaviors, which exacerbates post-trauma symptoms.

A common example of pendulation without sufficient titration is when a clinician asks a client to dive into the details of a traumatic event too soon. When titration is sufficient, clients are able to slowly engage with traumatic memories or uncomfortable sensations in the body without becoming overwhelmed. While memories or sensations may be unpleasant, they are not unbearable.

However, when titration is not used and the client is encouraged to engage with traumatic memories (or accompanying sensations associated with those memories) too soon, the client's amygdala may activate too much, making it impossible for them to manage their stress response. This is because the amygdala activation shuts down the cortical thinking center (prefrontal cortex) of the brain. This is a frightening and out-of-control feeling that, for some clients, resembles the feeling of being traumatized, since trauma occurs when something terrible and too much happens without a person's consent.

Without a sense of control, there can be a feeling of re-traumatization that leads to increased avoidance of trauma reminders because the thoughts and feelings related to the trauma feel dangerous and unmanageable. When teaching clients the techniques described in this book it is recommended that pendulation and titration be used in tandem.

THE BRAIN ON PENDULATION AND TITRATION

Integrating pendulation and titration in trauma treatment approaches can change the brain in at least **four key ways**, all of which help clients reduce and better manage post-trauma symptoms.

Bottom-Up Re-Regulation After Pendulation:

1. **Fear Center (Amygdala):** Initial slight increased activation of the fear center during pendulation. After pendulation, bottom-up techniques can be practiced in order to de-activate the amygdala. Eventually, this can lead to greater regulation of, and sense of control over, the amygdala.

2. **Interoception Center (Insula):** Normalized insula activation. During pendulation, the client "feels into" the body and notices physical sensations. In PTSD, the insula is often dysregulated. When it is over-activated, there is emotional reactivity and outbursts (emotion under-modulation); when it is under-activated, there is dissociation and numbing. Both extremes are common in PTSD. With a more regulated insula, individuals improve interoception, and they experience fewer emotional outbursts and dissociative symptoms (including numbing).

Top-Down Re-Regulation After Pendulation:

3. **Thinking Center (Prefrontal Cortex):** Initial slight decreased activation of the thinking center during pendulation due to activation of the amygdala. After pendulation, top-down techniques can be practiced to activate and strengthen the prefrontal cortex. Increased activation of the thinking center of the brain leads to improved attention and concentration, self-awareness (ventromedial prefrontal cortex), and awareness of others (dorsolateral prefrontal cortex).

4. **Self-Regulation Center (Cingulate):** Initial slight decreased activation of the self-regulation center during pendulation due to activation of the amygdala. After pendulation, top-down techniques can be practiced to activate and strengthen the cingulate, resulting in improved self-regulation (including both thought and emotion regulation) and decision-making.

The Distress Thermometer

The distress thermometer is a tool often used in anger management and anxiety protocols. It can be extremely useful in trauma treatment as well, since traumatized clients' distress can become so overwhelming that it is difficult to think or function well.

It is recommended that the distress thermometer worksheet be completed with clients before beginning any pendulation (emotion induction) exercise. While the distress thermometer can represent any specific emotion (anger, sadness, fear, etc.), in this workbook it is presented simply as "distress." The clinician can modify this to be more specific when desired.

The distress thermometer is similar to the fear hierarchies commonly used in anxiety treatments, in which the clinician helps the client identify situations, places, people, memories, etc. that are distressing to varying degrees. However, unlike the fear hierarchies of anxiety treatments, the goal is not to have the client identify distressing situations to prepare them for later exposure to those situations. Rather, the objective of the distress thermometer is to help clients build self-awareness, noticing how it *feels* to be distressed, and to identify levels of distress that cause feelings of overwhelm. The points at which distress becomes overwhelming are referred to as clients' boiling and freezing points. These are the points at which the fear center (amygdala) fires so intensely that it hijacks the thinking center (prefrontal cortex), causing the client to dissociate, fight, flee, or freeze.

To help clients complete the distress thermometer, it is recommended that the clinician do the following:

1. Explain the purpose of the distress thermometer. Use the language here as a guided script, if desired.

    Before moving forward, I would like us to spend some time discussing the distress thermometer. The point of completing this worksheet is to identify things, people, situations, etc. that you find to be distressing, in order to become more aware of how distress manifests in your body and your mind. I will not try to make you do any of the things we discuss. Rather, this is just for us to better understand how you experience distress. The benefit of this exercise will be an improved self-awareness of how you experience distress, even at a subtle level. Once you are aware of even low level distress in your body and mind, you can intervene earlier to manage that stress response so that it does not overwhelm you!

2. Next, explain how the distress thermometer works.

    The distress thermometer goes from 0-100, where 0 stands for total relaxation and no distress at all, and 100 stands for the most distress possible. You can see that the numbers appear in increments of 10. I want you, with my help, to identify situations, people, places, or even memories that you would categorize as distressing at these different levels. You will write these examples to the right of the thermometer. It is okay if "total relaxation" is not something you prefer – we are not measuring what feels "good" or "bad;" rather, we are identifying what feels "distressing" versus "relaxing."

3. Begin by identifying a stressor that the client rates as 100. Next, identify a situation, place, or person that is not distressing at all (score of 0 on the thermometer). These are the client's upper and lower limits.

> **Keep in mind that a client's lower limit, which represents total relaxation, may not actually feel good or safe to the client, as some clients will not like the feeling of relaxation. This is okay, and how to work with this is explained later in this chapter.**

4. After identifying examples of the client's upper and lower limits, help the client identify a situation that falls roughly in the 50 range, and from there fill in the other number ranges as well as possible. Ideally, the client will be able to identify situations that fall at nearly every increment of 10 on the thermometer.

Distress Thermometer Worksheet

Identify situations, people, places, or memories that are distressing to varying degrees (0-100), and write them down next to the number that best represents how distressing you experience them to be. To the best of your ability, try to provide an example on every line (broken into increments of 10).

100 – Worst distress _____

90 – Severe distress _____

80 – Strong distress _____

70 – Moderate distress _____

60 – Mild distress _____

50 - Neutral _____

40 – Mild relaxation _____

30 – Moderate relaxation _____

20 – Strong relaxation _____

10 – Very strong relaxation _____

0 – Total relaxation _____

Identifying Boiling and Freezing Points

Once the client has completed the Distress Thermometer Worksheet, the next step is to help the client identify their "boiling" and "freezing" points. These are the points at which the client becomes overwhelmed and feels out of control. Common reactions to reaching a boiling or freezing point include dissociation, becoming spacey, blacking out, withdrawing (which could include refusing to speak or ending the session), or becoming agitated. Many clients will describe their boiling and freezing points as the point at which they lose [themselves], or lose [their] mind.

Being aware of a client's boiling and freezing points is critical. If a client engages in a trauma-focused intervention that involves going into detail about traumatic events, it is important to know the client's boiling (distress) point ahead of time in order to avoid re-traumatizing the client. Additionally, understanding a client's freezing point is important when practicing many of the bottom-up, amygdala de-activating (relaxation-inducing) exercises, since some clients will not feel safe when too relaxed.

To better help clients identify their freezing and boiling points, it is recommended that you introduce the following concepts. If desired, you can use the information below as a guided script that you can read:

1. Explain boiling and freezing points.

   Next, we are going to identify two things on this thermometer: your boiling point, and your freezing point. The boiling point is the number at which you begin to feel out of control and overwhelmed by distress. It is the place at which you feel incompetent to manage your stress response. Everyone's boiling point is different, just like water. Water boils at different temperatures depending on factors such as altitude, and our emotional boiling points vary depending on different factors as well. What is important is for you to know your own boiling point - the level of distress at which your stress level becomes unmanageable. In addition, we are going to identify your freezing point, if you have one. This is the point at which your relaxation becomes so uncomfortably high that it actually stresses you out. When this happens, you may feel restless or unsafe, and notice that your distress skyrockets. Not everyone has a freezing point, but if you do have one, it is important to know about it!

2. Help the client identify their boiling point.

   On your thermometer, you have several examples of things that cause you distress. At about what point would you say your distress starts to feel unmanageable or out of control? For instance, your example at level 50 was _____. When faced with this, do you feel able to manage your distress, meaning, do you feel able to calm yourself down with some effort? At what point on this thermometer does this become more difficult?

3. Help the client identify their freezing point.

   As your distress rises on the thermometer, your relaxation response lowers, and vice versa. At the very bottom of the thermometer, at 0, is an example of something that makes you feel totally relaxed. Some people can endure being at a zero, and like this feeling. Conversely, some people can endure being at a 100 without "losing their mind." For other people, however, it is not comfortable to be too relaxed, as it can make them feel anxious or unsafe. What is your experience of relaxation? Is there a point at which you feel too relaxed? If so, where would that be on the thermometer?

Your Boiling and Freezing Points

Now that you have completed the Distress Thermometer Worksheet, it can be helpful to identify your boiling point and your freezing point.

The boiling point is the number at which you begin to feel out of control and overwhelmed by distress. It is the level at which you feel unable to manage your stress response. Everyone's boiling point is different depending on the conditions. Just as water boils at different temperatures depending on factors such as altitude, an individual's emotional boiling point varies depending on different factors as well.

Your freezing point, on the other hand, is the point at which intense feelings of relaxation become too uncomfortable. For some people, being too relaxed actually stresses them out. While this may not apply to you (not everyone has a freezing point), it is important to know if you do have one.

Using the thermometer, with the help of your therapist, try to identify both your boiling point and your freezing point. By getting familiar with your emotional thermometer, you'll be able to better identify when and to what extent you feel distressed—and what you need to do at that time to help yourself.

100 – Worst distress _____

90 – Severe distress _____

80 – Strong distress _____

70 – Moderate distress _____

60 – Mild distress _____

50 - Neutral _____

40 – Mild relaxation _____

30 – Moderate relaxation _____

20 – Strong relaxation _____

10 – Very strong relaxation _____

0 – Total relaxation _____

Identifying Degrees of Freedom

Once a client has identified their boiling and freezing points, determining their degrees of freedom is straightforward. The space between the freezing point and the boiling point is referred to as a client's degrees of freedom. This is the ideal range in which you can effectively work with a client without disengagement or re-traumatization. One goal of trauma treatment is to help clients expand their degrees of freedom over time so that they can endure and manage a wider range of feelings, including higher levels of distress and relaxation.

Understanding the degrees of freedom is an important starting point for clients. To help clients recognize why the degrees of freedom is an indispensable concept for trauma recovery, it is recommended that the clinician do the following:

1. Explain the concept of degrees of freedom as you review their boiling and freezing points with them on their Distress Thermometer Worksheet.

   You were able to identify your boiling point as being here, at _____ (the higher number they identified), and your freezing point (if they have one) as being here, at _____ (the lower number they identified). The space in between these two numbers, this range, is referred to as your degrees of freedom, which is the space in which you feel in control, able to manage your feelings, and be present. This is the space in which most people feel secure and safe. Our goal in therapy is to work within this space and expand it gradually over time, so that we increase your degrees of freedom and ability to tolerate and manage more intense feelings of both stress and relaxation. Do you have any questions at this point? How do you feel about starting here, in this safe and secure place? For some clients, it can feel relieving to know that we will not be pushing too hard, too fast.

2. Next, you'll introduce the client to the concept of pendulation and titration.

   The way we expand degrees of freedom is through practicing techniques that cause slight feelings of relaxation or stress over time. These techniques may include mindfulness or relaxation exercises, or exercises meant to stimulate an emotion—such as my asking you to recall a time when you felt a certain emotion (such as anger or joy). When you begin to feel the relaxation or stress, whichever experience we are trying to create, I will work with you to help you regulate that experience so that it feels more manageable. As we step through these types of exercises, we will refer back to the distress thermometer frequently and I will check in with you repeatedly about your current level of stress or relaxation. The idea here is for you to learn the skills necessary to begin working with distressing thoughts, memories, emotions, or sensations in a way that feels manageable but also challenging.

Your Degrees of Freedom

Between your boiling point and freezing point (if you have one) is a space. This space is referred to as your degrees of freedom. Your degrees of freedom represent the space in which you feel in control, safe, able to manage your feelings, and stay connected to the present moment.

One goal of therapy is to work within this space and expand it gradually over time, so that you expand your degrees of freedom, and also expand your ability to tolerate and manage more intense feelings of both stress and relaxation.

The way to expand a person's degrees of freedom over time is through practicing techniques that cause slight feelings of relaxation or stress. The intent is not to overwhelm you with relaxation or stress, but rather to ease you into these feelings while maintaining a sense of safety and control.

The techniques a therapist may use can include mindfulness or relaxation exercises, or emotion induction exercises in which you are asked to recall a time when you felt a particular emotion (such as anger or joy). When you begin to feel relaxed or stressed, the therapist will work with you to help you regulate that experience so that it feels more manageable.

Taking a Temperature Reading

Self-awareness for those experiencing trauma can be difficult. Clients may become overwhelmed without initially realizing it. For that reason, it is important for clients to remain inside of their degrees of freedom during techniques that elicit feelings of distress or discomfort. However, many traumatized clients will find it difficult to know when they have exited the boundaries of their degrees of freedom, since trauma teaches clients to focus outward instead of inward. In order to help clients monitor and regulate their distress levels, it is recommended to have clients frequently "take a temperature reading," in which they quickly evaluate their level of distress while completing various techniques.

For example, if a client is asked to complete a largely bottom-up, diaphragmatic breathing exercise aimed at reducing the stress response, it is helpful to have the client check in with their distress level every 30 seconds or so as they adjust to the technique. This helps the client avoid crossing into their freezing point, where their level of relaxation becomes unsafe-feeling. While this may seem excessive and disruptive to the practice, it is critical for the client to learn how to monitor internal experiences and sensations that indicate distress in order to avoid becoming overwhelmed.

Learning how to monitor and manage distress is helpful, more broadly, since traumatized clients often find themselves triggered and unable to manage the thoughts, feelings, and sensations that accompany triggers.

A temperature reading can be taken by simply asking for a subjective units of distress (SUDS) score, just as in traditional anxiety treatment. Using the same numbers as those presented on the thermometer (0-100) ask the client, "What is your temperature now?" It can be helpful to have the client's completed thermometer on hand for the client to refer to as they identify what number or range on the thermometer they feel best represents their current distress level.

It is recommended that clinicians ask for a temperature reading before, after, and multiple times during a bottom-up, top-down, or horizontal technique. This helps ensure that the client does not reach their boiling or freezing points, and teaches them to turn their attention inward to check in with themselves.

During a temperature reading, if a client appears to be approaching their boiling point (upper limit on the thermometer), it is best to lower the distress using a stress response-reducing, amygdala de-activation technique. If the client instead appears to be approaching their freezing point (lower limit on the thermometer), it is recommended to stop the stress response-reducing technique or reduce its intensity in order to slow the activation of the parasympathetic (relaxation) response.

Taking Your Temperature

Just as putting on the proper clothing during inclement weather keeps you safe and comfortable, remaining inside your degrees of freedom will keep you safe as you practice therapy techniques. In order to do this, you have to know when you're becoming overwhelmed, which can be difficult until it is too late and you've already become triggered.

To help you monitor and regulate your distress level, your therapist will frequently encourage you to take a temperature reading, in which you'll be asked to identify your current level of distress on the thermometer you completed. The reason for this is to ensure that you are still within your degrees of freedom. Learning how to monitor and manage distress is helpful in life in general, since this skill can help you better manage the thoughts, feelings, and sensations that accompany triggers.

In order to take a temperature reading, your therapist will ask you to rate your current distress (usually while engaging in a therapy exercise) on the thermometer scale of 0-100, where 0 is no distress and 100 is the most distress you can imagine experiencing. It is likely that your therapist will ask you to take a temperature reading before, after, and during therapy exercises (such as deep breathing, while talking about distressing memories, etc.).

If you take your temperature and notice that you are approaching your boiling point (upper limit on the thermometer), it is best to disengage from the technique you were just engaged in, and lower your distress using a stress response-reducing technique. If you instead appear to be approaching your freezing point (lower limit on the thermometer), it is recommended that you stop the stress response-reducing technique or reduce its intensity in order to slow the activation of the relaxation response.

Locating Distress in the Body

It can be challenging for traumatized clients to recognize early indications of physical distress since traumatic experiences encourage external awareness (for safety), and because trauma can change a person's relationship with their body. This is especially true if the site of the traumatic event was the body. Individuals whose bodies have been traumatized may feel disconnected from the body, and unsafe or otherwise distressed when connected to the body. This may lead to a lack of awareness about what is occurring in the body, including sensations or experiences that indicate distress. These sensations may include rapid heart rate, shallow breathing, the feeling of butterflies in the stomach, etc.

In order to heal trauma, it is important for clients to reconnect with the body and learn how to feel, monitor, and modify internal experiences. This is sometimes referred to as "felt sense" in Peter Levine's somatic experiencing approach (Levine, 1997). This improved self-awareness helps clients identify, manage, and reduce the impact of trauma triggers. To help clients begin to reconnect with the body and notice physical indications of distress, follow the instructions on the handout, Distress in Your Body, on the next page. For sensory awareness techniques that can further help clients learn how to reconnect with the body, refer to the body-based tools presented in Chapter 6.

Distress in Your Body

To notice distress in your body, you first need to connect with it. Ask yourself the following questions to connect with the surface and internal sensations of your body. While you can feel into the surface sensations described below any time, it is recommended that you practice these exercises at times when you are *not* feeling distressed, so that you can begin to connect with the body in its natural state and gain a greater awareness of your body's sensations.

Surface Sensations

- **Air Flow:** "Is there anywhere on the surface of my body that I can feel air?" This might be wind while standing outside, or where the air meets the skin while sitting still. For a moment, be still and notice any air current you may feel on the surface of your body.

- **Pressure:** "Can I feel any pressure on the surface of my body?" Starting at the bottom of the body, with the feet, scan upward, noticing any pressure that may be present. It may be noticed, for instance, that there is pressure on your legs and backside if you are sitting down.

- **Sensations:** "Can I feel any sensations on the surface of my body?" External sensations may include tingling, itching, or other experiences.

- **Temperature:** "Can I feel the temperature of my body?" Starting at the bottom of the body, with the feet, scan upward, noticing the temperature of various regions of the body and noting how they differ (for instance, the feet may be cooler than the stomach).

Internal Sensations

- **Air Flow**: "Can I feel the air current flow into my body through my nose or mouth?" Instead of feeling the air on the surface of the skin, now notice how the air feels as it enters your body through your mouth or nose. Notice where, inside of your mouth or throat, the sensation of the air disappears and it flows down to your lungs.

- **Sensations:** "Can I feel any sensations on the inside of my body?" Internal sensations may include stomach rumbling, head pulsating, "butterflies," a buzzing feeling (which may indicate anxiety), or the feeling of a pounding heart.

- **Temperature:** "Can I feel the temperature inside my body?" To notice internal temperature, consider focusing on the abdomen area and inside the mouth, feeling into these areas and noticing feelings of warmth that might be present.

- **Tension:** "Can I detect any tension in my muscles?" Some areas of the body tend to hold tension, such as the neck, back, and jaw.

Next, check in to your body for the following sensations in order to detect physical indications of distress in your body. If you answer yes to some of the following questions, it is likely that you are experiencing distress or anxiety, as all of the following signal stress in the body.

Distress Questions

1. Do I feel pressure in my head?

2. Do I feel pounding in my head?

3. Do I feel like there is a tight band around my head?

4. Does my head feel hot?

5. Does my face feel hot?

6. Do the muscles around my eyes feel tense?

7. Does my jaw feel tense or tight, like I am clenching my teeth?

8. Is there a ringing in my ears?

9. Does it feel difficult to swallow?

10. Does my neck feel stiff or sore?

11. Do my shoulders feel stiff or sore?

12. Does my back feel stiff or sore?

13. Does my chest feel tight?

14. Do I feel pressure in my chest?

15. Is my heart pounding or beating fast?

16. Does it feel like it is difficult to take deep breaths right now?

17. Is my breathing fast and shallow?

18. Does my stomach feel like it is "in knots"?

19. Does my stomach hurt?

20. Does my stomach feel like it is dropping?

21. Do my hands or feet feel cold?

22. Do my hands or feet feel shaky?

23. Does any part of my body feel shaky?

The above are examples of how distress can impact the body. When you experience some of these sensations, it may mean that your body has entered the stress response. The more you experience these sensations, the higher your temperature will be on your distress thermometer. One way to assess your distress temperature is to check in with your body and notice whether you are experiencing these symptoms.

When you are under stress, it can be helpful to refer back to this list and check in with yourself, noticing which of the above you experience at those times. While these sensations can be very uncomfortable and aversive, it is important to recognize and acknowledge them when they arise so that you can learn to manage and reduce those sensations!

Noticing Distress in the Mind

In addition to noticing physical sensations that indicate distress, it can be helpful to also recognize thoughts that indicate stress. Oftentimes, the thoughts a client experiences during distress serve to worsen their anxiety. Thoughts experienced during distress may be both a cause of, and a result of, the distress. However, most of the time, these thoughts go undetected and the individual is unaware of the impact they may have on their distress level.

Helping clients tune in to some of the common thoughts that are produced during times of distress encourages them to think differently about these thoughts. Instead of fusing with the thoughts and assuming the thoughts reflect reality at that moment, the client can begin to view these thoughts simply as an indication of distress, and a sign that they need to actively manage and reduce that distress with techniques that promote activation of the relaxation response (parasympathetic nervous system).

By using the following handout, clients will gain the ability to notice common thoughts they experience while feeling distressed or overwhelmed.

Your Distressed Thoughts

Just as distress is stored in the body, it is stored in the mind, too. It is often the case that when we experience distress, our mind produces thoughts, even if we are unaware of them. These thoughts can cause our distress to worsen, and the distress in turn can produce even more intensely distressing thoughts! As this handout will show you, just because you have a thought doesn't make it a fact or true.

For example, imagine you have a friend who suffers from panic attacks. Whenever she starts to feel the physical sensations of panic, such as racing heart and chest tightening, her mind begins to interpret what is happening to her body. Her mind might tell her, "Oh my gosh, what is happening? Can you breathe? Oh my gosh, you cannot breathe!!!" Naturally, anyone who believes they cannot breathe is going to become *even more distressed*, so once she has that thought about not breathing, her anxiety skyrockets higher.

As her panic worsens, her thoughts become even more catastrophic and begin to spin out of control. Now, not only does she have thoughts about not being able to breathe, she begins thinking that she is dying. This makes her panic even worse (if you can imagine that to be possible). As you can tell, her thoughts play a role in her distress in that they can both result from her distress and also cause it. It can be a frustrating cycle, and one that she is not even consciously aware of.

To avoid this type of spiraling, it is important to recognize the thoughts you tend to experience when you become distressed. If you can learn how to do this, you can view your thoughts simply as indications or warning signals of distress—such as when you're driving and see a flashing yellow light that is telling you to slow down. This awareness puts you in the driver's seat, so you don't have to instantly believe these thoughts or react strongly to them. To begin noticing these thoughts, read and complete the following, and try to fill in the blanks with your own thoughts.

My Distressed Thoughts About Myself: When I become stressed or overwhelmed, I tend to think the following about myself...

1. _____

2. _____

3. _____

Examples of common thoughts individuals may experience about themselves during stressful times include...

1. I am always messing up.

2. I will never succeed/get this done.

3. I am so dumb!

4. What was I thinking?

5. I'm never going to be able to handle/fix this.

My Distressed Thoughts About Others: When I become stressed or overwhelmed, I tend to think the following about others...

1. _____

2. _____

3. _____

Examples of common thoughts individuals may experience about others during stressful times include...

1. He/She doesn't like me.

2. I'm done with him/her.

3. He/She thinks I'm crazy/an idiot/incompetent!

4. I wish they would leave me alone.

5. I don't like him/her.

My Distressed Thoughts About Situations: When I become stressed or overwhelmed, I tend to think the following about the situation I'm in...

1. _____

2. _____

3. _____

Examples of common thoughts individuals may experience about their situation during stressful times include...

1. I can't handle this situation.

2. Why is this happening?

3. I wish this would end.

4. I want to get out of this situation.

5. This is terrible/awful.

Pendulation Strategies

Once a client is able to identify their boiling and freezing points and degrees of freedom, and to recognize indications of distress that change their temperature, they are ready to begin practicing pendulation. As stated earlier in this chapter, pendulation is the intentional shifting between emotional regulation and dysregulation, or amygdala de-activation and activation, for the purpose of training clients how to regulate emotion and lower their temperature.

Pendulation is accomplished through emotion induction, top-down exercises in which the therapist asks the client to either 1) remember something that happened in the past that elicited a distinct emotion (joy, anger, etc.), or 2) imagine something happening that would elicit that emotion. Oftentimes, imaginal exposure asks clients to do the latter, in order to promote desensitization to feared situations (while trauma processing techniques may emphasize the former). Imaginal exposure is just one example of pendulation.

Depending on whether the goal is to activate or de-activate the amygdala, the therapist may choose to pendulate the client toward regulation or dysregulation. When clients pendulate toward dysregulation, they move toward their boiling or freezing points. In other words, they begin to challenge their comfort zones.

If a client becomes too close to their boiling or freezing point, the therapist can work to help them move more toward the center of their degrees of freedom, helping them to re-regulate their temperature. Four types of emotion inductions that can pendulate clients include fear, anger, happiness, and love. Example instructions for how to induce these emotions appear on the following handouts. Additionally, trauma-focused techniques, such as those used in prolonged exposure, trauma-focused CBT, EMDR, or cognitive processing therapy are examples of high-level, high-distress pendulation techniques. **It is recommended that clients master lower level distress pendulation techniques before progressing to trauma-focused methods.**

To integrate titration with pendulation, begin with emotion inductions that aim to just slightly increase or decrease amygdala activation (distress). In the examples on the following handouts, it is recommended to start with emotion inductions that elicit distress temperatures around 35. As clients are able to successfully and confidently down-regulate this level of distress, the therapist can incrementally induce more intense distress (titration), helping the client to learn how to down-regulate these higher levels of distress with bottom-down techniques.

Anger Induction

To induce feelings of anger, follow the instructions below, trying to imagine the situation vividly and in detail.

1. Bring your thoughts to a memory of something that happened recently that can bring up moderate feelings of anger for you when you think about it. The goal here is to remember an event that raises anger temperature to approximately a 35. Be careful not to choose an event that is too angering, as it may be triggering and lead you past your boiling point.

2. In one sentence, summarize the situation. For instance, you may say, "That time last week I got that speeding ticket," or "That customer service representative who was so rude."

3. State the sentence out loud if you are completing this during a therapy session, so that the therapist can interact with you and help you connect with this memory.

4. After identifying the anger-inducing memory, begin to bring this memory to mind, starting with the beginning. Identify:
   a. Who was there
   b. Where it was
   c. What was happening
   d. And why it was happening (if possible)

5. Next, recall the memory to the therapist as you remember it unfolding, including as much detail as possible.

6. As you recall the memory, the therapist may discuss it with you, asking you for additional information about what happened. As you discuss the memory with the therapist, include the following:

   a. How you felt at the time
   b. What you were thinking at the time
   c. How you feel now when you think about it
   d. And what you think about it now

7. Once you have connected with the memory, notice any sensations in your body that indicate distress (fast heart rate, shallow breathing, etc.) and note these to the therapist.

8. After you have identified what the anger feels like in your body as you discuss this memory, take a temperature reading of your current anger.

9. If your anger is under a 25, you may need to connect more closely with the memory or choose another memory in order to activate feelings of anger more effectively. If your anger distress approaches your boiling point (or passes it), begin to disengage from the memory in order to lower your distress level.

10. Once your anger level is above 25, but still at a manageable level, you are ready to perform a bottom-up technique to practice lowering your anger distress.

11. After some practice with pendulation, you may develop the ability to titrate your distress level upward, to a temperature above 35, and down-regulate it using the same process.

Fear Induction

To induce feelings of fear, follow the instructions below, trying to imagine the situation vividly and in detail.

1. Bring your thoughts to a memory of something that happened recently that can bring up moderate feelings of fear for you when you think about it. The goal here is to remember an event that raises fear temperature to approximately a 35. Be careful not to choose an event that is too fear-inducing, as it may be triggering and lead you past your boiling point.

2. In one sentence, summarize the situation. For instance, you may say, "That time I saw a spider" or "That time last week I almost got into an accident."

3. State the sentence out loud if you are completing this during a therapy session, so that the therapist can interact with you and help you connect with this memory.

4. After identifying the fear-inducing memory, begin to bring this memory to mind, starting with the beginning. Identify:
   a. Who was there
   b. Where it was
   c. What was happening
   d. And why it was happening (if possible)

5. Next, recall the memory to the therapist as you remember it unfolding, including as much detail as possible.

6. As you recall the memory the therapist may discuss it with you, asking you for additional information about what happened. As you discuss the memory with the therapist, include the following:

    a. How you felt at the time
    b. What you were thinking at the time
    c. How you feel now when you think about it
    d. And what you think about it now

7. Once you have connected with the memory, notice any sensations in your body that indicate distress (fast heart rate, shallow breathing, etc.) and note these to the therapist.

8. After you have identified what the fear feels like in your body as you discuss this memory, take a temperature reading of your current fear. If your fear is under a 25, you may need to connect more closely with the memory or choose another memory to activate feelings of fear more effectively. If your fear distress approaches your boiling point (or passes it), begin to disengage from the memory in order to lower your distress level.

9. Once your fear level is above 25, but still at a manageable level, you are ready to perform a bottom-up technique to practice lowering your fear distress.

10. After some practice with pendulation, you may develop the ability to titrate your distress level upward, to a temperature above 35, and down-regulate it using the same process.

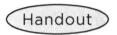
Love Induction

To induce feelings of love, follow the instructions below, trying to imagine the person or animal vividly and in detail.

1. Bring your thoughts to a person or animal that can bring up feelings of love when you think about them. The goal here is to remember an individual who, when you think of them, lowers your distress temperature.

2. Name the person or animal. For instance, you may say, "my sister," or "my dog."

3. Name the individual out loud if you are completing this during a therapy session, so that the therapist can interact with you and help you connect with this memory.

4. After identifying this individual, begin to bring them to mind, starting with the beginning. Next:
   a. State who they are
   b. Describe them
   c. State how you feel about them
   d. And say what you like most about them

5. Once you have connected with the thought of this individual, notice any sensations in your body that indicate your distress is lowering (slowing heart rate, deeper breathing, etc.) and note these to the therapist.

6. After you have identified what love feels like in your body as you discuss this individual, take a temperature reading of your current distress. If your distress is over a 25, you may need to connect more closely with the thought of this individual, or choose another individual you love, in order to activate feelings of love more effectively.

Happiness Induction

To induce feelings of happiness, follow the instructions below, trying to imagine the situation vividly and in detail.

1. Bring your thoughts to a memory that can bring up feelings of happiness when you think about it. The goal here is to remember an event that, when you think of it, lowers your distress temperature.

2. In one sentence, summarize the situation. For instance, you may say, "When I graduated from school," or "my birthday party last year."

3. State the sentence out loud if you are completing this during a therapy session, so that the therapist can interact with you and help you connect with this memory.

4. After identifying the happiness-inducing memory, begin to bring this memory to mind, starting with the beginning. Identify:

   a. Who was there
   b. Where it was
   c. What was happening
   d. And why it was happening (if possible)

5. Next, recall the memory to the therapist as you remember it unfolding, including as much detail as possible.

6. As you recall the memory the therapist may discuss it with you, asking you for additional information about what happened. As you discuss the memory with the therapist, include the following:

   a. How you felt at the time
   b. What you were thinking at the time
   c. How you feel now when you think about it
   d. And what you think about it now

7. Once you have connected with the memory, notice any sensations in your body that indicate your distress is lowering (slowing heart rate, deeper breathing, etc.) and note these to the therapist.

8. After you have identified what the happiness feels like in your body as you discuss this memory, take a temperature reading of your current distress. If your distress is over a 25, you may need to connect more closely with the memory or choose another memory in order to activate feelings of happiness more effectively.

How to Integrate Pendulation and Titration into Bottom-Up Techniques

The main goal of bottom-up techniques is to *go through the body*, bottom-up, to change the brain, especially the lower, subcortical areas of the brain including the amygdala. Sometimes the goal with bottom-up techniques is to activate or regulate specific areas of the brain (such as the insula to improve one's ability to feel into internal sensations). At other times, the goal may be to de-activate or reduce activation of a brain area (such as reducing amygdala activation to calm the stress response).

Most often, pendulation and titration techniques that increase distress (through anger or fear emotion inductions, for example) are paired with bottom-up techniques to achieve the goal of reducing distress (the stress response) and amygdala activation. While it may seem counterintuitive to induce distress with pendulation techniques when the ultimate goal is to reduce distress, this process can be more helpful for teaching clients emotional regulation than utilizing bottom-up techniques alone.

In the context of a therapy session, a client may feel more relaxed than usual. While their temperature read may still indicate distress, it is likely that with a safe and supportive therapist, their distress level is lower than it is in other situations. For a bottom-up technique to be most effective, however, a little bit of distress can be helpful, as it teaches the client how to reduce amygdala activation not just when it is low anyway, but when it is slightly elevated. Down-regulating the amygdala during times of distress is a difficult skill to develop, and a therapist's participation in helping a client to self-regulate in real-time can be immensely valuable.

To integrate pendulation and titration into bottom-up techniques, follow the instructions on the handout, Using Bottom-Up Techniques to Manage Distress.

Using Bottom-Up Techniques
to Manage Distress

To integrate pendulation and titration into bottom-up techniques, follow these instructions:

1. Identify the bottom-up technique, such as deep breathing, that will be used to self-regulate, or de-activate the amygdala in order to reduce distress.

2. Take a temperature reading, identifying your level of distress on the distress thermometer. Ask:
    a. Am I currently within my degrees of freedom?
    b. Am I close to my boiling or freezing point right now?

3. If you determine you are already too close to your boiling point, do not practice pendulation right now, as a negative emotion induction will likely push you past this boiling point.

4. If you determine you are already too close to your freezing point, do not engage in a bottom-up technique right now, as it will likely push you past your freezing point.

5. If your temperature is located safely within your degrees of freedom, now is a good time to practice pendulation.

6. To pendulate, follow the instructions for the anger or fear induction, as outlined on the Fear Induction and Anger Induction handouts.

7. When you have reached your target level of distress, let go of the thought of the memory you engaged with for the emotion induction, and begin to focus on the bottom-up technique you selected to practice.

8. As you practice the bottom-up technique, your therapist may occasionally interject and ask you to take a temperature read, to ensure you are either staying within your degrees of freedom or coping well with pushing those limits.

9. If you are practicing pendulation and bottom-up techniques on your own, consider setting an alarm to chime every minute or so, at which time you take a quick temperature reading of your distress to ensure that your distress level is still manageable.

PART II

Bottom-Up Tools

4

Focused Breathing Tools

Focused breathing is one of the first skills clinicians may teach clients who suffer from stress-based conditions. However, the reason for the effectiveness of these techniques is often not discussed. The breath can be used as a powerful tool to create change in both the brain and the body, as focused breathing is both a bottom-up and top-down approach. Let's take a closer look at this important tool.

Focused breathing exercises typically include the following two elements: 1) Diaphragmatic breathing, with an emphasis on elongating exhales, and 2) occupying the mind by focusing on counting, imagery, physical sensations in the body, or a mantra (such as a word or statement) while engaging in diaphragmatic breathing. Sometimes focused breathing exercises also involve holding the breath for a few seconds after fully inhaling or exhaling.

The top-down component of focused breathing is element 2 described above, in which clients focus on attending to a word, sensation, or image. This cognitive control activates cortical regions, changing the brain "from the top down." The bottom-up component of focused breathing is the activation of the vagus nerve, which is a result of breathing fully through the diaphragm (element one above).

VAGUS NERVE ACTIVATION AND THE BRAIN-BODY CONNECTION

The "brain-body connection" and "mind-body connection" are terms commonly used by clinicians, and for good reason, as the brain and body are intimately connected and influence one another bi-directionally. The brain-body connection provides a strong rationale for the use of focused breathing techniques to reverse the stress response and de-activate subcortical brain regions involved in anxiety and stress, such as the amygdala.

The vagus nerve is one way the brain is literally, physically connected to the body. This nerve is the 10th and largest cranial nerve, and runs from the medulla oblongata (subcortical region of the brain) and down the spine, at which point it branches off and wraps around several internal organs in the abdomen area. When activated, the vagus nerve initiates the relaxation response (parasympathetic nervous system arousal) in the body and sends the message to the brain that it is time to calm down. This process usually takes less than a minute.

While there are many ways to activate the vagus nerve, an easy and straightforward way to do this is through diaphragmatic breathing. When a client takes a deep breath through the diaphragm, the diaphragmatic wall expands downward as it fills with air. As the wall drops downward, it leads to a slight compression of the internal organs, around which the vagus nerve is wrapped. Compressing these organs leads to vagus nerve activation through pressing the nerve, which is like pressing a button.

When pressed, the vagus nerve activates and sends the signal back up to the spine and to the brain to relax. In order for breathing exercises to induce the relaxation response, it is critical for clients to breathe through the diaphragm, as opposed to shallower chest breathing.

Breathe Through the Diaphragm

It has become a cliché to say, "Take a deep breath!" However, when done correctly, breathing techniques can be extremely powerful. The reason diaphragmatic breathing can quickly calm the stress response, and amygdala activation, is because it activates the vagus nerve (see the following handout for a visual depiction of this nerve). When the vagus nerve is pressed, it quickly activates the parasympathetic nervous system and can reverse the stress response, making the individual feel calmer and more in control. To ensure clients are breathing through the diaphragm, refer to the poses recommended in Tool 4-3.

Vagus Nerve Activation Through the Breath

The breath is a very powerful tool that can reverse the stress response and activate the relaxation response in both the body and the brain. However, to achieve the relaxation response through the breath, it is critical to engage in *diaphragmatic breathing* (breathing deeply through the diaphragm as opposed to shallow chest breathing). This type of deep breathing is effective at reducing the stress response, and the areas of the brain involved in stimulating the stress pathway, because it activates the vagus nerve (shown below). The vagus nerve is the largest cranial nerve, running from the brain down the spinal cord, and then wrapping around several internal organs.

When activated, the vagus nerve activates the parasympathetic nervous system, known as the relaxation response, and calms the signals from the brain that activate the stress response and make us feel nervous, panicked, and jittery. But, in order to activate the vagus nerve, we must breathe through the diaphragm. Here's why!

When we breathe through the diaphragm, it expands. As it fills with air, the wall of the diaphragm expands downward, into the abdomen area. As it continues to expand, it begins to compress the internal organs lying below the diaphragm, slightly pressing on them.

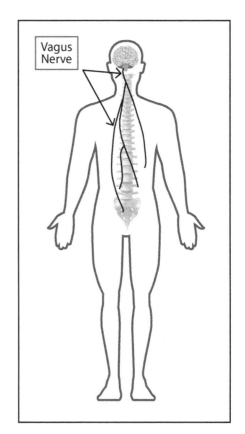

Wrapped around all of these organs is the vagus nerve. By compressing the organs, the vagus nerve also becomes compressed. When this happens, it is as though we are pushing a "relaxation button," by pressing on the vagus nerve. The result is that the vagus nerve activates, sending the signal back up the spine and to the brain to relax.

This process is extremely fast, and only takes about 45 seconds! We have already built inside of us the ability to induce the relaxation response very quickly – this a tremendous gift that we too often overlook!

The Brain on Focused Breathing

Focused breathing techniques change the brain in at least **four** key ways. These brain changes help clients reduce and better manage post-trauma symptoms, including arousal and reactivity, trauma re-experiencing, and negative alterations in cognition and mood symptoms.

1. **Fear Center (Amygdala):** Decreased activation of the fear center. De-activation of this area helps to reduce reactivity when trauma triggers arise. It also reduces the stress response (sympathetic nervous system arousal) and results in a decrease in arousal and reactivity symptoms, such as hypervigilance, feeling on guard, etc.

2. **Interoception Center (Insula):** Reduced insula over-reactivity. In PTSD, the insula is often dysregulated. When it is over-activated, there is emotional reactivity and outbursts (emotion under-modulation); when it is under-activated, there is dissociation and numbing. Both extremes are common in PTSD. With a more regulated insula, individuals improve interoception, and they experience fewer emotional outbursts and dissociative symptoms (including numbing).

3. **Thinking Center (Prefrontal Cortex):** Increased activation of the thinking center of the brain, including areas involved in attention and concentration, self-awareness (ventromedial prefrontal cortex) and awareness of others (dorsolateral prefrontal cortex).

4. **Self-Regulation Center (Cingulate):** Increased activation of the self-regulation center of the brain, which is involved in thought and emotion regulation and decision-making.

Your Brain on Focused Breathing

Focused Breathing techniques change the brain in **four** important and useful ways:

1. **Less activation in fear center (amygdala) of the brain:**
   ° Reduces how strongly you react to trauma triggers
   ° Reduces the stress response and increases the relaxation response
   ° Decreases hypervigilance and the feeling of "always being on guard"

2. **Less over-reactivity of the interoception center (insula) of the brain:**
   ° Reduces how strongly you react to trauma triggers
   ° Reduces anger and other emotional outbursts
   ° Reduces dissociation
   ° Reduces numbing

3. **Increased activation of the thinking center (prefrontal cortex):**
   ° Improves concentration and attention
   ° Improves self-awareness
   ° Improves social awareness and "social intelligence"

4. **Increased activation of the self-regulation center (cingulate):**
   ° Improves emotion regulation and self-regulation
   ° Improves decision-making

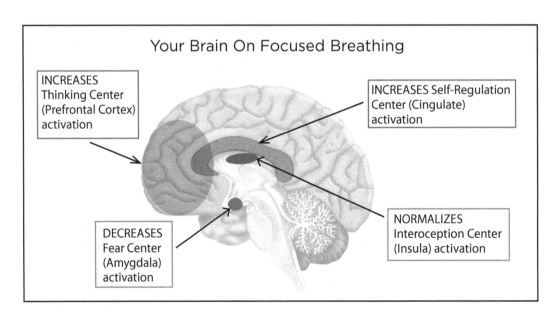

Diaphragmatic Breathing

Symptoms Addressed

- Emotional awareness and regulation
- Concentration and attention
- Dysregulated interoception
  (the ability to feel into internal states of one's body)
- Stress response
- DSM-5® PTSD arousal and reactivity symptoms

Diaphragmatic breathing, or abdominal breathing, is a type of deep breathing believed to be a healthy alternative to the shallow, chest breathing commonly associated with anxiety and panic. In diaphragmatic breathing, an individual breathes through their diaphragm, a muscle located between the chest and abdominal cavities, below the rib cage and above the belly button. Diaphragmatic breathing is a widely supported anxiety and stress management technique that is believed to induce a state of relaxation and reduce autonomic system arousal.

DIAPHRAGMATIC BREATHING TIPS

- Instruct clients to breathe through the diaphragm, as opposed to engaging in shallow chest breathing.
- This exercise can be completed standing, lying down, or sitting.
- If participants feel comfortable closing their eyes during this practice, this is recommended. If not, they may find a place on the floor to gently focus their eyes on.
- It is recommended that this technique be practiced for approximately 5 minutes, multiple times per day.

KEY RESEARCH FINDINGS

- Reduced stress and anxiety (Fried, 1993; Rowe, 1999; Wehrenberg, 2008)
- Increased quality of life (Hagman et al., 2011)
- Reduced blood pressure and improved self-regulation (Russell, 2014)
- Reduced inflammation (Rosas-Ballina et al., 2011)

Diaphragmatic Breathing

Strike a Pose

To ensure you are breathing through the diaphragm, thereby activating the vagus nerve (which then stimulates the relaxation response in the body and the brain), consider assuming these poses:

1. Lay-Z-Boy Pose: Sitting or lying down, place your hands behind your head, elbows facing out. If you are sitting in a chair, lean back slightly, expanding your rib cage a bit. Now begin taking long, deep, full breaths. As you do this, you will notice your rib cage expanding with each inhale.

2. Totem Pole Pose: Sitting upright in a chair, straighten your back and bring your shoulders down and back. Now place your hands under your thighs so that you are sitting on your hands. In this position begin taking long, deep, full breaths. As you do this, you will notice that it is difficult to move your chest, and the breath will feel as though you're blowing up a balloon in your lower stomach area.

3. Hands-On Pose: Sitting upright in a chair or lying down, place your left hand on your chest and your right hand on your stomach, just above your belly button. Begin taking long, deep, slow breaths in and out. As you breathe deeply, intentionally try to breathe in such a way that your left hand remains still, and your right hand moves upward/outward with each inhale, and downward/inward with each exhale. When you see your right hand moving more than your left, it is a good indication that you are breathing through your diaphragm.

Instructions

Sit or lie in a comfortable position.

Assume one of the above poses to ensure you are breathing through your diaphragm.

Begin to inhale slowly through your nose, allowing your diaphragm to fill with air.

As you exhale, breathe through your nose, and allow the air to exit your diaphragm slowly. If possible, elongate the exhale so that it is longer than your inhale.

Noticing what it feels like in your body to breathe, continue diaphragmatic breathing for approximately 2-3 minutes. As you repeat this practice over time, you may increase it to five, or even 10 minutes. Consistent practice over time, even if the practice is just for a few minutes, will be necessary to begin changing the brain.

If during this practice you begin to feel lightheaded, or start hyperventilating, stop the practice immediately until the symptoms subside. When you resume the practice, try inhaling and exhaling slightly less deeply/fully, and slow the pace of the breath a bit.

To end this practice, relax your hands at your sides and take two deep, diaphragmatic breaths.

Ocean Breath

```
Symptoms Addressed

• Emotional awareness and regulation
• Concentration and attention
• Dysregulated interoception
• Stress response
• DSM-5 PTSD arousal and reactivity symptoms
```

When practicing diaphragmatic breathing, it can sometimes be difficult to breathe slowly, elongating the breath, due to running out of breath too quickly during the exhale. This common problem can be addressed by utilizing Ocean Breath, which helps to lengthen the breath, intensifying the relaxation response. This is accomplished by constricting the epiglottis, as instructed on the Ocean Breath Handout.

OCEAN BREATH TIPS

- Instruct clients to breathe through the diaphragm as they practice Ocean Breath.
- If a client begins to feel lightheaded or dizzy, recommend that they stop Ocean Breath or take slightly more shallow breaths.
- This exercise can be completed standing, lying down, or sitting.
- If participants feel comfortable closing their eyes during this practice, this is recommended. If not, they may find a place on the floor to gently focus their eyes on.
- It is recommended that this technique be practiced for approximately 5 minutes, multiple times per day.

KEY RESEARCH FINDINGS

- Reduced stress and anxiety (Fried, 1993; Rowe, 1999; Wehrenberg, 2008)
- Increased quality of life (Hagman et al., 2011)
- Reduced blood pressure and improved self-regulation (Russell, 2014)
- Reduced inflammation (Rosas-Ballina et al., 2011)

Ocean Breath

Sit, lie, or stand in a comfortable position.

If you have difficulty breathing slowly and run out of breath too soon while exhaling, try this Ocean Breath practice. Gently open your mouth and begin breathing long, slow deep breaths in and out through the mouth.

As you inhale through the mouth, feel at the back of your throat where the cool air makes contact with the throat and tongue. Now, gently constrict the muscles in the epiglottis area by bringing the back part of your tongue up and back slightly.

When you constrict these muscles and exhale, it will create a fog breath effect, similar to when you huff on a pair of sunglasses to clean them, or huff to fog up a mirror. You will also notice a sound as you do this, like white noise.

Now, still constricting your epiglottis as you breathe through the diaphragm, gently close your mouth and breathe instead through your noise. This will produce a sound similar to the ocean (hence the name, Ocean Breath) as it helps you to exhale more slowly.

Continue Ocean Breath for approximately five minutes, attending to the sensations of breathing and the sound of your breath.

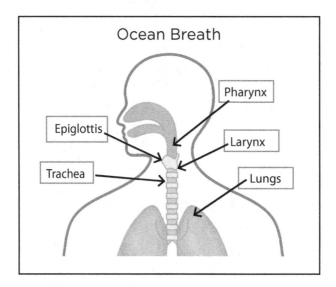

The Five-Count Breath

```
Symptoms Addressed

  • Emotional awareness and regulation
  • Concentration and attention
  • Dysregulated interoception
  • Intrusive memories
  • Stress response
  • DSM-5 PTSD arousal and reactivity symptoms
```

The Five-Count Breath is a focused breathing technique in which clients direct their attention to the breath, counting to five as they inhale, then holding the breath for five counts, and then exhaling for five counts. As they engage in this sequence, they concurrently visualize these counts as forming the outline of an upside-down triangle, such that on the inhale they visualize a line moving upward and to the left, then as they hold the breath they visualize a line going straight across from left to right, and then on the exhale they visualize the line moving down and to the left, connecting at the point where the line first began. This sequence is repeated for several minutes. The Five-Count Breath should be practiced in conjunction with diaphragmatic breathing.

FIVE-COUNT BREATH TIPS

- Instruct clients to breathe through the diaphragm, as opposed to engaging in shallow chest breathing.
- This exercise can be completed standing, lying down, or sitting.
- If participants feel comfortable closing their eyes during this practice, this is recommended. If not, they may find a place on the floor to gently focus their eyes on.
- It is recommended that this technique be practiced for approximately five minutes, multiple times per day.

KEY RESEARCH FINDINGS

- Reduced stress and anxiety (Fried, 1993; Rowe, 1999; Wehrenberg, 2008)
- Increased quality of life (Hagman et al., 2011)
- Reduced blood pressure and improved self-regulation (Russell, 2014)
- Reduced inflammation (Rosas-Ballina et al., 2011)
- May reduce intrusive memories (Kemps, Tiggemann, & Christianson, 2008)

The Five-Count Breath

Sit, lie, or stand in a comfortable position.

Begin to practice diaphragmatic breathing, focusing first on the sensations of the breath. If you would like to add structure to your breathing practice and give your mind something to focus on as you breathe, it is recommended to try the Five-Count Breath.

To begin the Five-Count Breath, inhale slowly and fully for a count of five.

Next, hold your breath for a count of five, counting at the same pace.

Finally, begin to exhale slowly and fully for a count of five.

Now, as you continue this sequence, begin to concurrently visualize these counts as forming the outline of an upside-down triangle (see below image).

On each inhale visualize a line moving upward and to the left.

When you hold the breath, visualize a line going straight across from left to right.

As you exhale visualize the line moving down and to the left, connecting at the point where the line first began.

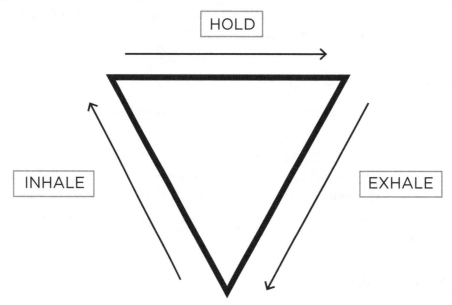

Repeat this sequence for approximately five minutes, bringing your mind back to the counting sequence when it wanders.

Balanced Brain Breath

Symptoms Addressed

- Emotional awareness and regulation
- Concentration and attention
- Dysregulated interoception
- Stress response
- DSM-5 PTSD arousal and reactivity symptoms

At any given time, one nostril is more constricted than the other. In other words, there is always one nostril that is a bit more "stuffy" than the other (more open) one (Hasegwa & Kern, 1977). Throughout the day, each nostril takes turns being open or stuffy, and this is related to brain activity. When the left nostril is open and dominant, for instance, the opposite (right) hemisphere of the brain is more active, and vice versa (Block, Arnott, Quigley, & Lynch, 1989). In order to balance activation of the two hemispheres of the brain, one can purposefully alternate breathing through each nostril, thereby activating each hemisphere and alternating dominance of hemispheric activity.

BALANCED BRAIN BREATH TIPS

- Instruct clients to breathe through the diaphragm as they engage in Balanced Brain Breath, as opposed to engaging in shallow chest breathing.
- This exercise can be completed standing, lying down, or sitting.
- If participants feel comfortable closing their eyes during this practice, this is recommended. If not, they may find a place on the floor to gently focus their eyes on.
- It is recommended that this technique be practiced for approximately five minutes, multiple times per day.

KEY RESEARCH FINDINGS

- Increased parasympathetic nervous system activation (relaxation response) (Upadhyay et al., 2008)
- Improved balance between the two hemispheres of the brain (Stancak & Kuna, 1994)
- Improves concentration (Telles, Singh, & Puthige, 2013)
- Reduced inflammation (Rosas-Ballina et al., 2011)

Balanced Brain Breath

Sit in a comfortable position.

Begin to practice diaphragmatic breathing, focusing first on the sensations of the breath.

Next, begin to engage in the Five-Count Breath, slowing inhaling, holding, and exhaling for counts of five. Repeat this sequence for a couple of breaths.

To begin Balanced Brain Breath, bring your right hand up to your face after inhaling, as you hold the breath for five counts. While holding the breath, press lightly on your right nostril with your right thumb, gently closing off that nostril.

Now exhale slowly and fully for a count of five, exhaling only through the left nostril.

Continuing to close off your right nostril, begin to inhale through your left nostril for a count of five. At the end of the inhale, hold your breath for a count of five just as before.

As you hold your breath, release your right nostril by removing your thumb, and now begin to lightly compress your left nostril with your right ring finger, closing it off. Exhale through the right nostril for a count of five.

Continuing to close off your left nostril, begin to inhale through your right nostril for a count of five. At the end of the inhale, hold your breath for a count of five just as before.

Once again, as you hold your breath, alternate nostril constriction, now pressing on the right nostril again and repeating the sequence described above.

Repeat this sequence for approximately five minutes, bringing your mind back to the counting sequence when it wanders.

Alternate Nostril Breathing

5-5-8-2 Breath

```
Symptoms Addressed
─────────────────────────────────────────
  • Emotional awareness and regulation
  • Concentration and attention
  • Dysregulated interoception
  • Stress response
  • DSM-5 PTSD arousal and reactivity symptoms
```

The 5-5-8-2 Breath is a focused breathing technique in which clients direct their attention to the breath, counting to five as they inhale, then holding the breath for five counts, and then exhaling for eight counts, and then holding for another two counts. This sequence is repeated for several minutes. The 5-5-8-2 Breath is like the Five-Count Breath, except with an elongation of exhalation and a brief holding of the breath after exhalation. Extended exhalations are often preferable, as they emphasize longer parasympathetic (relaxation response) activation. During inhalation, the sympathetic nervous system becomes slightly activated; during exhalation, the parasympathetic nervous system becomes slightly activated, which is why longer exhales are encouraged in diaphragmatic breathing techniques.

5-5-8-2 BREATH TIPS

- Instruct clients to breathe through the diaphragm, as opposed to engaging in shallow chest breathing.
- This exercise can be completed standing, lying down, or sitting.
- If participants feel comfortable closing their eyes during this practice, this is recommended. If not, they may find a place on the floor to gently focus their eyes on.
- It is recommended that this technique be practiced for approximately five minutes, multiple times per day.

KEY RESEARCH FINDINGS

- Reduced stress and anxiety (Fried, 1993; Rowe, 1999; Wehrenberg, 2008)
- Increased quality of life (Hagman et al., 2011)
- Reduced blood pressure and improved self-regulation (Russell, 2014)
- Reduced inflammation (Rosas-Ballina et al., 2011)

5-5-8-2 Breath

Since the parasympathetic nervous system becomes slightly activated on the exhale, longer exhales are encouraged in diaphragmatic breathing techniques. This practice will help you achieve those desirable longer exhales.

Sit or lie in a comfortable position.

Begin to practice diaphragmatic breathing, focusing first on the sensations of the breath.

To begin the 5-5-8-2 Breath, inhale slowly and fully for a count of five.

Next, hold your breath for a count of five, counting at the same pace.

Then, begin to exhale slowly and fully for a count of eight.

Finally, hold the breath briefly, for a count of two.

Repeat this sequence for approximately 5 minutes, bringing your mind back to the counting sequence when it wanders.

Body Breath

Symptoms Addressed

- Emotional awareness and regulation
- Concentration and attention
- Dysregulated interoception
- Intrusive memories
- Stress response
- DSM-5 PTSD arousal and reactivity symptoms

This technique combines several elements which, together, can address multiple trauma symptoms. First, the Body Breath practice incorporates interoceptive training, helping the individual become more aware of their internal states through feeling into the heart and other areas of the body. Second, this diaphragmatic breathing exercise includes visual imagery, which activates the right hemisphere of the brain. This is important, as it is common for traumatized individuals to show right hemisphere *under-activation* (and, as a result, perhaps lose their sense of creativity, experience spiritual crisis, and feel overwhelmed by intrusive thoughts produced by the left hemisphere). Finally, this breathing technique includes a positive emotion induction (love), which aims to reduce feelings of fear associated with the activation of the amygdala (fear brain).

BODY BREATH TIPS

- Instruct clients to breathe through the diaphragm as they engage in Body Breath, as opposed to engaging in shallow chest breathing.
- This exercise can be completed standing, lying down, or sitting.
- If participants feel comfortable closing their eyes during this practice, this is recommended. If not, they may find a place on the floor to gently focus their eyes on.
- It is recommended that this technique be practiced for approximately 5-15 minutes per day.
- During the emotion induction portion of this exercise, in which the participant chooses a person or pet to bring to mind, they should try to focus on a person or pet that elicits simple and pure feelings of love. Try to refrain from choosing a person, for instance, who elicits mixed feelings, such as love and anger.

KEY RESEARCH FINDINGS

- Reduced stress and anxiety (Fried, 1993; Rowe, 1999; Wehrenberg, 2008)
- Increased quality of life (Hagman et al., 2011)
- Reduced blood pressure and improved self-regulation (Russell, 2014)
- Reduced inflammation (Rosas-Ballina et al., 2011)
- May reduce intrusive memories (Kemps, Tiggemann, & Christianson, 2008)

Body Breath Script

Begin to close your eyes and draw your attention to the breath, beginning to breathe through the diaphragm. Now bring an image of your heart into your mind's eye. Visualize your heart as it is in your chest, and feel into this area of the body.

Develop a clear vision of what your heart looks like, and try to focus on it, noticing its size, shape, color, and texture. In this exercise, your heart, and other areas of the body, can look any way you wish. It does not have to appear "realistic."

Now, still visualizing your heart, begin to imagine that the air you are breathing is flowing through the heart, such that when you inhale, it flows through the heart in one direction, and as you exhale, it flows back through the heart in the other direction. The color of the breath may be white, or any other color you prefer.

Continue breathing, fully in and fully out, taking long, deep breaths, and as you do this keep the vision of your heart in your mind, watching the breath flow through the heart with each inhale and exhale.

As you continue to breathe through the heart, bring into your mind the thought of a person, or a pet, that elicits strong feelings of love. Identify this person or animal by name in your mind, connect with them mentally, and allow yourself to feel the love you have for them. Connect with that love.

Staying connected to that love, gently let go of the thought of that special person or animal, holding on to the love you feel for them. Imagine this love is a color, perhaps purple, or any color that feels right.

Imagine this love is flowing through the heart along with the breath. As you breathe through the heart, the love flows through the heart along with the breath. Visualize both colors flowing up through the heart with each inhale, and back down through the heart with each exhale. Continue breathing love through your heart for a few moments, continuing to visualize your heart, breath, and emotion.

Next, begin to shift your focus away from your heart and onto your brain, visualizing your brain inside of your head and feeling into this area of the body. Imagine that you are breathing the love and air through the brain, once again watching the colors flow up through the brain with each inhale, and back down the brain with each exhale. Continue this visualization for several breaths.

Finally, shift your attention to your stomach, visualizing your stomach inside of your abdomen area and feeling into this area of the body. Imagine that you are breathing the love and air through the stomach, watching the colors flow up through the stomach with each inhale, and back down the stomach with each exhale. Continue this visualization for several breaths.

Moving Breath

> ## *Symptoms Addressed*
>
> - Emotional awareness and regulation
> - Concentration and attention
> - Dysregulated interoception
> - Stress response
> - DSM-5 PTSD arousal and reactivity symptoms

Moving Breath combines movement with diaphragmatic breathing, simultaneously creating a calming and energizing experience. This approach to focused breathing is often preferred by children, adolescents, or adults with a history of ADHD-hyperactive/impulsive type, as it does not require the body to be still as with other breathing techniques. During Moving Breath, the individual engages in diaphragmatic breathing, breath-counting, and physical movement (see Moving Breath Handout for instructions), all at the same time.

MOVING TIPS

- Instruct clients to breathe through the diaphragm as they engage in Moving Breath, as opposed to engaging in shallow chest breathing.
- If possible, have clients complete this exercise lying down. Lying down is preferable because, when this technique is executed while lying on the back, it can improve lower rib mobility and discourages engagement of the neck muscles while breathing. This, in turn, trains participants to become better at breathing through the diaphragm (which requires good lower rib mobility and minimal tension of neck muscles).
- If it is not feasible to lie down, this practice can be done standing. Moving Breath will be executed slightly differently depending on the participant's position.
- Unlike other breathing exercises, it is recommended that eyes be kept open during this practice, gently gazing downward.
- It is recommended that this technique be practiced for approximately 5 minutes per day, multiple times per day.

KEY RESEARCH FINDINGS

- Reduced stress and anxiety (Fried, 1993; Rowe, 1999; Wehrenberg, 2008)
- Increased quality of life (Hagman et al., 2011)
- Reduced blood pressure and improved self-regulation (Russell, 2014)
- Reduced inflammation (Rosas-Ballina et al., 2011)

Moving Breath

Lie down on a comfortable surface, with your head flat and arms resting to your side, palms up. If possible place a pillow under your knees to remove pressure from your lower back.

Before starting the practice, direct your gaze to a spot directly above your eyes, perhaps on the ceiling, for the duration of the exercise.

Begin Moving Breath by slowing inhaling for a count of five through the diaphragm. As you inhale slowly raise your arms toward the sky, with your palms up.

Now begin to exhale slowly for a count of eight, making a large circle with your arms, grazing the floor as you lower your arms back down to your sides.

Continue this movement sequence for several breaths.

Other Ways to Activate the Vagus Nerve

While using the breath to activate the vagus nerve is fast and effective, there are also many other ways to "go to vagus," some of which are practices people enjoy integrating into their lives. These commonly overlooked vagus-activation methods can be informally or formally practiced as a matter of habit, to achieve small parasympathetic boosts as needed.

Ways to Activate the Vagus Nerve

While diaphragmatic breathing is one of the fastest, easiest techniques to practice to activate the vagus nerve, there are several other ways to "go to vagus." Here are four additional ways you can activate the vagus nerve!

Do yoga. Begin by sitting on the floor, with your back straight and your legs stretched out in front of you. Next, gently move your knees up toward your abdomen. As they approach your abdomen, still keeping your back straight, allow your knees to begin to separate and point outward, entering butterfly pose with your heels near your pelvis. Now, slowly move your hands behind, helping you to gently lie down, flat on your back.

If preferable, you may also lie inclined by putting a pillow under your head, neck, and back. As you lie down, focus on relaxing your shoulders, moving them downward away from your ears, and slowly lift your arms above your head, allowing them to rest above you. Finally, begin to take deep breaths, which will activate the vagus nerve when you are in this position.

Wear a relaxing eye pillow. When you wear an eye pillow, it gently presses on your eyeballs, and this pressure activates the oculocardiac reflex. Twelve eye muscles, which together hold your eyeballs in place, regulate the oculocardiac reflex. When pressure is applied to these muscles, they communicate with the vagus nerve, communicating a signal to activate the relaxation response (Barrett, 2013).

An alternative way to activate the oculocardiac reflex is to practice eye convergence and divergence. This can be done by holding one finger, pointing upward, in front of your nose, focusing your eyes on it (convergence), and then watching your finger as you move it away from your nose (divergence).

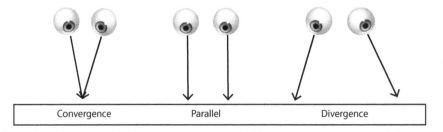

Sing: Singing activates the vagus nerve, as it tenses the muscles in the back of the throat and gets the vagal pump moving. In addition to singing, humming and chanting can also activate the vagus nerve (Vickhoff et al., 2013).

Pray. Prayer – including rosary reading - and other types of compassion meditation, such as Loving-Kindness Meditation, activate the vagus nerve by increasing heart rate variability (HRV) [Bernardi et al., 2001]. HRV refers to the variation in time intervals between heartbeats. When inhaling, heart rate speeds up a bit, whereas when exhaling, heart rate slows. This means there is variation in the time interval between each heartbeat. Generally speaking, high HRV is associated with low stress and anxiety, and low HRV is considered an indicator of high stress. With prayer, connecting with feelings of love and gratitude toward ourselves, others, and a higher power can activate the relaxation response through increasing HRV.

Power Breath

┌───┐
│ ### *Symptoms Addressed*
│
│ • Concentration and attention
│ • Energy
│ • Stress response
└───┘

Most breathing techniques, including diaphragmatic breathing exercises, aim to reduce the stress response, de-activate the amygdala, and activate the relaxation response as quickly as possible. However, the breath can also be used to energize and stimulate. Vigorous, rapid breathing exercises such as Power Breath (also called Bhastrika Breath or Bellows Breath) actually slightly *increase* the stress response in the short-term (in a way similar to exercise), but can be extremely beneficial because they improve concentration, increase energy, decrease stress, and lead to longer-term, sustained increased activation of the relaxation response.

POWER BREATH TIPS

- Have clients consult with their physician before practicing Power Breath, especially if they are pregnant or suffer from a medical condition.
- This technique is not recommended for individuals suffering from panic disorder.
- If participants become lightheaded while practicing Power Breath, instruct them to slow down or deepen their breathing, or stop the exercise.
- This exercise can be practiced standing up or sitting down.
- The eyes can be kept open during this exercise if preferred.
- It is recommended that this breathing technique be practiced in increments of 30 breaths, multiple times per day.

KEY RESEARCH FINDINGS

- Improved concentration (Shavanani & Udupa, 2003)
- Increased energy (Veerabhadrappa et al., 2011)
- Increased oxygen intake (Couser, Martinez, & Celli, 1992)
- Reduced stress response (Veerabhadrappa et al., 2011)

Power Breath

Sit in a chair with your spine vertical, or stand up straight to practice this exercise.

To begin, keeping your back straight, bend your elbows and lift your hands up to your shoulders, palms closed and facing out (see Power Breath diagram below). Take one slow, deep breath in and out.

As you begin to slowly inhale again, raise your arms up straight up and slowly open your palms, completing inhalation when your arms are completely extended and palms are open.

Now begin to exhale slowly, lowering your arms back to the original position as you exhale.

Repeat this sequence a couple of times slowly, inhaling as you lift your arms, and exhaling as you lower your arms.

Next, begin to breathe faster, moving your arms faster as well.

Continue speeding up your breath until you are inhaling for no longer than about one second, and exhaling for the same amount of time.

Continue this movement sequence for 30 breaths, multiple times per day.

5

Body-Based Tools

INTEROCEPTION

Interoception is the ability to "feel inside" the body and to be aware of internal states. Interoception can include things like detecting hunger, but it also includes awareness of internal states that tell individuals which emotions they are feeling. For instance, a client may notice their heart beating faster (an interoceptive ability), which may be an indication of stress or anxiety. With improved interoceptive abilities, clients become able to feel into their bodies in order to know how they feel, both physically and emotionally! Without interoceptive abilities, it is difficult to identify emotions, and even harder to regulate them.

THE BRAIN ON INTEROCEPTIVE EXPOSURE

Interoceptive exposure techniques change the brain in **five** key ways, all of which help clients reduce and better manage post-trauma symptoms.

1. **Fear Center (Amygdala):** Decreased activation of the fear center. De-activation of this area helps to reduce reactivity when trauma triggers arise. It also reduces the stress response (sympathetic nervous system arousal) and results in a decrease in arousal and reactivity symptoms, such as hypervigilance, feeling on guard, etc.

2. **Interoception Center (Insula):** Normalized insula activation. In PTSD, the insula is often dysregulated. When it is over-activated, there is emotional reactivity and outbursts (emotion under-modulation); when it is under-activated, there is dissociation and numbing. Both extremes are common in PTSD. With a more regulated insula, individuals improve interoception, and they experience fewer emotional outbursts and dissociative symptoms, including numbing.

3. **Memory Center (Hippocampus):** Increased activation of the memory center of the brain (hippocampus). This activation helps remind the individual that they are safe in the present moment, and it is involved in the extinction of fear responses when trauma triggers arise. The increased competence the individual experiences in managing negative memories can reduce the avoidance symptoms of PTSD.

4. **Strengthened connectivity:** Connections running from the emotion regulation and thinking areas of the brain (prefrontal cortex and anterior cingulate cortex) down to the fear brain (amygdala) become stronger, making it easier to down-regulate and control negative emotions. This also results in an enhanced ability to manage trauma triggers and cope with painful memories without being overwhelmed.

5. **Weakened connectivity:** Bidirectional connections between the amygdala and insula weaken. Strong connections between these two structures lead to exaggerated fear responses. The insula interprets aversive bodily sensations, and the amygdala detects threat, and when these two areas are too strongly connected, they tend to create high, chronic anxiety for the individual, even when there is no danger present. Weakening this connectivity reduces the arousal and reactivity symptoms of PTSD.

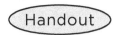

What is Interoception?

Did you ever notice your heart beating faster? Or, maybe you've noticed that your face suddenly feels hot?

This ability to "feel inside" of yourself and to be aware of internal states is called interoception. When you improve your interoceptive abilities, you can feel into your body and be more aware of how you feel, both physically and emotionally! Interoception can include things like detecting hunger or pain, but it also includes awareness of internal states that tell us which emotions we are feeling.

With strong interoceptive abilities, we can detect and monitor internal states and sensations, which in turn alert us to early signs of emotions, since all emotions are experienced in the body (as well as in the mind).

When we can feel into our bodies and become aware of how we are feeling, even at subtle levels, we are then better able to manage those emotions by intervening early! Interoceptive exposure exercises help us build the ability to notice internal states, and use that information to regulate emotions before they become overwhelming.

Your Brain on Interoceptive Exposure

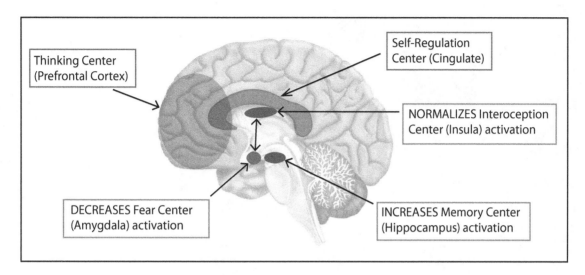

Interoceptive Exposure techniques change the brain in **five** ways:

1. **Less activation in the fear center (amygdala) of the brain:**
   - Reduces how strongly you react to trauma triggers
   - Reduces the stress response and increases the relaxation response
   - Decreases hypervigilance and the feeling of "always being on guard"

2. **More regulated activation of the interoception center (insula) of the brain:**
   - Reduces how strongly you react to trauma triggers
   - Reduces anger and other emotional outbursts
   - Reduces dissociation
   - Reduces numbing

3. **More activation of the memory center (hippocampus) of the brain:**
   - Increases feeling of safety
   - Reduces fear, especially when faced with trauma triggers
   - Increases ability to cope with negative memories

4. **Stronger connection from self-regulation (cingulate) and thinking (prefrontal cortex) centers to fear center (amygdala):**
   - Reduces how strongly you react to trauma triggers
   - Increases ability to regulate negative emotions
   - Increases ability to de-activate the fear center of the brain

5. **Weaker connection from fear center (amygdala) to interoception center (insula):**
   - Decreases feelings of fear
   - Decreases the feeling of chronic anxiety or being on guard

Anchoring into the Present

Symptoms Addressed

- Awareness of physical sensations
- Dysregulated interoception
- Stress response
- DSM-5 PTSD arousal and reactivity symptoms

Our sense of touch is like a bridge, connecting our internal environment to the external world. While traumatized individuals often find it difficult to connect to internal states and sensations, they tend to be extremely skilled at understanding and monitoring the external world in which they live. Anchoring into the Present uses this honed external awareness to help individuals learn to connect with their internal world, building awareness of physical and internal sensations. In Anchoring into the Present, participants connect with external surfaces and objects, noticing how they feel on the skin in order to connect the outside world to internal, physical sensations. This technique can also be conceptualized as a grounding exercise.

ANCHORING INTO THE PRESENT TIPS

- Because clients may not readily recognize the benefit of this practice, it is recommended that therapists discuss the rationale behind sensory awareness techniques. This will help clients understand the purpose of the techniques and how they strengthen the brain.

- It is recommended that this technique be practiced for approximately 10 minutes per day (total).

- Instruct clients to try this technique with a variety of surfaces and objects that vary in temperature, texture, color, size, and shape to become skilled in sensory awareness.

KEY RESEARCH FINDINGS

- Improved cognitive control and pain management (Gard et al., 2012)
- Improved attention and concentration (Malinowski, 2013)

Anchoring into the Present

This exercise can be practiced in most places, as a fast and simple way to increase internal awareness. Follow these instructions to practice Anchoring into the Present:

1. Place your hand on one surface. This can be a table, a chair, your own body (your arm, for instance), or any other surface. With your hand on the surface and your eyes open, ask yourself the following questions:
   a. Is this surface cold, cool, warm, or hot?
   b. Is this surface hard or soft?
   c. If I put pressure on this surface, does it move, or give?
   d. What color is this surface?
   e. What does this surface look like?
   f. When I move my hand on this surface, what does the texture of this surface feel like?

2. Remove your hand from that surface and immediately place your hand on a second, different surface. Ask yourself the following questions:
   a. Does this surface feel different from the first one?
   b. Is this surface cooler or warmer than the first surface?
   c. Is this surface harder or softer than the last?
   d. If I put pressure on this surface, does it move, or give?
   e. What color is this surface?
   f. What does this surface look like?
   g. When I move my hand on this surface, what does the texture of this surface feel like? Is the texture of this surface different from the last surface?

3. Finally, remove your hand from that surface and immediately place your hand on a third surface. Ask yourself the following questions:
   a. Does this surface feel different from the last one?
   b. Is this surface cooler or warmer than the last surface?
   c. Is this surface harder or softer than the last?
   d. If I put pressure on this surface, does it move, or give?
   e. What color is this surface?
   f. What does this surface look like?
   g. When I move my hand on this surface, what does the texture of this surface feel like? Is the texture of this surface different from the last surface?

4. To end this exercise, review the three surfaces in your mind, noting how they differed from one another.

Other Ideas for Anchoring into the Present

Tool 5-1 emphasized connecting with surfaces in order to help clients move from heightened external awareness to improved internal awareness. However, this is only one type of sensory awareness exercise that can help clients develop better internal awareness. Specifically, sensory awareness exercises that utilize *any* sense can be incorporated to work toward this goal. The next handout provides some examples of ways clients can improve internal awareness through sensory experiences.

Handout

Other Ideas for Anchoring into the Present

In the Anchoring into the Present Handout, the focus was on connecting with external surfaces and noticing what they felt like (promoting sensory awareness) in order to develop internal awareness. There are several other ways in which internal awareness can be improved utilizing the external environment. Read through the list below, noticing which techniques appeal to you. Try as many as you would like to, with the aim of expanding internal awareness:

- Notice multiple objects of one category, such as cups, bowls, books, etc. and note how they differ.

- Connect with your sense of smell by smelling different perfumes, foods, candles, incense, etc. and note how they differ.

- Connect with various regions of your body, noting how they differ (for instance, how your abdomen feels different from your foot).

- Break down a daily practice, such as taking a shower, into components, noticing what each component feels like on your skin. For example, a shower may be broken down into the following components:

  o Feel the hot water beating on your back (2 minutes)

  o Feel the sensation of shampoo in your hands (10 seconds)

  o Notice what it feels like to move the shampoo through your hair (30 seconds)

  o Experience the feeling of water washing the shampoo out of your hair (30 seconds)

Sensory Sensitization Training

> ## *Symptoms Addressed*
>
> - Awareness of physical sensations
> - Dysregulated interoception
> - Stress response
> - DSM-5 PTSD arousal and reactivity symptoms

Sensory sensitization training uses this honed external awareness to help individuals learn to connect with their internal world, building awareness of physical and internal sensations. In sensory sensitization training, participants engage in a mindfulness practice using "sensitizing objects" that connect the outside world to internal, physical sensations.

Sensitizing objects are those that engage one or more of the senses (touch, smell, sight, hearing, taste). For this type of exercise, small objects or surfaces that engage touch, such as stones, silly putty, or coins, tend to be utilized. Surfaces may include tabletops, the side of a water glass, an armrest, or carpet.

SENSORY SENSITIZATION TRAINING TIPS

- Because clients may not readily recognize the benefit of this practice, it is recommended that therapists discuss the rationale behind sensory awareness techniques, to help clients understand the purpose of the techniques and how they strengthen the brain.
- If possible, have the client complete this exercise while sitting upright in a chair.
- If clients feel comfortable closing their eyes during this practice, this is recommended. If not, have them gently gaze at the object they are holding during the exercise.
- It is recommended that this technique be practiced for approximately 10 minutes per day (total).
- Try this technique with a variety of objects that vary in weight, shape, and texture, to become skilled in sensory awareness.

KEY RESEARCH FINDINGS

- Improved cognitive control and pain management (Gard et al., 2012)
- Improved attention and concentration (Malinowski, 2013)

Sensory Sensitization Training

Before beginning this practice, select a small object that can easily be held in one hand. This will be referred to as the "sensitizing object." Ideally, this object will be complex in some way (with varying curves or textures, for example) and lightweight. Follow these instructions to complete sensory sensitization training:

1. Begin by picking up the sensitizing object with your right hand and placing it in the palm of your left hand (your left palm should be facing up). With the object in your hand, close your eyes and begin to sense it.

2. With your eyes closed, move the object around in your left hand, allowing your fingers and thumb to touch various parts of it.

3. As you connect with the object, notice its shape. Stay with this awareness for a moment, focusing just on the shape of the object.

4. Now notice the size of the object. Stay with this awareness for a moment, focusing just on the size of the object.

5. Next, notice the weight of the object. Stay with this awareness for a moment, focusing just on the weight of the object.

6. Now notice the texture of the object, and any variations in the texture as you feel different parts of the object.

7. Finally, gently squeeze the object, noticing any effect this might have on it (if, for instance, it compresses) or on your hand (feeling additional pressure on your fingers and palm, for example).

8. Next, remove the object from your left hand with your right hand, and set it down. Allow your empty left palm to remain facing upward. Position your right hand as you have your left hand – empty, with your right palm up.

9. Now, with two empty upward-facing palms, begin to check in with each hand, noticing any sensations or experiences in those hands.

10. Checking in with your left hand, notice what it feels like without the object. You may notice, for example, that your left hand still senses traces of the object, and feels different from your right hand (which was not holding the object). Observe any differences in sensation that you notice in the left hand, compared to the right hand.

11. Place the object back in your left hand, and once again sense it, noticing how it feels, its shape, weight, size, and texture. Keep the object in your left hand for a moment.

12. With the object again removed, hold out both empty palms, upward, and allow your awareness to move from palm to palm, noticing any similarities or differences.

13. Repeat steps 1-12, but with the object in the right hand.

Breath Connection

> ## *Symptoms Addressed*
>
> - Emotional awareness
> - Dysregulated interoception
> - Stress response
> - DSM-5 PTSD arousal and reactivity symptoms

Interoceptive training, wherein the individual connects with internal bodily sensations, is a key component of trauma treatment, broadly, and building emotional awareness, specifically. However, traumatized individuals often have difficulty feeling into their bodies and becoming aware of internal sensations. Breath connection is an evidence-informed technique that helps traumatized individuals build interoceptive awareness by connecting external movement and sensations with internal experiences. This technique, along with the next technique, described in Tool 5-5, encourages clients to feel into or connect with internal functions of the body by touching the external surface of different areas of the body. In this technique, clients connect with the breath through placing their hands on the abdomen as instructed below.

BREATH CONNECTION TIPS

- This exercise can be completed standing, lying down, or sitting.
- If participants feel comfortable closing their eyes during this practice, this is recommended. If not, they may find a place on the floor to gently focus their eyes on.
- It is recommended that this technique be practiced for approximately 5-10 minutes.

KEY RESEARCH FINDINGS

- Improved self-regulation and sense of well-being (Herbert & Pollatos, 2012; Gu & Fitzgerald, 2014)
- Improved emotional balance (Seth, 2013)
- Increased ability to be in the present moment and to focus (Seth et al., 2011)

Handout

Breath Connection Script

If possible, complete this exercise sitting in a chair or lying down. Begin by closing your eyes, if you feel comfortable doing this, and draw your attention to the breath, beginning to breathe through the diaphragm. If you wish to keep your eyes open, find a place directly above your eyes, perhaps on the ceiling, to gently focus on.

Now begin to connect more deeply with the breath by placing both hands on your abdomen area, feeling your stomach expand with each inhale, and then collapse with each exhale.

As you feel each breath, keeping your hands on your abdomen, begin to notice the quality of the breath. Is the breathing fast? Slow? Are the breaths deep? Shallow? Without changing the breath, just notice what it feels like, inside of your body, to breathe in and breathe out, allowing your hands (still resting on your abdomen) to more deeply connect you to your breath.

Shifting the attention to your hands, also notice what your hands feel like as they rest on your abdomen. Notice the movement of the hands, and the rhythm created as the breath and the abdomen move in sync.

Next, gently direct your attention to your nostrils, noticing what the cool air feels like as it enters your nose on each inhale. As the air enters your nose, note where it seems to disappear (perhaps at the back of your nose), the point at which you cannot feel the air anymore as it enters down into your lungs.

Finally, as you continue breathing, gently open your mouth, inhaling and exhaling through the mouth. As you do this, notice what the air feels like as it enters your mouth. Note how it feels against your teeth and your tongue, and feel where it seems to disappear as it enters your throat.

Continue to connect with the breath through the abdomen, nose, and mouth, and as you feel yourself breathing in and out, think of this breath, flowing effortlessly through your body, as an anchor to keep yourself grounded or present. Imagine this anchor to be ever-present, a resource that is always with you when you need it.

Continue this practice for approximately 5-10 minutes. To end this practice, release your hands down to your sides and take two deep, diaphragmatic breaths.

Heart Connection

Symptoms Addressed

- Emotional awareness
- Dysregulated interoception
- Stress response
- DSM-5 PTSD arousal and reactivity symptoms

Heart Connection is an evidence-informed technique that helps traumatized individuals build interoceptive awareness by connecting external movement and sensations with internal experiences. This is primarily done by physically connecting with the heartbeat using the hands, as instructed below.

HEART CONNECTION TIPS

- This exercise can be completed standing, lying down, or sitting.
- If participants feel comfortable closing their eyes during this practice, this is recommended. If not, they may find a place on the floor to gently focus their eyes on.
- It is recommended that this technique be practiced for approximately 10 minutes.

KEY RESEARCH FINDINGS

- Improved self-regulation and sense of well-being (Herbert & Pollatos, 2012; Gu & Fitzgerald, 2014)
- Improved emotional balance (Seth, 2013)
- Increased ability to be in the present moment and to focus (Seth et al., 2011)

Heart Connection Script

Begin to close your eyes and draw your attention to the breath, beginning to breathe through the diaphragm.

Now, with your eyes closed, begin to shift your awareness to your heart, checking in with your heart and noticing any sensations you may be experiencing in your heart.

To connect more deeply with the heart, take the fingers of your right hand and press gently on the inside of your left wrist, locating your pulse. When you feel the pulse, begin to imagine the beating that you feel as occurring both in your wrist, where you can feel it with your fingers, but also in the heart region of your chest. Continue connecting with your pulse for a few moments, imagining your pulse to be located in your wrist and your heart.

Finally, begin to integrate the breath, pulse, and heart. To do this, continue to connect with your heartbeat by pressing your right fingers on the inside of your left wrist. Next, begin to inhale slowly for 10 beats. After inhaling for 10 beats, begin to slowly exhale for 10 beats. You may notice that as you inhale, beats are slightly faster than when you exhale.

Keep breathing in and out, counting to 10 beats on each inhale and each exhale. To physically connect with the breath at the same time, with your right fingers still on your left wrist, slowly move your left hand down to your abdomen area, allowing your left pinky finger to rest against your abdomen. This allows you to physically connect with the movement of the breath in your abdomen, while also remaining physically connected to your heartbeat.

Stay here for a few moments, remaining fully connected to the breath and heartbeat.

To end this practice, release your hands down to your sides and take two deep, diaphragmatic breaths.

Find Your Center

Symptoms Addressed

- Emotional awareness
- Dysregulated interoception
- Proprioception

In proprioceptive training, the main objectives are for clients to improve their sense of balance and to become aware of their body's position relative to the environment. Body awareness is a key component of trauma treatment, as stated in previous tools, but this is a skill many traumatized clients find difficult to develop. Find Your Center is an evidence-informed technique that helps traumatized individuals build proprioception by slightly tipping the body off balance and then re-balancing it (helping them find their center).

The instruction find your center is commonly used in formal mindfulness practice, but may be difficult for clients to understand. In this technique, a client's center is defined as the physical position of their body at which they feel most stable and balanced. Defining center in a more concrete manner is helpful to clients who may struggle connecting to their bodies, and who may not readily grasp the abstract concept of becoming centered.

FIND YOUR CENTER TIPS

- Instruct clients to complete this exercise while standing, or as they slowly sit down in a chair.
- It is recommended that clients keep their eyes open during this practice.
- It is recommended that this technique be practiced for approximately 3 minutes.

KEY RESEARCH FINDINGS

- Improved sense of self (Damasio, 2003)
- Improved emotional balance (Seth, 2013)

Find Your Center

The following mini-exercises can be used to build proprioception, or the sense of your body's position relative to the environment. This can help you learn how to find your center.

Rocking: Standing up, separate your feet so that they are approximately hip width apart. Hold your spine and head upright, gazing forward and slightly downward. Next, slightly tip yourself off balance by gently rocking forward and backward. Keep rocking back and forth for about 10 seconds and then find your center, defined as the spot at which you feel most balanced and stable. You will recognize your balance when you reach it.

Swaying: While standing, separate your feet so that they are approximately hip width apart. Hold your spine and head upright, gazing forward and slightly downward. Next, slightly tip yourself off balance by gently swaying side to side. Keep swaying for about 10 seconds and then find your center, defined as the spot at which you feel most balanced and stable.

Sitting: Stand in front of a chair and slowly lower yourself to sit in it. Slowly sit in the chair, rocking your torso a bit forward and back until you can locate your center in that chair. As before, center is defined as the spot at which you feel most balanced and stable. After finding your center in this chair, repeat this exercise with every chair, sofa, and bed in your house, finding your center in each one, noting how center feels a bit different in each.

Scanning for Strength

> ## *Symptoms Addressed*
>
> - Stress response
> - DSM-5 PTSD avoidance symptoms
> - DSM-5 PTSD arousal and reactivity symptoms

Scanning for Strength is a body scan that helps individuals connect with their body and locate areas of the body containing strength. When an individual can identify and connect to their own strength, they become resourced and able to use that strength during difficult emotional times. In this exercise, participants focus their attention on different parts of their body, one at a time. As Kabat-Zinn (1990) instructs, the participant must, "maintain awareness in every moment, a detached witnessing of your breath and body, region by region, as you scan from your feet to the top of your head" (p. 89).

The purpose of a body scan is to teach participants to notice and fully experience any sensations – neutral, painful, or pleasant – that are occurring in their body, without judgment. Moreover, participants will learn over time not only to notice bodily sensations without judgment, but also to gain an awareness and acceptance of accompanying emotions and thoughts (Teasdale et al., 2000). With this awareness, it becomes easier to shift attention away from unhelpful or maladaptive thoughts, while still remaining connected to areas of strength in the body.

Finally, Scanning for Strength helps participants regulate physical sensations and emotions, which can reduce feelings of emotional numbness or dissociation that are common in PTSD.

SCANNING FOR STRENGTH TIPS

- The entire exercise should take participants 10-15 minutes.
- If possible, participants should complete this exercise sitting in a chair or lying down.
- If participants feel comfortable with closing their eyes during this practice, this is recommended. If not, they can find a place on the floor to gently focus their eyes on.
- An alternative way to practice this tool is to have clients imagine that they are breathing into each area of the body. For instance, while attending to the sensations in the feet, they can imagine that they are breathing into the feet during the inhales or exhales.
- When participants have completed this exercise for the first time, it can be helpful for them to write down the areas of the body that contained strength, so that they can remember these areas in the future.

- Connecting to areas of strength in the body can be helpful when in stressful situations, when completing trauma-focused therapy sessions, or when participants need the courage to try something new or difficult.

- Clients who have experienced trauma to certain parts of their body, either sexual or physical, often feel symptoms of the trauma when that part of the body is focused on. It's recommended that clients be given permission to stop this exercise, or skip certain areas of the body, if they feel uncomfortable or unsafe.

KEY RESEARCH FINDINGS

- Reduces overreaction to anxiety signals in the body (Wald & Taylor, 2008)
- Improves concentration and attention abilities (Kabat-Zinn, 1991)
- Increases the relaxation response (Ditto, Eclache, & Goldman, 2006)

Scanning for Strength Script

Begin by closing your eyes or gently gazing downward on one spot. Focus your attention on your breath, breathing effortlessly, not trying to change your breath. Notice what it feels like as you breathe in, and as you breathe out.

Now begin Scanning for Strength. As you go through this exercise, you may notice various sensations. When this happens, simply experience and acknowledge the sensations, as well as any accompanying thoughts or emotions you may notice.

To begin, shift your focus to the soles of your feet, just noticing any sensations that may arise as you attend to this area. Feel into the soles of your feet, without judgment, noticing what the heels, balls, and arches of your feet feel like. Stay here for a moment.

Still focusing on the soles of your feet, ask yourself, "Is there strength in this area?" If the answer is no, begin to redirect your awareness to the next area of the body – the toes and tops of your feet. If the answer is yes, remain focused here for a few moments, connecting more deeply with this area of the body and intentionally experiencing the strength this area is providing. Remember that you can connect with this strength whenever you need it.

Now gently shift your awareness to your toes, and the tops of your feet, noticing what this area feels like, without judgment. Notice any sensations that are present in your toes or the tops of your feet. Stay here for a moment.

Still focusing on your toes and the tops of your feet, ask yourself, "Is there strength in this area?" If the answer is no, begin to redirect your awareness to the next area of the body – the lower part of the legs. If the answer is yes, remain focused here for a few moments, connecting more deeply with this area of the body and intentionally experiencing the strength this area is providing. Remember that you can connect with this strength whenever you need it.

Let awareness begin to shift upward to the lower part of the legs, above the feet but below the knees. Notice the sensations occurring in your calf muscles, and in the front areas of your legs. Just feel into these areas with a calm awareness. Stay here for a moment.

Still focusing on the lower part of your legs, ask yourself, "Is there strength in this area?" If the answer is no, begin to redirect your awareness to the next area of the body – the upper parts of your legs. If the answer is yes, remain focused here for a few moments, connecting more deeply with this area of the body and intentionally experiencing the strength this area is providing. Remember that you can connect with this strength whenever you need it.

As you complete this exercise it is okay to stop, or skip certain areas of the body, if a region does not feel safe or comfortable to connect with.

Withdraw your attention from your lower legs, and begin focusing on the upper parts of your legs, above your knees but below your hips, noticing what your hamstrings and quads feel like. Become a non-judgmental observer of these areas, simply accepting any sensations that may be present. Stay here for a moment.

Continue this exercise, moving your awareness through several major muscle groups and different regions of the body. Which specific areas you choose to focus on is up to you, but it is recommended that most of the following areas be scanned in this exercise:

- *Feet*

- *Lower legs*

- *Upper legs*

- *Buttocks/hips/pelvic area (any or all of these areas)*

- *Abdomen*

- *Lower and/or upper back, or entire back*

- *Arms*

- *Hands*

- *Chest area (with a focus on the breath)*

- *Shoulders*

- *Neck*

- *Head*

Tense and Release

Symptoms Addressed

- Emotional awareness
- Reactivity to trauma triggers
- Stress response
- DSM-5 PTSD arousal and reactivity symptoms

Muscle tension is commonly associated with stress, anxiety, and PTSD symptoms as part of a process that helps the body prepare for potentially dangerous situations. One method of reducing muscle tension is by practicing a technique called Tense and Release, a form of progressive muscle relaxation (PMR). In PMR, muscles are intentionally tensed and then fully released/relaxed.

When clients practice Tense and Release, they will tense each region for approximately 5-7 seconds, and then relax that area for approximately 10 seconds. When participants squeeze each area, instruct them to tense their muscles at approximately 40% of the hardest they could possibly squeeze. Do not instruct them to squeeze each muscle group as hard as they can, as one of the goals of Tense and Release is to learn how to detect *subtle* muscle tension. Also, if a specific area is painful, instruct the client to squeeze only at 10%, or not at all.

TENSE AND RELAX TIPS

- If possible, have participants complete this exercise sitting in a chair or lying down.
- If participants feel comfortable with closing their eyes during this practice, this is recommended. If not, they can find a place on the floor to gently focus their eyes on.
- It is recommended that this technique be practiced for approximately 10 minutes.
- If participants have any injuries, or a history of physical problems that may cause muscle pain, always have them consult with their doctor before starting this practice.
- Be aware that trauma can be stored in the body. It may happen that when participants focus on specific areas of the body, there may be accompanying emotions. If this happens, instruct the participants to simply notice the link between physical sensations and emotions, honoring these experiences.
- Clients who have experienced trauma to certain parts of their body, either sexual or physical, often feel symptoms of the trauma when that part of the body is focused on. It is recommended that clients be given permission to stop this exercise, or skip certain areas of the body, if they feel uncomfortable or unsafe.

KEY RESEARCH FINDINGS

- Normalizes low-frequency heart rate variability and reduces other cardiovascular indices of stress (Green, 2011)
- Normalizes cortisol levels (Dolbier & Rush, 2012)
- Reduces depression (Lolak et al., 2008) and anxiety (Chen et al., 2009)
- Reduces headaches (Sanjiv & Apurva, 2014)

Tense and Release

Begin to close your eyes as you assume a comfortable position, either lying down or sitting up. Gently shift your focus to the breath, just noticing what it feels like to breathe in and out, breathing deeply through the diaphragm. As you complete this exercise, you may skip certain areas of the body that do not feel safe or comfortable to connect with, or that experience pain.

Now extend you awareness to your entire body. As you attend to any sensations arising in your body, make note of any tension you may be experiencing in your body. However, do not try to change this tension right now, just be aware of it, without judgment.

Begin Tense and Release following the relaxation (Tense and Release) sequence presented below. For each area, do the following:

1. *Feel into the area, noticing any sensations or experiences that might be there.*

2. *Tense the area at 40% (10% or not at all if there is pain) for 7 seconds.*

3. *Relax the area for 10 seconds. While relaxing the area, complete the following:*

   a. *Feel into the area and notice what it feels like to be relaxed after having been tense.*

   b. *State the name of the body region you are attending to, silently to yourself, along with the number associated with that area (see below – upper legs = 3, neck = 8, etc.). For example, you may state to yourself, "Lower legs, 2" or "Face, 10."*

4. *After completing the Tense and Release sequence following these instructions, expand your awareness to your entire body, noticing any sensations or experiences present in the body.*

5. *Optional: Complete Conditioned Relaxation (refer to Tool 5-9) before ending this exercise.*

6. *Take one deep breath through the diaphragm and open your eyes, slowly coming back into the room.*

Tense and Release Sequence

1. Feet
2. Lower legs
3. Upper legs
4. Hands
5. Abdomen
6. Arms
7. Upper back
8. Shoulders
9. Jaw
10. Face

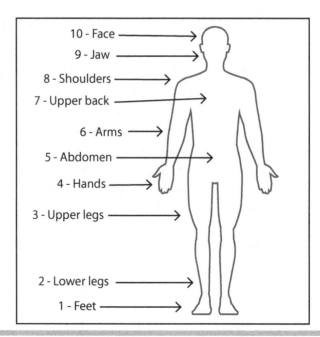

Conditioned Relaxation

```
╔══════════════════════════════════════════════════════╗
║              Symptoms Addressed                      ║
║  ──────────────────────────────────────────────     ║
║  • Reactivity to distressing sensations in the body ║
║  • Stress response                                  ║
║  • DSM-5 PTSD arousal and reactivity symptoms       ║
╚══════════════════════════════════════════════════════╝
```

Conditioned Relaxation is a type of body scan intended to be used in conjunction with Tense and Release. In this exercise, the client slowly, silently counts backward from 10 to 1, feeling into and intentionally relaxing a different region of the body with each number. The body regions that correspond with each number are shown in the Conditioned Relaxation handout. The objective of this technique is for clients to learn how to relax on command by feeling into and releasing tension from various regions of the body, starting at the top of the body (with the face) and working their way down (to the feet).

CONDITIONED RELAXATION TIPS

- It is recommended that this technique be practiced immediately after the previous technique (Tool 5-8), Tense and Relax, as a way to end that formal practice.

- Additionally, it is recommended that Conditioned Relaxation be practiced alone on a regular basis, perhaps multiple times per day for 1-2 minutes.

- If possible, have participants complete this exercise sitting in a chair or lying down.

- If the client feels comfortable with closing the eyes during this practice, this is recommended. If not, have the client find a place on the floor to gently focus her or his eyes on.

- Be aware that trauma can be stored in the body. It may happen that when a client focuses on specific areas of the body, there may be accompanying emotions. If this happens, simply have the person notice the link between physical sensations and emotions, honoring these experiences.

KEY RESEARCH FINDINGS

- Reduces reactivity to distressing physical sensation, improves psychological well-being, and reduces interpersonal sensitivity (Carmody & Baer, 2008)

- Reduces cravings (Cropley & Ussher, 2007)

- Improves pain management (Ussher et al., 2014)

Conditioned Relaxation

To practice Conditioned Relaxation, follow the directions below:

1. *Take a moment to review each region of the body that will be covered in this exercise, and the number that is associated with each area. A visual depiction of each region, and the number with which it is associated, appears below.*

2. *Gently begin to close your eyes, bringing your awareness to area 10, the face. Feeling into your face, state to yourself, "10, relax."*

3. *Next, move your awareness to the area associated with the number 9 (the jaw). Feel into this area and state to yourself, "9, relax."*

4. *Continue moving your awareness downward to the next area of the body, the shoulders, which is associated with the number 8. Feel into this area and state to yourself, "8, relax."*

5. *Continue this process, progressively moving your awareness down the body as you count down to the number 1 (feet).*

6. *After completing the body scan, pause for a moment, noticing what it feels like for your entire body to be relaxed. Take one deep breath through the diaphragm before opening your eyes and coming back into the room.*

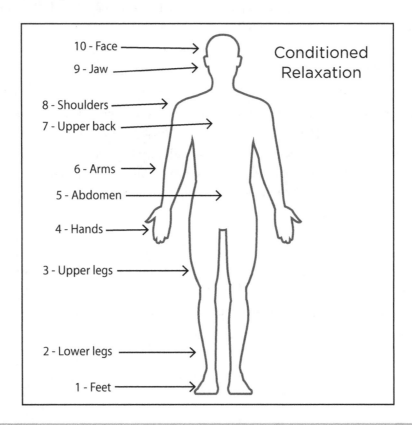

Autogenic Training

```
┌─────────────────────────────────────────────────────────┐
│                                                         ·
│                  Symptoms Addressed                     ·
│            ──────────────────────────────              ·
│                                                         ·
│         •  Emotion regulation                           ·
│         •  Reactivity to trauma triggers                ·
│         •  Stress response                              ·
│         •  DSM-5 PTSD arousal and reactivity symptoms   ·
│                                                         ·
└─────────────────────────────────────────────────────────┘
```

Autogenic training is a mindfulness practice where the participant focuses on selected sensations in the body as a way of achieving a state of deep relaxation (Stetter & Kupper, 2002). Autogenic training improves self-regulatory capacities and trains individuals to modify the functioning of their autonomic nervous system by repeating a sequence of statements about warm and heavy sensations felt throughout the body.

AUTOGENIC TRAINING TIPS

- It is recommended that participants practice this meditation multiple times per day for short periods of time (5-10 minutes). If possible, encourage clients to try to practice 2-3 times per day.

- It is best to practice in a quiet space or room, without distractions.

- Clients may complete this exercise while sitting or lying down. If the participant is seated in a chair, instruct them to try to straighten their back, with their feet flat on the floor.

- If a participant suffers from heart disease or high blood pressure, use caution in practicing this exercise and have them speak with their physician before engaging in autonomic training.

KEY RESEARCH FINDINGS

- Increases heart rate variability and improves vagal heart control (Miu, Heilman, & Miclea, 2009), thereby reducing individuals' levels of stress and anxiety

- Reduces anxiety (Bowden, Lorenc, & Robinson, 2012; Dhiman & Bedi, 2010)

- Improves self-monitoring and self-regulation (Shinozaki et al., 2010)

- Reduces insomnia, depression, and a variety of health conditions (Bowden et al., 2012)

Autogenic Training

Begin to slowly close your eyes and draw your attention to the breath, starting to breathe deep into the diaphragm.

ARMS

Begin autogenic training by stating to yourself: *I am completely calm.*
Now gently direct your focus to your arms, feeling into your arms, noticing any sensations or experiences in this area.
   State to yourself: *My arms are heavy* (repeat 6 times).

And now state to yourself: *I am completely calm.*
Maintaining focus on your arms, once again feel into your arms, noticing any sensations that may be present.
   Still focusing on your arms, state: *My arms are warm* (repeat 6 times).
   Finally, state to yourself: *I am completely calm.*

LEGS

Now gently direct your focus to your legs, feeling into your legs, noticing any sensations or experiences in this area.
   State to yourself: *My legs are heavy* (repeat 6 times).
   And now state to yourself: *I am completely calm.*

Maintaining focus on your legs, once again feel into your legs, noticing any sensations that may be present.
   Still focusing on your legs, state: *My legs are warm* (repeat 6 times).
   Finally, state to yourself: *I am completely calm.*

HEART

Now gently direct your focus to your heart, noticing any sensations or experiences in this area.
   State to yourself: *My heartbeat is calm and slow* (repeat 6 times).
   And now state to yourself: *I am completely calm.*

BREATH

Now gently direct your focus to your breath, noticing any sensations or experiences in this area.
   State to yourself: *My breath is calm and steady* (repeat 6 times).
   Now state to yourself: *I am completely calm.*

STOMACH

Now gently direct your focus to your stomach, noticing any sensations or experiences in this area.

    State to yourself: *My stomach is soft and warm* (repeat 6 times).

    Now state to yourself: *I am completely calm.*

Now gently direct your focus to your forehead, noticing any sensations or experiences.

    State to yourself: *My forehead is cool and relaxed* (repeat 6 times).

    Now state to yourself: *I am completely calm.*

Shift your attention back to the breath for a moment, practicing focused, diaphragmatic breathing. Enjoy the feeling of relaxation before ending this exercise.

Integrated Systems Check

```
┌─────────────────────────────────────────────┐
│              Symptoms Addressed                │
│  ─────────────────────────────────────────    │
│                                                │
│    • Memory                                    │
│    • Self-regulation                           │
│    • Reactivity to trauma triggers             │
│    • DSM-5 PTSD avoidance symptoms             │
│    • DSM-5 PTSD arousal and reactivity symptoms│
│                                                │
└─────────────────────────────────────────────┘
```

The Integrated Systems Check, which is an open awareness mindfulness technique, increases self-awareness by teaching participants to check in with themselves at three levels, or systems: body, emotions, and thoughts. When these systems are in check, clients become fully aware of what they are experiencing and how these different domains may be influencing one another. For example, a client might realize that an anxious thought produces rapid heart rate.

It is very common for clients to experience thoughts, feelings, or sensations without awareness, and to only notice when they become overwhelming. As a method to effectively manage stress and anxiety, however, it is important to know when and how stress is experienced, and to be able to detect it early. Frequent check-ins of these three systems can help individuals become more aware of the presence of stress and anxiety.

INTEGRATED SYSTEMS CHECK TIPS

- The entire exercise should take 5-10 minutes, as it is meant to be a short formal practice.
- If participants feel comfortable with closing their eyes during this practice, this is recommended. If not, they may find a place on the floor to gently focus the eyes on.
- It is recommended that this technique be incorporated into everyday life. Practice the Integrated Systems Check between tasks, during a break, or when stress increases.

KEY RESEARCH FINDINGS

- Boosts immune functioning (Davidson, Kabat-Zinn, et al., 2003)
- Reduces depression, anxiety, and chronic pain (Goyal et al., 2014)
- Decreases cortisol, a stress hormone (Turakitwanakan, Mekseepralard, & Busarakumtragul, 2013)

Integrated Systems Check

To begin, close your eyes, or find a spot down in front of you that you may gaze at.

Begin the Integrated Systems Check by first attending to your breath. Notice its qualities, what it feels like. Breathe in, and breathe out, noticing how your abdomen rises with each inhale and falls with each exhale. Engage in this focused breathing practice for a moment.

Body Awareness: *Now extend your awareness of the breath to your entire body, being present with your body and noticing any sensations that arise. Allow your focus to drift to any area(s) of the body requesting your attention, simply noticing any experiences. Maybe you feel a little relaxation in some area, or some tension. Just be with these experiences for a moment, without judgment.*

Emotional Awareness: *Now shift your attention to your emotions, and any feelings you may be having, no matter how subtle or strong. If there is a specific place in your body that you experience emotions, you may shift your attention there now. As you become more aware of your emotions, you may notice the presence of multiple emotions, perhaps to varying degrees of intensity, or no emotions at all. This is okay. Just stay with your emotions here for a moment.*

Thought Awareness: *Now gently shift your awareness to your thoughts. As you do this, imagine your thoughts as trains, where each train represents one thought. Visualize these trains coming into, flowing through, and exiting your mind, just observing the thought trains. As you do this, be mindful of any attempt to prevent the trains, stop them, or "jump on the trains." If you notice that you have attached to, or "jumped on" one of your thought trains, congratulate yourself on this awareness, jump off that train, and take your observer stance again, just watching the thoughts as they flow through your mind.*

Connecting Mind, Body, and Emotion: *Finally, as you continue to watch your thought trains, begin to simultaneously open your awareness, noticing any physical sensations or emotions that may be attached to those thoughts. You may notice that some thoughts produce specific emotions, or sensations throughout the body.*

When you are ready, slowly and gently open your eyes and re-enter the room.

6

Movement-Based Techniques and Poses

Movement-based techniques are (largely) bottom-up exercises designed to help clients become more connected to their bodies, reduce the stress response and amygdala activation, and strengthen the memory and cortical areas of the brain. While most mental health professionals will not have completed rigorous training in movement-based approaches such as qigong, tai chi, or yoga, there are simple and straight forward ways to incorporate movement into psychotherapy. The goal of this chapter is to present simple ways of adding movement into the therapy setting, without the requirement of additional space, time, or therapist training.

These techniques tend to resonate with clients who have attention difficulties or who struggle with exercises that require them to sit still. While these techniques can be practiced on their own, their effects can be intensified by integrating movement with breathing techniques, other bottom-up exercises, or even top-down methods.

One theory, by renowned trauma expert Peter Levine (1997), asserts that unresolved trauma results in energy becoming "stuck" in the body. When this happens, the nervous system becomes disrupted and the individual has a difficult time recovering from the event due to the trapped energy in the body. Incorporating movement into therapy is one way to help your client become connected to the body and begin to restore awareness of, and trust in, the body. It may also help clients begin to discharge traumatic energy, allowing them to rebalance their nervous system.

THE BRAIN ON MOVEMENT-BASED TECHNIQUES

Movement-based techniques may change the brain in **seven** key ways, all of which help clients reduce and better manage post-trauma symptoms.

1. **Fear Center (Amygdala):** Decreased activation of the fear center. De-activation of this area helps to reduce reactivity when trauma triggers arise. It also reduces the stress response (sympathetic nervous system arousal) and results in a decrease in arousal and reactivity symptoms, such as hypervigilance, feeling on guard, etc.

2. **Stress Response:** Related to amygdala de-activation, multiple movement-based exercises have been shown to reduce allostatic load, which is the wear and tear the body experiences due to a dysregulated stress response system. The stress response system is located in both the brain (such as the amygdala and hypothalamus) and the body (such as the adrenals).

3. **Interoception Center (Insula):** Normalized insula activation. In PTSD, the insula is often dysregulated. When it is over-activated, there is emotional reactivity and outbursts (emotion under-modulation); when it is under-activated, there is dissociation and numbing. Both extremes are

common in PTSD. With a more regulated insula, individuals improve interoception, and they experience fewer emotional outbursts and dissociative symptoms (including numbing). Additionally, movement-based techniques have been shown to increase insular volume.

4. **Memory Center (Hippocampus):** Increased activation of the memory center of the brain (hippocampus). This activation helps remind the individual that they are safe in the present moment, and it is involved in the extinction of fear responses when trauma triggers arise. The increased competence an individual experiences in managing negative memories can reduce the avoidance symptoms of PTSD. Moreover, movement-based exercises have been shown to increase the volume of the hippocampus.

5. **Thinking Center (Prefrontal Cortex):** Increased prefrontal cortex activation, resulting in improved attention, problem-solving, and decision-making. A strong prefrontal cortex can help traumatized individuals maintain presence of mind during stressful or triggering situations, and can help them evaluate, reframe, or shift unhelpful thinking patterns that contribute to their PTSD symptoms.

6. **Self-Regulation Center (Cingulate Cortex):** Increased activation of the cingulate cortex, resulting in better thought and emotion regulation and conflict monitoring. Cingulate activation may help traumatized individuals respond more adaptively and appropriately to triggering stimuli and situations, and down-regulate negative emotions when needed.

7. **Connectivity:** Movement-based exercises have been shown to improve connectivity between key brain areas (such as the prefrontal cortex and hippocampus), leading to better brain integration and functioning.

What are Movement-Based Techniques?

Movement-based exercises integrate movement and mindful awareness of the body, and can be practiced alone or with other techniques (such as breathing techniques, or even while engaging in trauma-focused work). The main objective of movement-based techniques is to help individuals become more aware of the body, and to engage in movement that is self-soothing, promotes self-awareness, and reduces the stress response.

Movement-based exercises can help individuals strengthen both interoception (our ability to "feel inside" of ourselves) and proprioception (our ability to sense body position, movement, and balance), which activates brain areas that tend to be dysregulated after trauma.

Research has shown several movement-based techniques to be very helpful for reducing post-trauma symptoms. Some examples of movement-based approaches that may be beneficial for survivors of trauma include:

- Yoga

- Tai chi

- Qigong

- Exercise

- Dance

- Walking meditation

- Martial arts

Your Brain on Movement-Based Techniques

Movement-based techniques change the brain in **five** ways:

1. **Less activation in fear center (amygdala) of the brain:**
   - Reduces how strongly you react to trauma triggers
   - Reduces the stress response and increases the relaxation response
   - Decreases hypervigilance and the feeling of "always being on guard"

2. **Increased activation and increased volume of the interoception center (insula) of the brain:**
   - Reduces how strongly you react to trauma triggers
   - Reduces anger and other emotional outbursts
   - Reduces dissociation
   - Reduces numbing

3. **More activation and increased volume of the memory center (hippocampus) of the brain:**
   - Increases feeling of safety
   - Reduces fear, especially when faced with trauma triggers
   - Allows traumatic memories to be experienced as past events, as opposed to reliving them as though they are occurring in the present
   - Increases ability to cope with negative memories

4. **More activation in the thinking center (prefrontal cortex) of the brain:**
   - Allows for clear thinking, better problem-solving, and improved decision-making
   - Improves concentration and attention

5. **More activation in the self-regulation center (cingulate) of the brain:**
   - Improves emotion regulation
   - Improves ability to respond to triggers in a healthy way
   - Improves ability to manage distressing thoughts

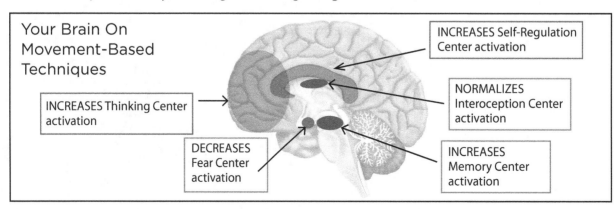

Your Brain On Movement-Based Techniques

INCREASES Thinking Center activation

INCREASES Self-Regulation Center activation

NORMALIZES Interoception Center activation

DECREASES Fear Center activation

INCREASES Memory Center activation

Incorporating Movement and Poses into Psychotherapy

Clients can learn formal movement-based exercises and poses, such as those taught in yoga or tai chi classes, but these types of techniques can also be incorporated into psychotherapy sessions. While it can be beneficial to become an expert in a practice such as qigong or various types of exercise, the benefits of simple movement and easy-to-learn poses can be experienced by anyone.

Traditional psychotherapy evokes images of clients and therapists sitting still, usually across from one another, while talking. However, depending on the setting, the techniques utilized, and the abilities and preferences of the client and the therapist, it is possible to incorporate movement and poses into psychotherapy. Specifically, movement and poses can be used in conjunction with bottom-up or top-down techniques. Here are some examples of ways to use movement in therapy:

- **Combining breath work (bottom-up) with movement:** Lifting arms during inhales, and lowering arms slowly during exhales, or making circles with the arms while engaging in a breath exercise.

- **Combining body awareness techniques (bottom-up) with movement:** Bringing awareness to the legs, and sensations in the legs, while lifting each leg. Bringing awareness to the lungs while walking briskly.

- **Combining trauma processing (top-down) with movement:** EMDR and tapping are examples of combining movement with top-down approaches. Additionally, therapists and clients may walk while completing some types of top-down techniques, such as cognitive restructuring (keeping in mind the importance of confidentiality, of course).

- **Combining cognitive therapy (top-down) with movement:** Engaging with distressing thoughts while gently moving different regions of the body, especially areas where uncomfortable sensations are experienced. Movement of these areas may be soothing to clients.

Incorporating Movement and Poses into Psychotherapy

Some therapists prefer to incorporate movement in psychotherapy sessions due to the brain-changing, recovery-promoting benefits of movement. For example, movement can decrease stress and anxiety and it has been shown to help clients become more aware of, and comfortable in, their bodies. Your therapist may recommend that you engage in more movement outside of session by taking a yoga or aerobics class, but it is also possible to use movement as a part of psychotherapy.

Here are some examples of how movement may be used in therapy:

- **With breathing exercises:** Walking, or movement of the arms or legs, can be combined with breathing exercises.

- **With mindfulness exercises:** Movement may be combined with techniques in which attention is brought to the body, emotions, or thoughts.

- **With cognitive methods:** Movement may be combined with techniques in which clients think or talk about distressing memories. An example of this is presented in the following Handout entitled Example of Incorporating a Pose and Movement into a Top-Down Approach.

Example of Incorporating a Pose and Movement into a Top-Down Approach

Begin to recall a memory of a recent event, incident, or interaction that made you feel anxious or stressed out. This will not be a traumatic experience; rather, it is a recent event that brought up feelings of mild to moderate anxiety (perhaps at a level of 35 or so on a distress thermometer).

Incorporate a Pose

Once you have identified the anxiety-provoking event, lie down (on the floor or on a couch) and prop your lower legs and feet up, angling your knees at 90 degrees. You may also put a pillow under your head if that is more comfortable for you. This position will induce relaxation of the psoas muscles, which tense whenever an upsetting event is experienced. In this exercise, the idea is to intentionally relax an area of the body that tenses during stressful experiences, and by inducing relaxation, create a new emotional experience from the memory of a negative event.

In this position, without discussing the details of the event, select three words that summarize either 1) how the event made you feel ("scared, anxious, upset") or, 2) what happened during the event ("brother, argument, holidays, fall"). This is a method commonly used to contain distressing memories. State the three words out loud to the therapist. At this time, you may "take your temperature" to check in with your distress level.

Next, release these three words and feel into your lower body, intentionally relaxing the hip flexors, quadriceps, lower legs, and feet. Take a deep breath in, and as you exhale, state the word "relax" silently to yourself. Repeat this process with a few more breaths, taking long, deep, slow breaths in and out, repeating the word "relax" on each exhale. Check in with your temperature again, noting any change in your level of distress.

Incorporate Movement

Now begin to close your eyes and bring into your mind's eye a visual image related to this memory and, as you do this, focus about 40% of your attention on your heels as you press the edges of your heels into the surface your feet are propped on. Press your heels hard into this surface, creating a slight movement. This is a grounding technique.

Keeping 40% of your attention on your heels as they press into the surface, assign about 60% of your attention to the image of the recent anxiety-provoking event. Stay here for a few moments before gently relaxing your heels as you open your eyes. Once again, check in with your temperature.

Next, with your eyes open, once again intentionally relax your hip flexors, quadriceps, lower legs, and feet. Take a deep breath in, and as you exhale, state "relax" silently to yourself.

Finally, with your lower body still completely relaxed, begin to slowly inhale, stating the three summary words related to the event silently to yourself as you take the breath in, and then as you exhale state "relax" silently to yourself.

Repeat this sequence for a few breaths, and then release all of the words, now focusing on your hip flexors, imagining that you are breathing air through your relaxed hip flexors as you inhale and exhale. Stay here for a moment before ending this exercise.

| Tool 6-2 | Trauma-Informed Instruction |

Somatic experiencing practitioners often refer to trauma as an event that happens "too much, too fast, too soon." In other words, traumatic events overwhelm an individual's capacity to cope. When treating trauma, it is important to keep this definition in mind and to facilitate experiences in therapy that produce the opposite effect. In other words, mental health professionals should be mindful not to create experiences for clients that produce feelings of out-of-control overwhelm, or push for clients to engage in techniques too much, too fast, too soon. This applies to movement-based techniques, as well as other bottom-up or top-down methods.

When helping clients connect with their bodies (through movement, sensation, or otherwise), it can be useful to incorporate language commonly used in trauma-informed yoga approaches. Just as with trauma-informed yoga, when incorporating movement into psychotherapy, a main goal is to help clients slowly, safely, gently enter their own bodies with a sense of curiosity and compassion (Khouri & Haglund, 2016). Therapists can facilitate clients' reconnection with the body by using language emphasizing 1) inquiry, and 2) invitation (Emerson & Hopper, 2011) while guiding clients' movements.

"Inquiries," or permission questions, signal to clients that they are the decision-makers of their own bodies and experiences, while "invitation" statements communicate to clients that they maintain control over the intensity of their movement. Note that permission and invitation are two components that are not present during traumatic experiences, which occur without consent or control. To heal after trauma, it is critical for clients to re-establish a sense of safety, control, and consent.

Below are examples of trauma-informed statements and questions that can be used in the context of movement-based techniques (adapted from Khouri & Haglund, 2016).

Invitation Statements

Gently allow your (arm/leg/breath/head/etc.)…

If it feels right to you…

When you are ready...

Begin to notice, with curiosity…

At some point, you might notice…

With kindness, gently allow...

You may invite yourself to become aware…

Consider (reaching your arm up, lowering your leg, etc.)…

You may give yourself permission to feel...

With curiosity, notice where you mind is, and gently redirect it (to your breath, arms, etc.)…

Inquiry Questions

Where, if anywhere, do you feel strong?

Which area feels stronger, your [shoulders] or [legs]?

What does it feel like to you when you…?

Can you detect a space within your body that feels safe?

Is it possible to send compassion to the areas of your body that feel less safe, or unstable?

How might you describe the feeling of [sharpness, coldness, tension] in the body?

As you engage in this pose, what do you notice in the body? In your emotions? In the mind?

How would you describe your breathing right now? What quality does it seem to possess (jagged, shallow, smooth, etc.)?

What areas of the body feel at peace right now? Which areas feel tense, or unsafe?

Can it be okay to still connect with the areas of the body that feel unsafe or tense?

Is it okay to lose balance?

Is there a place in the body it would feel okay to send compassion and kindness to right now?

Handout

Trauma-Informed Movement Tips

A goal of movement-based techniques is to help individuals reconnect with, and feel safe in, the body. To encourage this sense of safety and reconnection, it is important to refrain from forcing movement or engaging in movement that feels painful or unsafe.

The objective of these techniques is not to attain a higher level of fitness. Rather, we want to learn more about the body, feel into it, and practice compassion toward it. The language we use with ourselves during movement-based exercises can facilitate safe reconnection with the body when we focus on: 1) making inquiries into our own experiences, and 2) inviting ourselves to fully experience the body. Here are some inquiry questions you may ask yourself as you engage in movement-based techniques, such as yoga:

Inquiry Questions

Where, if anywhere, do I feel strong?

Which area feels stronger, my [shoulders] or [legs]?

What does it feel like when I move…?

Is there a space within my body that feels safe?

Can I allow myself to send compassion to the areas of my body that feel less safe, or unstable?

How would I describe the feeling of [sharpness, coldness, tension] in my body?

What do I notice in my body as I settle into this pose/move in this way? What emotions begin to arise? What thoughts begin to surface?

What is my breathing right now? What quality does it seem to possess (jagged, shallow, smooth, etc.)?

What areas of my body feel at peace right now? Which areas feel tense, or unsafe?

Can it be okay to still connect with the areas of my body that feel unsafe or tense?

Is it okay to lose balance?

Is there a place in my body it would feel okay to send compassion and kindness to?

Poses and Movement for Grounding

Symptoms Addressed

- Emotional awareness and regulation
- Concentration and attention
- Dysregulated interoception
- Memory
- Stress response
- DSM-5 PTSD arousal and reactivity symptoms

Grounding poses and movements help clients focus attention downward, attuning to what it feels like for the body to connect with the ground/floor. During these exercises, the client intentionally focuses on one or more areas of the body (the feet, or sit bones) making contact with the earth. Focusing on the connection between the ground and the body creates a sense of stability and is a way, metaphorically, to "come back down to Earth" and into the present moment. Each of the poses and accompanying movements presented here may be practiced with clients in the context of psychotherapy, with little space and no equipment required.

Trauma often results in clients feeling anxious, lost, out of control, and stuck in the past. When this happens, dissociation may occur, and clients may report feeling "spacey" and ungrounded. Additionally, trauma can create a sense of uncertainty about the body, which may feel unsafe and untrustworthy after trauma. Grounding techniques reconnect clients with their bodies, the earth, and the present moment in ways that feel safe and stable.

Over time, a client's connection with the body and the earth can provide them with resources, a sense of support, and improved inner strength. As with trauma treatment in general, one goal of grounding techniques is to shift a client's tendency to avoid the body (and the self) to engage in escape behaviors, and instead turn inward during times of distress.

Please Note: The Partner Grounding Exercise requires a partner and can best be conducted in a group context. This allows for discussion between group members about their experiences with the exercise. It is recommended that this exercise only be conducted with individuals who fully consent to being touched, and who feel safe having a partner with whom to complete this exercise. This exercise will not feel safe to all trauma survivors, so use it with caution.

POSES AND MOVEMENT FOR GROUNDING TIPS

- The therapist may practice these poses and movements along with the client, especially as the client is learning them, in order to model the correct form.

- While in grounding poses, instruct clients to focus on the point at which their body makes contact with the earth, feeling the weight of the body on the ground, creating a sense of stability and connection with the present moment.

- During these exercises, attention may simultaneously be brought to the breath, focusing on long, slow, steady inhales and exhales.

- It is also recommended to have clients imagine that they are breathing into the poses and movements as they engage in them.

- If appropriate, these techniques can also be utilized with top-down, cognitive techniques, including trauma-focused approaches. For instance, while in a grounding pose, clients may be asked to access information regarding a traumatic memory. They remain in the pose as they do this, and continue to focus on pressing their feet or pelvis (or other body parts connected to the ground) into the earth as they discuss some aspect about the memory.

- Whenever a client experiences an unexpected, uninvited distressing memory, they may keep grounded in the present moment by pressing their feet (or other body parts connected to the ground) into the floor, again noticing the sensation of connecting with the earth.

KEY RESEARCH FINDINGS

- Reduced stress and allostatic load (which is the wear and tear on the body due to stress) (Streeter et al., 2012)

- Increased ability to concentrate (Kerr et al., 2011)

- Increased volume of several brain areas, including the hippocampus (Hariprasad et al., 2013), the dorsolateral prefrontal cortex (Wei et al., 2013), and insula (Villemure et al., 2014)

Easy Pose

Gently enter a sitting position on the floor, meditation cushion, or chair. If you are seated on the floor or on a cushion, enter a cross-legged position. If you opt to complete this pose in a chair, plant your feet firmly on the ground.

Next, rest both of your hands (palm up) on the inside of your knees, or just above your knees, and allow your arms to fully relax. Notice what it feels like for your sit bones (and any other area of the body touching the floor or chair) to connect with the floor (or chair).

Begin to gently close your eyes and maintain continued focusing on what it feels like for your sit bones to make contact with the earth. As you do this, imagine your sit bones (and feet, if applicable) pushing further into the ground, creating a sense of strength and stability.

Now, as you continue to push your sit bones into the ground, begin taking long, deep breaths, maintaining focus on the connection between your body and the earth. Take three deep breaths while maintaining this awareness.

Next, as you continue to take long, deep breaths, begin to imagine that you are breathing into the sit bones, which remain firmly pressed into the ground. As you exhale, imagine breathing that air through the sit bones, into the ground, further stabilizing your connection to the earth. Maintain this focus and continue breathing in this way for a few moments.

Incorporate Movement

Finally, begin to incorporate movement into this pose by gently rocking back and forth, shifting your weight from one sit bone to the other. Notice what it feels like to pendulate, or sway slightly off balance onto your left sit bone, and then rebalance at the center before swaying to your right sit bone. Continue to sway back and forth for a few moments, continuing to focus on the connection between your sit bones and the ground, breathing through the sit bones into the earth. When you are ready, you may gently begin to open your eyes and end this practice.

Mountain Pose

This yoga pose is called "mountain pose" because it creates the opportunity for the participant to feel strong, steady, and "grounded" into the earth, like a mountain. This beginner pose can be used as a foundation for other standing yoga poses, or can be practiced alone, to help you feel stable and strong.

To enter mountain pose, remove your shoes and stand up slowly from the chair, placing your feet hip distance apart. Direct your toes straight ahead and feel into the feet, noticing what it feels like for the feet to make firm contact with the ground (see figure below). At the same time, gently engage your hamstrings and quadriceps, and slightly tense the lower muscles of your abdomen area. During this pose it is recommended that you keep your eyes slightly open, gazing downward (but keeping your head upright) at a point on the floor about six feet in front of you.

Next, return the focus back down to your feet, continuing to feel into the feet. Focus on pressing into the balls of each foot, the little toe mounds near the outside of the feet, and the heels. Imagine that these three areas of the foot form a triangle, and as you maintain this pose, concentrate on pressing into the three corners of the triangle. Imagine now that the corners of these triangles have nails, or roots coming out of them, extending down into the earth to ground and stabilize you. Stay here for a moment, continuing to notice the connection between your feet and the ground.

Now, as you continue to focus on this connection with the earth, begin taking long, deep breaths, visualizing the breath flowing upward through the body as you inhale, and back downward through the body and out the triangles of the feet, into the earth as you exhale. Maintain this focus and continue breathing in this way for a few moments.

Incorporate Movement

To incorporate movement into this pose, begin to gently rock back and forth, shifting your weight from one foot to the other. Notice what it feels like to pendulate, or sway slightly off balance onto your left foot, and then rebalance at the center before swaying to your right foot. Continue to sway back and forth for a few moments, continuing to focus on the connection between the triangles of your feet and the ground, breathing through the triangle points into the earth. Come back to center, holding this pose once more, grounding into the earth.

Once you have re-grounded your feet into the earth, begin to pendulate once more, this time by gently swaying forward and backward, slightly tipping yourself off balance as you do this. Continue this for a few moments before coming back to center, feeling once more into the earth with your feet. When you are ready, you may gently begin to open your eyes and end this practice.

Warrior II Pose

Warrior II pose is an intermediate yoga pose used to help you feel grounded and stable, both physically and mentally. Engaging in this pose even briefly can help you refocus and redirect racing thoughts, nervous energy, and scattered attention, so you become calm, grounded, and present.

To enter right-facing Warrior II pose, gently stand (preferably barefoot) with your feet very wide, approximately 3 feet apart. Extend your arms straight out from your sides, lifting them until they are parallel to your shoulders. Extend your hands and your fingers as well, creating a straight line from your fingers all the way to your shoulders. This is referred to as "center pose," a prerequisite to Warrior II Pose.

Next, turn your head 90 degrees to the right, gently gaze at a point out in front of you (on a wall, or something up at eye height). Point the toes on your right foot 90 degrees to the right, the same direction as your head. Keep your left toes pointing in their original direction; do not move your left foot. Now, begin to gently bend your right knee, lowering your entire body as your knee bends. Bend your knee until it creates a 90-degree angle, keeping the knee stacked squarely over the ankle. Gently engage the abdomen muscles, simultaneously rotating your buttocks downward (see figure below).

Now that you have fully entered right-facing Warrior II pose, begin taking long, deep breaths, and as you breathe, focus on pressing your feet into the ground, noticing the connection between your feet and the earth. As you inhale, imagine the air flowing upward through your body. As you exhale, long and slow, imagine that the air is flowing downward, through your feet and into the earth below, further stabilizing and grounding you. Stay here for a moment, continuing to take long, deep breaths, emphasizing long exhales and breathing through your feet into the earth.

Incorporate Movement

To incorporate movement, begin to exit Warrior II pose by straightening your right knee, turning your head 90 degrees to the left, and pointing your right toes 90 degrees to the left, now parallel to your left foot. This is the center pose you assumed before entering right-facing Warrior II pose.

Next, turn your head another 90 degrees to your left, and shift your left toes 90 degrees to the left, now facing the opposite direction as when you first engaged in Warrior II pose. Gently begin to bend your left knee, lowering to a 90-degree angle, entering Warrior II pose again, but this time facing the opposite direction (left-facing Warrior II pose).

Breathe into this pose, imagining that during the exhales, the breath is flowing downward through your feet into the earth. Hold this pose for a couple of breaths before gently coming out of left-facing Warrior II pose, passing through center pose, and once more entering right-facing Warrior II pose, holding this pose for two breaths before moving through center pose again and into left-facing Warrior II pose. Repeat this sequence of movements for a few moments before gently returning to center pose, holding this position, and taking two last deep breaths before ending the exercise.

Partner Grounding Exercise

The partner grounding exercise, which is adapted from an aikido practice, demonstrates the power of focusing inward on the self and the body as a way to stay strong and grounded. This exercise requires a partner; to complete the exercise, one person of the partner dyad volunteers to be lifted by the other person. The exercise can be completed in two short steps:

1. The volunteer stands facing away from the "lifter," legs straight and at shoulder width apart, and arms straight, down at the sides. In this position, the volunteer is instructed, "Focus on your partner, who is standing behind you, and if possible, do not allow your partner to lift you off up off the ground. Just focus on resisting your partner's efforts to lift you."

   The partner, who is standing behind the volunteer, now can wrap their arms around the volunteer and attempt to slightly lift them upward.

2. After completing step one, have the volunteer resume their stance, facing away from the lifter with their legs straight and arms down. Now, have the volunteer gently bend their knees, and instruct them to do the following: "With your knees bent, and chest still upright, imagine that you are directing your energy and breath downward, through your knees, through your feet, into the ground. Imagine that your energy is flowing downward, strongly, like nails going from your feet into the earth."

   The partner, who is once again behind the volunteer, will now try to lift the volunteer again, noticing any differences between this stance and the previous stance.

   Now, partners switch positions, so that the volunteer is now the lifter, and vice versa. Complete this short exercise with the partners in their new roles.

Discussion

After completing this exercise, talk about what was experienced. Was there a difference between the first stance and the second one? Which stance was easier to lift the volunteer from? What was it like to focus on grounding your feet into the earth, as opposed to focusing on something external like the partner?

Most people will agree that when a volunteer assumes the second stance, and focuses inward, it is much more difficult to pick them up or "unground" them. A main take-home message from this exercise is that when we focus on controlling things or people outside of us, it makes us feel less stable, less grounded, and more out of control. When we focus inward, on our own grounding and stability, we feel more powerful and in control, and are less likely to be swayed or thrown off balance.

(Adapted from Khouri & Haglund, 2016)

Poses and Movement for Calming

Symptoms Addressed

- Emotional awareness and regulation
- Concentration and attention
- Dysregulated interoception
- Memory
- Stress response
- DSM-5 PTSD arousal and reactivity symptoms

Calming poses and movements, which often involve stretching, help clients de-stress and relax. These techniques can be used alone, to promote mindful relaxation, or in conjunction with other bottom-up or top-down practices, to train the body to relax while experiencing distressing thoughts or to intensify the effects of other stress-reducing practices (such as mindful breathing). **Each of the poses and accompanying movements presented here may be practiced with clients in the context of psychotherapy, but they require more space and sense of safety with the therapist than grounding poses and movements.**

POSES AND MOVEMENT FOR CALMING TIPS

- To introduce calming poses and movements to clients, discuss the poses and show the client a picture of the pose(s) you propose they try. If possible, also consider doing these along with the client, to demonstrate for them the proper form. This will help ensure that the client feels confident and safe about attempting these poses both in and out the context of therapy.

- Before practicing calming poses and movements, ensure that the client has completed a recent physical with their physician and that the physician does not believe these practices are contraindicated for the client.

- During these exercises, attention may simultaneously be brought to the breath, focusing on long, slow, steady inhales and exhales.

- It is also recommended to have clients imagine that they are breathing into the poses and movements as they engage in them.

- If appropriate, these techniques can also be utilized with top-down, cognitive techniques, including trauma-focused approaches. For instance, while in a calming pose, clients may be asked to access information regarding a traumatic memory. As they do this, they remain in the pose, and continue to focus on feeling into a specific area as they discuss some aspect about the memory.

- After practicing these poses, follow up with the client about their experience and discuss when, and for how long, they will practice these poses outside of session. A short daily practice of approximately five minutes is a common recommendation.

KEY RESEARCH FINDINGS

- Reduced stress and allostatic load (which is the wear and tear on the body due to stress) (Streeter et al., 2012)
- Increased ability to concentrate (Kerr et al., 2011)
- Increased volume of several brain areas, including the hippocampus (Hariprasad et al., 2013), dorsolateral prefrontal cortex (Wei et al., 2013) and insula (Villemure et al., 2014)

Child's Pose

This beginner's yoga pose helps individuals reduce stress and induce relaxation. To enter child's pose, begin by gently lowering onto the ground, onto your hands and knees. While on your hands and knees, bring your feet together behind you so that your big toes touch. Begin to lean back, putting your weight on your heels, feeling the front of your feet pushing into the ground. As you lean back a bit, ensure that your knees are approximately hip distance apart, keeping your feet together under your weight.

Next, sit upright, spine straight, and take a deep breath in and out. Now, begin to lean forward, extending your arms to the ground and moving them outward, away from the body, stretching as far out in front of you as possible. Keep the lower part of your body in the same position as it was when you were seated upright; push your sit bones into your heels as you simultaneously extend your arms out as far as you can, beginning to feel the lower (and perhaps the upper) parts of your arms touching the floor.

If you find it difficult or uncomfortable to keep your sit bones pressed into your heels, you may place a blanket or pillow in the fold of your knees, providing you with extra support. Gently allow your head to drop down, lowering your forehead to the ground. Press your palms gently into the floor as you continue to press your sit bones into your feet (see figure below).

Begin to breathe deeply into this position and, as you breathe, focus on continuing to press your sit bones and palms downward. Stay here for a few moments, continuing to take long, deep breaths, emphasizing long, deep exhales.

Incorporate Movement

To incorporate movement into child's pose, gently begin to transition from child's pose to upward dog pose, using the instructions in the following Upward Facing Dog Pose Handout. You may enter upward dog pose, remain there for a few moments, and then slowly transition back to child's pose, alternating between the two poses a few times.

Upward Facing Dog Pose

This beginner's yoga pose helps individuals open the chest and reduce tension. To enter upward facing dog pose, begin by gently lowering your entire body onto the ground, stomach down. Lift your head slightly, bend your elbows, and position your hands firmly on the floor between your chest and shoulders. As you do this, ensure that your elbows and arms remain close to the sides of your body, as opposed to allowing them to flare out away from your body. With your hands pressed into the floor, begin to push through your palms, lifting your head and chest off the floor upward as you slowly straighten your arms. There is no requirement to completely straighten your arms; rather, focus on opening the chest, stretching the back, and lifting the head and chest up toward the sky.

As you continue to lift the head and chest, palms pushing into the floor, set your intention to gently shift your hips forward and, if possible, push upward a bit more with your palms, beginning to lift your hips off the floor while keeping your legs straight. Hold this position and take a deep breath, directing your gaze upward.

Begin to breathe deeply into this position and as you breathe, focus on continuing to press upward through the palms. Stay here for a few moments, continuing to take long, deep breaths, emphasizing long, deep exhales.

Incorporate Movement

To incorporate movement into upward facing dog pose, gently begin to transition from this pose back into child's pose, holding each pose for several breaths before transitioning between the poses.

Cat/Cow Pose

These yoga poses produce a calming response by lengthening the spine and relaxing the back, a place where the body commonly holds tension. Additionally, this exercise promotes circulation between back discs, which in turn releases tension from the back and improves flexibility.

Before entering cow pose, lower onto the floor, assuming a "tabletop position" with your palms on the floor, arms straight, and knees, lower legs, and tops of feet on the floor. As much as possible, equally distribute your weight between your hands, knees, lower legs, and feet. Gently engage the core muscles so that the center of your body, the abdomen, is not saggy. Additionally, ensure that the shoulders are directly over the wrists, and the hips are directly over the knees as you hold this position for a moment. From this position, you may enter cow pose or cat pose, and begin to alternate between the two, incorporating movement.

Enter Cow Pose

To enter cow pose, begin to inhale, while allowing your stomach to drop downward as you release the tension in your core muscles. As you do this, also lift your head, gaze, and chest upward, and imagine that you are simultaneously lifting your tailbone upward (figure below).

Begin to breathe deeply into this position and, as you breathe, focus on continuing to extend your head, chest, and tailbone up into the sky. Stay here for a few moments, continuing to take long, deep breaths, emphasizing long, deep exhales.

Enter Cat Pose

To enter cat pose from cow pose, take one more inhale while in cow pose, and as you start to exhale, begin to engage your core muscles, pulling your abdomen upward. Pass through the neutral position you assumed at the beginning of this practice, continuing to pull your core muscles upward, rounding your spine and tucking your tailbone under. At the same time, lower your head and gaze downward, allowing your chin to make contact with your chest. Now, with your spine still curved, breathe in this position for a moment, continuing to take long, deep breaths out.

Incorporate Movement

To incorporate movement, flow between cow pose and cat pose with each breath, moving into cow pose on each inhale, and transitioning into cat pose with each exhale. Continue this movement for several breaths.

Poses and Movement for Safety

Symptoms Addressed

- Emotional awareness and regulation
- Concentration and attention
- Dysregulated interoception
- Memory
- Stress response
- DSM-5 PTSD arousal and reactivity symptoms

Safety poses and movements help clients move their attention inward to the body in a safe and gentle manner. For many clients, trauma has caused the body to be experienced as dangerous, and this often results in clients avoiding the body, intensifying the disconnect between the mind and the body. This is especially true for clients who suffered physical trauma to the body (through violence, sexual assault, etc.). To heal trauma, a re-integration of the body and mind is necessary, and one way to work toward this is to help clients begin to re-enter the body in a safe, controlled way.

The following safety poses and movements help clients reconnect with the body in a way that promotes a sense of safety and security. Each of the poses and accompanying movements presented here may be practiced with clients in the context of psychotherapy, with little space and no equipment required.

POSES AND MOVEMENT FOR SAFETY TIPS

- During these exercises, attention may simultaneously be brought to the breath, focusing on long, slow, steady inhales and exhales.
- It is also recommended to have clients imagine that they are breathing into the poses and movements as they engage in them.
- If appropriate, these techniques can also be utilized with top-down, cognitive techniques, including trauma-focused approaches. For instance, while in a grounding pose, clients may be asked to access information regarding a traumatic memory. As they do this, they remain in the pose, and continue to focus on pressing their feet or pelvis (or other body parts connected to the ground) into the earth as they discuss some aspect about the memory.
- Whenever a client experiences an unexpected, uninvited distressing memory, they may remain in the safety pose or shift into a grounding pose by placing their feet onto the floor and pressing downward, into the earth.

KEY RESEARCH FINDINGS

- Reduced stress and allostatic load (which is the wear and tear on the body due to stress) (Streeter et al., 2012)

- Increased ability to concentrate (Kerr et al., 2011)

- Increased volume of several brain areas, including the hippocampus (Hariprasad et al., 2013), dorsolateral prefrontal cortex (Wei et al., 2013) and insula (Villemure et al., 2014)

Psoas Relaxation Pose

The Psoas Muscles

The psoas muscles connect the legs to the front of the spine, and the upper torso with the pelvis. These muscles function to stabilize and decompress the spine, and to help individuals walk upright and maintain a healthy posture. Chronic tension in, or injury of, the psoas muscles (which is a common outcome of sexual abuse specifically and trauma more broadly) can lead to lower back pain. If this occurs over a long period of time, neck and shoulder pain may also develop.

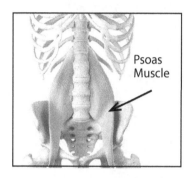

Psoas Muscle

An interesting fact about the psoas muscles is that they are involved in the experience and storage of traumatic experiences. We can work with this area of the body to facilitate recovery from trauma, including releasing traumatic energy from this region. As trauma expert Dr. David Berceli (2005) states, "The psoas muscles are considered the fight or flight muscles of the human species" (p.14). Specifically, the psoas muscles play a role in keeping us braced and protected when something very stressful or traumatic happens.

The psoas muscles contain the largest number of "fight or flight nerves" (sympathetic nervous system nerves) in the entire body, and these nerves become activated during traumatic events, causing strong tension in the psoas region. In other words, when there is trauma or a strong stress response, psoas tension is present, which can remain long after the trauma has subsided. One goal of body-based trauma treatment can include psoas muscle release, so that the body can enter a more relaxed state and a sense of safety can return to the body.

Enter the Psoas Relaxation Pose

To enter the psoas relaxation pose, you may lie down and rest your lower legs and feet on a chair as shown in the figure below. As you enter this position, ensure your lower back is pressed into the floor and allow your arms to fall gently at your sides, palms up. Next, feel your hip flexors begin to release as your femurs (the bones of the upper legs) relax into your hip joints.

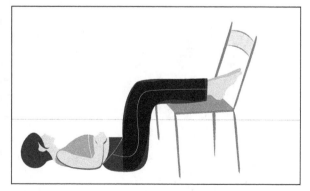

Begin to breathe deeply into this position and, as you breathe, focus on the sensation of your femurs relaxing into your hip joints, thereby reversing any tension in your psoas muscles. Stay here for a few moments, continuing to take long, deep breaths, imagining that you are breathing relaxation and health into your hip flexors.

Incorporate Movement

To incorporate movement, gently move one knee toward your chest, grasping the lower leg with your arms and gently pulling it into the chest. Breathe into this position for a moment before releasing the leg back to its original position on the chair, and repeating this motion with the other leg. Alternate legs every few breaths, for approximately 3-5 minutes.

Forward Bend Pose

To heal trauma, it is important for individuals to experience the body as a safe haven, and a protected space to which they can turn when feeling distressed. This pose creates a feeling of "folding into oneself" and promotes a sense of safety and protection. We have often noticed the tendency that many people have to curl up into a ball when extremely stressed or upset; this natural response to stress is meant to help the person feel safe and comforted within their own body. It can also be understood as a self-soothing strategy.

To enter forward bend pose, begin by sitting upright in a chair, feet flat on the floor shoulder width apart (or even slightly further apart), spine elongated upward with arms resting down at the sides of the body. Begin by slowing inhaling and, as you do this, extend the arms out, away from your sides, and then lift them straight up until they are close to your ears. Keeping the arms straight, begin to exhale very slowly and, as you do this, lean your torso forward, keeping the spine as straight as possible.

Continue to slowly bend forward as you exhale, slowly bringing your abdomen and chest down to the tops of the legs until the abdomen is resting on the legs. Do not force yourself to stretch more than feels comfortable, and ensure that while your abdomen is resting on your legs, it is not pushing hard into your legs so that you have difficulty breathing. Allow your arms to relax down to your sides and begin taking slow, long breaths while maintaining this pose.

Continue to breathe into this position and, as you inhale, straighten your spine just a little, making room for the breath to enter the diaphragm. Move slightly downward with each exhale, curving the back as the air exits your diaphragm.

Incorporating Movement

To incorporate movement, you can slowly, in rhythm with the breath, move between forward bend pose and sitting upright. To do this, start by sitting upright and move into forward bend pose using the instructions provided above. Once in forward bend pose, start to inhale slowly as you extend your arms out from your sides, straighten your spine a bit, and begin to lift your torso upward. As you continue moving your torso upward, lift your arms until they are straight above you, arms next to your ears. As you complete the inhalation, assume an upright seated position. Now, as you begin to exhale, slowly transition back into forward bend pose. You may flow through these two poses for a few moments, inhaling to come into an upright seated pose, and exhaling to fold into forward bend pose.

Walking Meditation

> ## *Symptoms Addressed*
>
> - Emotional awareness and regulation
> - Concentration and attention
> - Dysregulated interoception
> - Memory
> - Stress response
> - DSM-5 PTSD arousal and reactivity symptoms

Walking meditation is an effective way to maintain moment-to-moment awareness of the body and the external environment, activate thinking areas of the brain, and reduce autonomic arousal. Additionally, walking meditation can help participants integrate external and internal awareness, by strengthening both inward connection with the body and external, environmental awareness. Specifically, slow walking meditation emphasizes proprioceptive awareness (which is our sense of balance), while fast walking meditation emphasizes interoception (such as breath awareness) and environmental awareness.

WALKING MEDITATION TIPS

- When possible, it is recommended that walking meditation be completed outside in nature.
- If conducted in a group setting, ensure that each person engaging in walking meditation has sufficient personal space while walking.
- During this exercise, attention may be brought to the breath, the body, the external environment, or a combination of all three.
- If appropriate, walking meditation can also be utilized with top-down, cognitive techniques, including trauma-focused approaches. For instance, while focusing on something in the environment (a tree, flower, etc.), clients may be asked to access information regarding a traumatic memory. As they do this, they remain grounded in the external environment, which can help reduce dissociation.

KEY RESEARCH FINDINGS

- Reduced stress and allostatic load (which is the wear and tear on the body due to stress) (Streeter et al., 2012)
- Increased ability to concentrate (Kerr et al., 2011)
- Increased volume of several brain areas, including the hippocampus (Hariprasad et al., 2013), dorsolateral prefrontal cortex (Wei et al., 2013) and insula (Villemure et al., 2014)

Slow Walking Meditation

In slow walking meditation, the goal is to break down the process of walking into several steps, noticing what it feels like to move through each step. To begin slow walking meditation, find a location that feels safe and private. This place does not have to be large. In fact, you only need a path where you can walk approximately 10 steps before turning around and walking in the other direction. Note, however, that walking very slowly can compromise balance. To remain steady, you may want to do this exercise near a wall, balancing yourself by placing one hand on the wall to start until the slow walking pace feels safe enough to lower your hand and maintain balance.

Begin this exercise by standing up, spine straight, arms relaxed down to your sides. Starting at the beginning of the path, shift your weight to your right foot and begin to take a small step with your left foot by slowly lifting it off the ground. Focusing as much as you can on your feet, and the sensation of balance, move the lifted left foot forward. Start to gently lower the left foot back onto the ground parallel to, and in front of, the right foot, placing the heel on the ground first. Once the heel makes contact with the ground, allow the entire foot to be placed firmly on the ground.

Next, shift your weight a bit forward, distributing it equally on each foot. Now shift most of your weight to your left foot as you slowly begin to lift your right foot off the ground. Again, focusing as much as you can on your feet, and the sensation of balance, move the lifted right foot forward. Start to gently lower the right foot back onto the ground parallel to, and in front of, the left foot, placing the heel on the ground first. Once the heel makes contact with the ground, allow the entire foot to be placed firmly on the ground. Shift your weight slightly forward, distributing the weight equally on each foot.

Repeat the above process for the length of the walking path you have identified and when you reach the end of the path, slowly turn 180 degrees and begin walking back down the path in the other direction, continuing to walk very slowly and mindfully, attending to the sensations associated with each movement. Practice slow walking meditation for approximately 10 minutes. When the mind wanders, congratulate yourself on this awareness, acknowledge the thought your mind wandered to, let it go, and return the focus back to the sensations of the movements.

Fast Walking Meditation

In fast walking meditation, the objectives are to notice the feeling of air flowing in and out of the body, and to connect with the external environment, including sights, smells, and sounds. Before beginning fast walking meditation, identify a long path or sidewalk, preferably out in nature. Paths containing trees, water, flowers, birds, and perhaps even animals are best, as they allow for a richer connection with nature.

Begin fast walking meditation by beginning to slowly walk on the path you have chosen. If you would like, you may begin this practice with a brief slow walking meditation, and then gradually speed up to a comfortable pace.

Inward Focus

As you start walking the path, bring your awareness inward to the breath, noticing what it feels like as your pace slowly increases. Breathing through the nose, be mindful of the feeling of air flowing into your nostrils, down your throat, and into your diaphragm as you breathe in. You may notice that the breath feels cool as it enters your nose. When you breathe out, notice the inward movement of your abdomen as the air exits your diaphragm, flowing upward back through your nostrils, now warmer than when it entered. Continue walking briskly with mindful awareness of the breath for a few moments, breathing fully in, and fully out in a comfortable manner. As your pace increases, notice the intensity of the breath increasing as well.

Outward Focus

After focusing inward on the breath for a few moments, begin to shift your awareness to your external environment, noticing the sights, sounds, and smells around you, following these instructions:

1. **Sights:** Begin attending to your external environment by turning your head to the left, looking at what might be there, and then slowly scanning your gaze to the right, as far as is comfortable. When you notice something in the environment, such as a tree, state to yourself, "I am seeing a tree to my left." As your gaze fixes on various objects around you, sustain your focus on them for a moment and state to yourself what you see.

2. **Sounds:** Next, as you continue walking, notice any sounds that might be in your environment. Sounds may include birds chirping, the sound of leaves rustling, the sound of your feet making contact with the ground, or the sound of your breath. State to yourself what you hear ("I am hearing my feet make contact with the earth as I walk.").

3. **Smells:** Finally, take a moment to connect with any smells you might be experiencing as you walk the path. Smells can be more difficult to identify; if you experience difficulty identifying a smell, simply state to yourself, "I am experiencing this smell right now."

Fast walking meditation can be completed in as little as 10 minutes, or can last much longer, depending on one's preference.

Benefits of Exercise

> ## *Symptoms Addressed*
>
> - Concentration and attention
> - Memory
> - Stress response
> - DSM-5 PTSD arousal and reactivity symptoms

Exercise has many medical and psychological benefits, including brain-related benefits that can be especially helpful for clients with a history of trauma. Two noteworthy benefits of exercise include: 1) reduced stress, due in part to increased heart rate variability. (See p. 87 for an explanation of HRV), and 2) increased activation and volume of the memory center of the brain (the hippocampus).

Individuals suffering from anxiety or post-trauma symptoms experience a high level of activation of the stress response (sympathetic nervous system activation). When this happens, subcortical areas of the brain such as the amygdala (fear brain) activate, dulling the thinking areas of the brain and setting into motion the stress response in the body (via the HPA axis). When this occurs, hundreds of psychophysiological and biochemical reactions occur, including the release of cortisol; these reactions exhaust and break down the body and brain over time. This high level of stress can have many medical and psychological consequences.

Additionally, those who suffer from anxiety or post-trauma symptoms often experience memory difficulties, and this is partially explained by deficits in the memory center of the brain, the hippocampus. This is directly related to the problematic stress response described above, because the hippocampus is dense with cortisol receptors. When cortisol is released during times of high stress (which occurs on a very frequent basis when anxiety or post-trauma symptoms are present), the cortisol floods the cortisol receptors on the hippocampus, resulting in under-activation and even shrinkage of the hippocampus over time.

Because the hippocampus plays a critical role in memory, individuals who have suffered trauma, anxiety, and/or prolonged stress often report memory difficulties. Hippocampal under-activation is also the reason that trauma memories tend to be re-experienced instead of remembered; the hippocampus is responsible for putting the time stamp on events that happen, but when it is damaged or under-activated, it fails to do this, resulting in past events being experienced as if they are occurring in the present.

Exercise not only helps reduce the stress response and quiet the fear brain, but it promotes the growth of *brand new neurons* in the memory center by facilitating the production of brain-derived neurotropic factor (BDNF) (Wrann et al., 2013). BDNF, which is a protein found in the brain, acts on the stem cells of the hippocampus, leading to the generation of new neurons.

EXERCISE TIPS

- Ensure that clients consult with their physicians before beginning any exercise programs.
- Ask clients to complete yearly physical examinations to ensure an adequate level of physical health needed to engage in exercise.
- Advise clients to consider exercising with a friend if they find it difficult to stick to an exercise schedule.
- Encourage clients to maintain a healthy diet when possible, since a healthy diet in addition to exercise can further increase BDNF.

KEY RESEARCH FINDINGS

- Decreased depression (Craft & Perna, 2004)
- Increased production of BDNF (Sleiman et al., 2016)
- Neurogenesis (the growth of new neurons) of the hippocampus (Erickson et al., 2011)
- Increased heart rate variability, indicating decreased stress (Routledge et al., 2010)

Benefits of Exercise

You probably hear this so often that it has become a cliché to consider exercise. However, there are very good reasons to think about using exercise as a way to cope with trauma, if you have been cleared by your physician to engage in it. There are two brain-related benefits that can be especially helpful for reducing post-trauma symptoms: 1) Exercise reduces stress and activation of the fear brain (the amygdala) and 2) Exercise builds a bigger, stronger memory center of the brain (the hippocampus).

1. **Reduce stress and calm the fear brain (amygdala):** Individuals suffering from anxiety or post- trauma symptoms experience a high level of stress and fear, which is due to activation of the fear brain (see the amygdala in the figure below). When the fear brain fires, it starts the stress response in the whole body, and part of that response includes the release of a stress hormone, cortisol. Cortisol floods the body and brain and contributes to that "stressed out" feeling, and exercise can help calm that feeling! Those who exercise enjoy lowered stress and less activation in the "fear brain."

2. **Strengthen the memory center (hippocampus) of the brain:** Additionally, those who suffer from anxiety or post-trauma symptoms often experience memory difficulties, and this is because the memory center of the brain (the hippocampus, see figure below) is no longer working well. Specifically, the memory center de-activates and actually begins to shrink when there is intense or prolonged stress. The reason for this is that the cortisol that is released during the stress response floods into the hippocampus, causing it to shrink and activate less over time. This, in turn, means it becomes very difficult to learn and remember things, and sometimes terrible memories from the past occur as though they are happening in the present. These memory center errors can be addressed, however, with exercise, which has been shown to both strengthen AND grow new neurons in the hippocampus.

Exercise not only helps reduce the stress response and quiet the fear brain, but it also promotes the growth of *brand new neurons* in the memory center at the same time!

Other Movement Practices

This chapter has described several movement-based techniques and poses that may be conducted during a typical psychotherapy session. However, several other movement-based techniques may also be helpful to incorporate into the treatment of trauma as homework, general recommendations to a client, or during session (such as tapping or sensorimotor approaches).

Other movement-based practices to consider, along with resources to get you started, include the following:

- **Yoga.** For an explanation of the different types of yoga, go here: http://www.healthline.com/health/fitness-exercises/types-of-yoga#2

- **Tai Chi.** To learn about the impact of tai chi on stress, read this: http://www.mayoclinic.org/healthy-lifestyle/stress-management/in-depth/tai-chi/art-20045184

- **Qigong.** To learn more about this practice, visit the Qigong Institute here: https://www.qigonginstitute.org/category/4/getting-started

- **Aikido** (or other types of self-defense or martial arts). To understand the purpose of aikido, visit the Aikido Association of America here: http://www.aaa-aikido.com/about-aikido/

- **Dance.** To better understand how dance can help with trauma recovery, visit Dr. Jamie Marich's website on "Dancing Mindfulness" here: http://www.dancingmindfulness.com/

- **Tapping Techniques** (such as emotional freedom technique or meridian tapping techniques) are a set of psychosensory tools that aim to help clients alter reconsolidation of the link between trauma memories and accompanying distress through the use of distraction and touch. To learn more about tapping approaches, go here: http://www.eft-alive.com/eft-therapy.html

- **Havening Techniques®.** To learn about how havening techniques can help clients recover from trauma, read this: http://www.havening.org/about-havening/faqs

- **Sensorimotor Approaches to Therapy.** For an introduction to this approach, visit this website: https://www.sensorimotorpsychotherapy.org/articles.html

Other Movement Practices

Many different movement-based practices can be immensely helpful to individuals suffering from the aftereffects of trauma. If one practice does not resonate with you, do not worry; there are several ways to incorporate movement into your life (and perhaps even your therapy) in stimulating, healthy, and even fun ways! Some examples of movement-based practices that you may want to consider are listed below. As with any exercise practice, however, make sure your doctor has approved your participation in the exercise before beginning!

Some common movement-based practices enjoyed by some clients include the following:

- Taking **a walk** or going for a jog (it does not have to be vigorous).

- **Yoga**. For an explanation of the different types of yoga, go here: http://www.healthline.com/health/fitness-exercises/types-of-yoga#2

- **Tai Chi**. To learn about the impact of tai chi on stress, read this: http://www.mayoclinic.org/healthy-lifestyle/stress-management/in-depth/tai-chi/art-20045184

- **Qigong**. To learn more about this practice, visit the Qigong Institute here: https://www.qigonginstitute.org/category/4/getting-started

- **Aikido** (or other types of self-defense or martial arts). To understand the purpose of aikido, visit the Aikido Association of America here: http://www.aaa-aikido.com/about-aikido/

- **Dance**. To better understand how dance can help with trauma recovery, visit Dr. Jamie Marich's website on "Dancing Mindfulness" here: http://www.dancingmindfulness.com/9

PART III

Top-Down Tools

7

Meditations

Meditations typically contain both bottom-up and top-down components, but they are categorized here as top-down exercises, since they require intense cognitive monitoring, awareness, and/or attention. While meditation can change the brain bottom-up, impacting the activation of subcortical areas such as the amygdala, the main effects of meditation are largely top-down. Specifically, meditations are an effective way to strengthen the cortical thinking areas of the brain, such as the prefrontal and cingulate cortices.

The way "meditation" is defined has varied widely across time, culture, and tradition. In fact, there are likely upwards of 100 different definitions of this type of practice! The lack of consensus regarding the definition of meditation is in part due to the sheer number of different meditative practices that have been documented (well over 1,000), which makes it difficult to create a single definition that adequately describes all of these techniques. For the purpose of this workbook, meditation is defined as a set of practices that train the mind to focus on one or more experiences, sensations, emotions, thoughts, or external stimuli.

THE BRAIN ON MEDITATION

Meditations may change the brain in several ways, depending on the practice. However, there are certain brain changes this type of practice tends to elicit, some of which can be especially helpful to clients struggling with post-trauma symptoms:

1. **Fear Center (Amygdala):** Decreased activation of the fear center. De-activation of this area helps to reduce reactivity when trauma triggers arise, and lowers baseline fear center activation. Meditation down-regulates amygdala activation from the "top down," via increased activation of cortical areas such as the prefrontal and cingulate cortices and increased connectivity between the amygdala and cortical regions. This down-regulation results in a decrease in arousal and reactivity symptoms, such as hypervigilance, feeling on guard, etc.

2. **Memory Center (Hippocampus):** Increased volume of the memory center of the brain (hippocampus). This activation helps remind individuals that they are safe in the present moment, and it is involved in the extinction of fear responses when trauma triggers arise. The increased competence an individual experiences in managing negative memories can reduce the avoidance symptoms of PTSD.

3. **Thinking Center (Prefrontal Cortex):** Increased prefrontal cortex activation, resulting in improved attention, problem-solving, and decision-making. A strong prefrontal cortex can help traumatized individuals maintain presence of mind during stressful or triggering situations, and can help them evaluate, reframe, or shift unhelpful thinking patterns that contribute to their PTSD symptoms.

4. **Self-Regulation (Center Cingulate Cortex):** Increased activation of the cingulate cortex, resulting in better thought and emotion regulation and conflict monitoring. Cingulate activation may help traumatized individuals respond more adaptively and appropriately to triggering stimuli and situations, and down-regulate negative emotions when needed.

5. **Connectivity:** Meditation has been shown to improve connectivity between key brain areas (such as the prefrontal cortex and hippocampus, and the basal ganglia, thalamus, and prefrontal cortex), leading to better brain integration and functioning.

What is Meditation?

The way meditation is defined has varied widely across time, culture, and tradition. In fact, there are likely upwards of 100 different definitions of this type of practice! For the purpose of this workbook, meditation is defined as a set of practices that train the mind to focus on one or more experiences, sensations, emotions, thoughts, or external stimuli. Some meditations require an individual to focus just on one thing, or one experience, whereas others encourage individuals to simply watch their attention as it drifts from one thing to another (see Tool 7-1 for different types of meditations).

Meditations typically contain both bottom-up and top-down components, but they are categorized here as top-down exercises, since they require a lot of intense cognitive effort and attention. You can think of meditations as a type of cognitive therapy.

People across the world practice meditation for different reasons, a common one being that it is believed to enhance wellbeing. The following handout, entitled Your Brain on Meditation, outlines some key brain changes associated with meditation, each of which enhances mental health for those who meditate.

Your Brain on Meditation

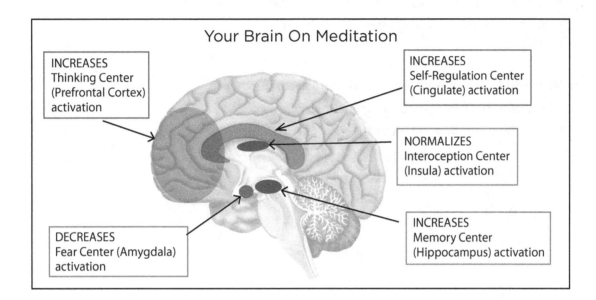

Meditations change the brain in **five** ways:

1. **Less activation in the fear center (amygdala) of the brain:**
   - Reduces how strongly you react to trauma triggers
   - Reduces the stress response and increases the relaxation response
   - Decreases hypervigilance and the feeling of "always being on guard"

2. **More activation and increased volume of the memory center (hippocampus) of the brain:**
   - Increases feeling of safety
   - Reduces fear, especially when faced with trauma triggers
   - Allows traumatic memories to be experienced as past events, as opposed to reliving them as though they are occurring in the present
   - Increases ability to cope with negative memories

3. **More activation in the thinking center (prefrontal cortex) of the brain:**
   - Allows for clear thinking, better problem-solving, and improved decision-making
   - Improves concentration and attention

4. **More activation in the self-regulation center (cingulate) of the brain:**
   - Improves emotion regulation
   - Improves ability to catch mind wandering during mindfulness practices or other times when concentration is required
   - Improves ability to respond to triggers in healthy ways
   - Improves ability to manage distressing thoughts

5. **More connectivity between critical brain areas:**
   - Improves brain integration and functioning
   - Speeds up communication between key brain areas

Types of Meditation

There are more than 1,000 meditative practices that have been described, and these practices can be categorized in many different ways. One way to classify meditations is to assign them to one of two main categories: Open awareness meditations, and closed concentration meditations (also called "open monitoring" and "focused attention" practices, according to Schmalzl, Powers, and Blom (2015)).

OPEN AWARENESS MEDITATIONS

Open awareness meditations are practices in which an individual allows their attention to drift within a specific domain (or domains). Examples of domains include the body, emotions, thoughts, or the external environment. For instance, in an open awareness meditation, an individual may set their intention to attend to the body, and within that domain (the body), they allow their attention to drift to whatever area of the body is calling their attention.

In open awareness practices, the individual is not trying to sustain attention to one specific area of the body (such as the feet, or heart), but rather the goals are to allow attention to drift anywhere within the body, and to simply notice where the attention goes. When the individual becomes aware that they have drifted into another domain (such as becoming lost in thought), they gently return the focus back to the intended domain (such as the body).

CLOSED CONCENTRATION MEDITATIONS

In closed concentration practices, the goal is to focus one's attention on one stimulus or experience at a time, committing all attentional resources to it. In advanced meditation practices, the focus may be split between two stimuli or experiences. For example, an individual may be instructed to put 60% of their attention to a specific area of the body, and 40% of their attention to a selected thought. More commonly, in closed concentration exercises, the objective is to maintain attention to one experience, thought, emotion, or region of the body. When the mind wanders, the goal is to become aware of this and gently redirect attention back to that one stimulus or experience.

This workbook presents four open awareness meditations, four closed concentration meditations, and one meditation containing both open and closed elements that can be helpful to clients suffering from post-trauma symptoms. Because meditation practices vary widely, it is recommended that clients be taught at least two meditation practices to get a sense of how different these techniques can feel. It is often the case that clients assume they will experience all meditations in the same way. However, different practices can result in radically different experiences, some of which may or may not resonate with clients.

Open Awareness vs. Closed Concentration Meditations

Meditations can be categorized into one of two categories: open awareness meditations, and closed concentration meditations. The easiest way to distinguish between these types of practices is that in closed concentration meditations *you bring your awareness to just one thing*, whereas in open awareness meditations *you allow your attention to drift to multiple things*. Here is a bit more information on these two types of techniques:

Open Awareness Meditations

Open awareness meditations are practices in which an individual allows their attention to drift within a specific domain (or domains). Examples of domains include the body, emotions, thoughts, or the external environment. For instance, in an open awareness meditation, an individual may set their intention to attend to the body, and within that domain (the body), they allow their attention to drift to whatever area of the body is calling their attention.

In this type of open awareness practice, the individual is not trying to keep their attention on one specific area of the body (such as the feet, or heart), but rather the goal is to allow attention to drift anywhere within the body. The objective with open awareness meditations is to allow the attention to drift to different things, and to simply track it and maintain awareness of it.

Closed Concentration Meditations

In closed concentration exercises, the objective is to maintain attention to one experience, thought, emotion, or region of the body. When the mind wanders, the aim is to become aware of this and gently redirect attention back to that one stimulus or experience. For example, in a closed concentration exercise, an individual may focus on different areas of the body, one at a time, in a distinct sequence, but the attention is on only one area at once (such as the foot)!

Trainspotting Meditation (Open Awareness)

Symptoms Addressed

- Concentration
- Emotion regulation
- Memory
- DSM-5 PTSD arousal and reactivity symptoms

Trainspotting Meditation is an exercise in which an individual checks in with and observes thoughts that are flowing into, passing through, and exiting the mind. This is accomplished by visualizing thoughts as trains that are running through the mind.

The main goal of this meditation is to observe and identify these trains of thought without becoming immersed in them. When an individual becomes completely immersed in a thought, this can be thought of as cognitive fusion, as the person's thought, emotions about this thought, and identity become fused. When there is cognitive fusion, it is difficult to examine or manage distressing thoughts because they are experienced as part of the self, true, and oftentimes emotional. This in turn can lead to rumination, anxiety, and suffering.

One way to manage thoughts is to practice cognitive defusion, in which thoughts are watched and identified from an observer standpoint. This allows the individual to make an intentional decision regarding how they wish to interact with the thought, if at all. For example, when an individual is able to observe the presence of a thought, they may state to themselves: "There is that thought again about failing that big exam."

During a cognitive defusion exercise, such as trainspotting meditation, the objective is to simply watch and identify thoughts without engaging or interacting with them. While the individual may choose to engage with the thought after this meditation, or take some action on it at that time, during this practice, the goal is to practice the skill of thought observation only, with no interaction or immersion. In this practice, cognitive fusion is referred to as "jumping on a train of thought," and individuals are trained to "jump off the train" (cognitive defusion) when they notice fusion occurring.

TRAINSPOTTING MEDITATION TIPS

- Because this technique incorporates mental imagery, intrusive images are less likely to occur, as mental imagery can reduce the presence of interfering images. However, if an individual tends to dissociate or experiences intrusive traumatic images, this meditation may be practiced with the eyes open, gently gazing downward to some static point.
- It is recommended that the therapist normalize the experience of "fusing" with thoughts, which occurs when an individual becomes immersed in a thought as opposed to observing it. When

this happens, the goal is to notice the fusion, let go of the thought, and return to an observer stance, simply noticing the thought that is present and labeling/identifying it.

- If a participant does not resonate with the idea of imagining thoughts as trains, thoughts may be visualized as cars, clouds, or anything that can be imagined as passing through the mind.

- This exercise can be practiced for small periods of time (5-10 minutes), multiple times per day.

KEY RESEARCH FINDINGS

- Increased creativity and divergent thinking, which is the ability to generate new ideas (Colzato et al., 2012)
- Greater pain relief (Zeidan et al., 2012)
- Improved body awareness (Holzel et al., 2011)
- Reduced substance use (Simpson et al., 2007)

Trainspotting Meditation
(Open Awareness)

Did you ever get so absorbed in anxious or negative thoughts that you couldn't control your feelings? That's where the Trainspotting Meditation can help put you back in control. Trainspotting Mediation is an exercise in which an individual observes thoughts that are flowing into, passing through, and exiting the mind by visualizing thoughts as trains. The main goal of this brain training exercise is to observe and identify these trains of thought without "jumping on the trains" and becoming immersed in them. Follow the instructions below to practice Trainspotting Meditation.

Begin to close your eyes, bringing your attention inward to the breath. Take a couple of deep breaths in and out, keeping the focus on the breath for a few moments.

Next, begin to shift your awareness to your mind, becoming aware of any thoughts entering, flowing through, or leaving the mind. As you observe these thoughts, begin to visualize them as trains, where each train represents one thought. Imagine that you are standing about 20 feet away from these thought trains, watching them from a slight distance as an observer. You may notice one thought train passing through your mind, or perhaps several. Some may move quickly, others more slowly, and some may stop for a while or appear to be on a loop.

As a curious observer of these trains, you are not the conductor, nor a passenger, of the trains, and therefore do not attempt to stop them, speed them up, or otherwise interact with them. Rather, as you become aware of each thought train, identify it in a single sentence. For example, you may state to yourself: "There is that thought train about [insert topic here]," or "This thought train is called [insert title here]." Your job is to watch these trains and allow them to enter, move through, and exit your mind at their own pace.

Continue to observe and name thought trains as you become aware of them. When you notice that you have jumped onto one of these trains, and have become a passenger or conductor of a train instead of an observer, congratulate yourself on this awareness, acknowledge the thought train, then jump off that train and resume your stance as an observer.

Continue trainspotting for a few minutes, watching and identifying thought trains and disengaging from thoughts that you have become immersed in by "jumping off" the thought trains as needed.

Mind-Body Connection Meditation (Open Awareness)

Symptoms Addressed

- Concentration
- Emotion regulation
- Memory
- DSM-5 PTSD arousal and reactivity symptoms

The Mind-Body Connection Meditation is an open awareness exercise in which an individual allows their attention to drift within one of these three domains (the body, emotions, or thoughts), simply noticing where their attention is drawn. The practice begins by attending to experiences within the body, followed by attending to emotions that may be present, followed by thought observation (referred to as trainspotting, as described in Tool 7-2).

In this exercise, the goal is not to focus intentionally just on one experience or stimulus. Here, attention is allowed to drift, and the individual observes where their attention is drawn. For instance, while attending within the domain of the body, an individual may notice their attention being drawn to sensations in the feet, and then the shoulders, and then the hands, etc. The objective is simply to notice where the mind wanders within each of the three domains. When the mind wanders outside of the intended domain, or fusion with a separate experience occurs, the individual gently redirects the attention back to the domain of interest.

After the individual has noticed, or checked in, with experiences occurring within each of the three domains, attention is brought to all three domains simultaneously. The individual is then prompted to notice how experiences within one domain, thoughts, are connected to emotional experiences and physical sensations. For example, an individual may notice that when they experience a thought about an upcoming exciting event, they experience a change in heart rate and notice the presence of an emotion such as happiness. The connection between the body, emotions, and mind is experienced in real-time, highlighting the mind-body connection.

MIND-BODY CONNECTION MEDITATION TIPS

- If an individual tends to dissociate, or experiences intrusive traumatic images, this meditation may be practiced with the eyes open, gently gazing downward to some static point.
- It is recommended that the therapist inform the client ahead of time that it is natural and expected for the mind to wander outside of the domain of interest (for example, the mind may wander from the body to thoughts).
- This exercise can be practiced for small periods of time (5-10 minutes), multiple times per day.

- Clients who have experienced trauma to certain parts of their body, either sexual or physical, often feel symptoms of the trauma when that part of the body is focused on. It is recommended that clients be given permission to stop this exercise, or skip certain areas of the body, if they feel uncomfortable or unsafe.

KEY RESEARCH FINDINGS

- Increased creativity and divergent thinking, which is the ability to generate new ideas (Colzato et al., 2012)
- Greater pain relief (Zeidan et al., 2012)
- Improved body awareness (Holzel et al., 2011)
- Reduced substance use (Simpson et al., 2007)

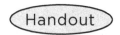

Mind-Body Connection Meditation

1. *Begin by closing your eyes (or gazing downward at a static object) and attending to your breath. Notice its qualities, and what it feels like. Breathe in, and breathe out, noticing how your abdomen rises with each inhale and falls with each exhale. Engage in this focused breathing for a moment.*

2. *Body Awareness: Now extend this awareness of the breath to your entire body, just being present with your whole body and noticing any sensations that arise. Do not judge these sensations; rather, just notice anything happening in your body. Maybe you feel some relaxation in some area, or some tension. Maybe there is some discomfort, or another distinct sensation. Just be with these experiences for a moment, allowing your focus to drift anywhere in the body that is calling your attention. As you complete this exercise it is okay to stop, or skip certain areas of the body, if a region does not feel safe or comfortable to connect with.*

3. *Emotional Awareness: Now, gently shift your attention away from the body, and onto your emotions. Notice any feelings you may be experiencing, no matter how subtle or strong. Again, do not judge these emotions, simply notice and accept their presence. As you connect with your emotions, you may notice the presence of multiple emotions, to varying degrees. Or, you may notice no emotions at all. Just stay here, with your emotions, for a moment.*

4. *Thought Awareness: Finally, shift your awareness to your thoughts.*

   a. *Without becoming attached to any of your thoughts, or getting wrapped up in them, simply notice them. Notice them as they arrive, observe them as they play out, and allow them to leave without trying to push them away or cling to them. Stay with your thoughts for a moment.*

   b. *As you continue to observe your thoughts, begin to visualize your thoughts as trains, where each train represents one thought. If possible, label or identify each thought train that passes by. Imagine that you are standing about 20 feet back from these trains, watching them. You are not the conductor of these trains, nor are you a passenger right now. You may notice one train of thought passing through your mind, or perhaps several. Some may move quickly, others more slowly, and some may stop for a while. This is okay. Your job is to watch these trains and allow them to enter, move through, and exit your mind at their own pace.*

   c. *If you notice at some point that you have jumped onto one of these trains, and followed or fused with one of your thoughts, congratulate yourself on this awareness, acknowledge the thought you were just having, then jump off that train and resume your stance as an observer.*

5. *Now, as you continue to watch the thought trains, start to open your awareness to include your emotions and body, so that you begin to notice any emotions or physical sensations that might be connected to your thoughts. These may be visualized as cargo attached to the thought trains. Simply notice the association between the thoughts, emotions, and physical sensations without judging or trying to alter them. You may notice, as you complete this exercise, that certain thoughts are associated with certain sensations and emotional experiences, and that these three domains (body, thoughts, emotions) can interact.*

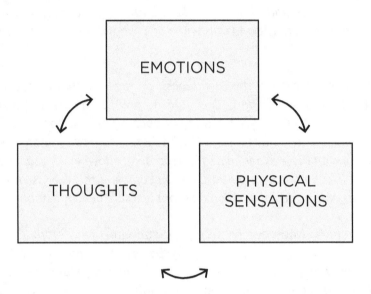

6. *To end this exercise, gently shift your attention back to your breath, taking two deep, diaphragmatic breaths before opening your eyes and re-entering the room.*

Emotional Awareness Meditation (Open Awareness)

Tool 7-4

Symptoms Addressed

- Concentration
- Emotion regulation
- Body awareness
- DSM-5 PTSD arousal and reactivity symptoms

Emotional Awareness Meditation helps individuals learn what different emotions feel like in the body. Every emotion has physical correlates, or specific physical sensations associated with it, and the objective of this open awareness practice is for individuals to notice how they experience various emotions in the body. This is accomplished via small emotion inductions intended to produce low-level emotions that can be noticed, examined, and managed.

Additionally, this practice improves interoception, which is one's ability to feel into the body and become aware of internal states and experiences. When interoceptive abilities are strong, an individual may learn to identify emotions by the profile of physical sensations the emotions produce. This in turn may help individuals regulate emotion, since physical sensations can be managed using bottom-up exercises. While this meditation is classified as a largely top-down practice, it contains the bottom-up element of feeling into, and connecting with, the body.

EMOTIONAL AWARENESS MEDITATION TIPS

- This exercise can be completed with the eyes open, directing the gaze to a static object, if an individual tends to dissociate or experiences intrusive traumatic images.

- It is recommended that this exercise be practiced for multiple emotions so that participants learn how different emotions feel in the body. However, recalling traumatic events during this exercise is not recommended unless the client is stabilized and resourced.

- This exercise can be practiced for small periods of time (5-10 minutes), multiple times per day.

KEY RESEARCH FINDINGS

- Increased creativity and divergent thinking, which is the ability to generate new ideas (Colzato et al., 2012)

- Greater pain relief (Zeidan et al., 2012)

- Improved body awareness (Holzel et al., 2011)

- Reduced substance use (Simpson et al., 2007)

177

Emotional Awareness Meditation

Emotional Awareness Meditation helps you learn how you experience various emotions in the body. This is done by inducing low-level emotions in the body by recalling past events that bring up those emotions. Before beginning Emotional Awareness Meditation, it is helpful to identify the emotions you will connect with during the exercise, as well as the memories you will recall in order to experience those emotions. Some examples of emotions you may choose to connect with, and types of memories that can aid in this process, include:

- **Happiness:** A time when you felt joy or happiness in your life.

- **Pride:** A time when you, or someone you love, succeeded and you felt pride.

- **Excitement:** A time in your life when you felt excited about something positive that was going to happen.

- **Contentment:** A time in your life when you were relaxed, content, and at peace.

- **Anger:** An incident that made you feel irked, frustrated, or angry.

- **Disappointment:** A time in your life when you felt let down or disappointed.

- **Embarrassment:** An incident that made you feel embarrassed, either for yourself or someone else.

- **Disgust:** An example of a time when you felt repulsed or disgusted by something.

To practice Emotional Awareness Meditation, begin to close your eyes and take a deep breath, connecting with the breath for a moment. Next, begin to bring to mind a time in your life when you felt [insert emotion here]. Imagine this event or time period clearly in your mind, remembering what happened, when it happened, who was there, and where you were. As you develop a clear picture in your mind of this event, try to also begin accessing the emotion you felt at that time. While you may not experience this emotion as intensely as you did during those moments, you may be able to experience a lower level of the emotion as you remember this event.

When you are able to access the emotion you experienced during this event, continue to connect with this memory for a moment, allowing the emotion to intensify a bit. Next, gently release the memory from your imagination, so that you are no longer intentionally focusing on this event. Instead, with your eyes still closed, shift your awareness from the emotional memory to the body, beginning to notice any physical sensations occurring in the body as you experience [insert emotion here].

As you check in with the body, allow your focus to drift anywhere in the body that calls your attention, simply noting any sensations or experiences that you notice as you experience this emotion. You may notice changes in your heart rate, sensations in your abdomen, temperature changes in the body, or feelings of heaviness or lightness. All sensations are acceptable and noteworthy in this practice. As you check in with the body, assume the role of a curious scientist, as opposed to a judge, and remain open to any physical sensations that might be occurring.

If it is difficult to detect any specific sensations in the body while maintaining an open awareness stance, wherein you allow your attention to drift to various areas without effort, you may set your intention to check in with broad regions of the body, beginning with the feet and moving upward.

Repeat this process with multiple different emotions, noting how different emotions feel in the body. If possible, pause after noticing what each emotion feels like in the body and write down what you experienced. For example, when experiencing fear, you might notice physical sensations such as tingling, shortness of breath, feeling hot, etc. These may be substantially different from the physical sensations associated with some other emotions, such as contentment.

Expansion Meditation (Open Awareness)

┌───┐
│   *Symptoms Addressed*   │
│ ───   │
│   │
│   • Concentration   │
│   • Emotion regulation   │
│   • Memory   │
│   • DSM-5 PTSD arousal and reactivity symptoms│
└───┘

Expansion Meditation is a type of mindfulness meditation wherein the goal is for the individual to expand their awareness from the breath to the entire body, and then to emotions, thoughts, and the external environment. As this is done, the individual observes where their attention is pulled. Much like in Mind-Body Connection Meditation, the individual allows their attention to drift wherever it is called, and simply notices where the mind travels.

The observation of attention can be a particularly challenging task in a technique such as Expansion Meditation, where the awareness expands so wide that it is eventually completely uncontained, allowing for attention to drift among many domains, experiences, and stimuli. Maintaining such an open awareness can lead to immersion in, or "fusion" with, a variety of experiences. When the individual notices that they have become lost in a distinct experience or stimulus, they are instructed to congratulate themselves on their awareness of the immersion, acknowledge the experience they became lost in, let go of it, and return to an expanded awareness state, watching their attention as it drifts between experiences, domains, and stimuli.

EXPANSION MEDITATION TIPS

• Because this technique incorporates intentional mental imagery, unwanted, intrusive images related to traumatic events may be suppressed, as intentional mental imagery can reduce the presence of unwanted, intrusive, trauma-related images. However, if an individual tends to dissociate or experiences trauma-related intrusive images, this meditation may be practiced with the eyes open, gently gazing downward to some static point.

• If it becomes overwhelming for a client to expand their awareness, it is recommended clinicians take a titrated approach to this practice, expanding to additional domains slowly over time. For instance, the clinician may not expand past the body to emotions right away, and may refrain from expanding to thoughts or the external environment until the client feels comfortable being in the body.

• This exercise can be practiced for small periods of time (5-10 minutes), multiple times per day.

KEY RESEARCH FINDINGS

- Increased creativity and divergent thinking, which is the ability to generate new ideas (Colzato et al., 2012)
- Greater pain relief (Zeidan et al., 2012)
- Improved body awareness (Holzel et al., 2011)
- Reduced substance use (Simpson et al., 2007)

Expansion Meditation

In Expansion Meditation, the objective is to gradually expand awareness from the breath to the entire body, and then keep expanding awareness to include emotional experiences, thoughts, and awareness of the external environment.

Begin this exercise by gently closing the eyes. If this is not comfortable for you, softly gaze downward at a static object. With your eyes now closed, begin to take a long, deep breath in through the diaphragm, and then exhale slowly and completely. Keep your attention here for a moment, at the breath, just noticing what it feels like to breathe in and out.

As you continue focusing on the breath, imagine that there is a bright yellow bubble appearing around the breath, containing it and highlighting it. This yellow bubble is your scope of awareness, and at this moment, the awareness is only as wide as the breath, meaning that you are solely focusing on, or aware of, the breath at this time.

Next, begin to slowly grow and expand your yellow awareness bubble, allowing it to expand outward to include the entire torso of your body. Visualize this yellow bubble encompassing your entire torso, such that your attention has now expanded past the breath to your entire torso. As you do this, continue to take deep breaths in and out of your diaphragm and keep your awareness contained to your torso for a moment.

Now begin to expand your awareness past the torso to the entire body from the neck down, envisioning the yellow awareness bubble expanding outward to encompass your whole body except your head. Allow your attention to drift anywhere within the awareness bubble it wishes to go.

In this exercise, you are not trying to force the attention to any one single place; rather, simply allow your attention to drift anywhere within the bubble that is calling your attention, and observe where your attention goes. Keeping your attention contained to the body, observe where in the body your mind is drawn, and what you notice about those experiences. Stay here for a moment.

As you stay connected to the body, imagine the yellow bubble expanding upward just a bit, now encompassing your head. At this point, your entire body is contained in the awareness bubble, and you can open your awareness to include sensations on the face or in the head.

Additionally, you may begin to expand your awareness to notice any thoughts or emotions that might be present. Thoughts and emotions may be experienced in any area of the body; open your awareness to these domains and observe where your attention flows and where in the body, if anywhere, these thoughts and emotions are experienced. Remain here for a few moments, allowing your attention to drift to any physical sensations, emotions, or thoughts that might be there.

Finally, with your eyes still closed, begin to expand your awareness to your external environment. Imagine that your bright yellow bubble of awareness has grown to encompass not only your body, but also the space all around your body, to include your immediate external environment. Although you are not looking at your environment, you may experience other aspects of your environment such as sounds and sensations.

Take a moment to notice any sounds that you may hear, just connecting with those sounds and observing their quality. You may also notice how external objects feel on the skin; for example, you may notice the softness of a chair, the ground making contact with your feet, or the feeling of an object in your hands.

With your awareness fully expanded, stay here for a few moments, allowing your attention to drift to any internal experiences, external sensations, emotions, thoughts, or aspects of your environment that may be calling your attention. As you allow your attention to drift, simply follow its path, noticing where it goes. After maintaining this wide-open awareness stance for a few moments, return the focus back to the breath and take two deep breaths through the diaphragm before opening your eyes and coming back into the room.

Focus Meditation (Closed Concentration)

> ## *Symptoms Addressed*
>
> - Concentration
> - Emotion regulation
> - Memory
> - DSM-5 PTSD arousal and reactivity symptoms

In Focus Meditation, the objective is to focus one's entire attention to just one word or phrase (called a mantra or affirmation), repeating it over and over. Focus Meditation can be conceptualized as a type of meditation that trains individuals to improve concentration abilities and prevent distracting thoughts from surfacing by restricting attention to only one stimulus. While this closed concentration technique can be very challenging to practice for even short periods of time, it has extensive research support for its use in helping individuals reduce stress, improve concentration, and improve well-being.

FOCUS MEDITATION TIPS

- If an individual tends to dissociate or experiences intrusive traumatic images, this meditation may be practiced with the eyes open, gently gazing downward to some static point.
- This exercise can be practiced for small periods of time (5-10 minutes), multiple times per day.
- If possible, encourage clients to begin forming a habit of redirecting their awareness back to the mantra/affirmation if the mind wanders from it during focus meditation.

KEY RESEARCH FINDINGS

- Greater pain relief (Zeidan et al., 2012)
- Improved body awareness (Holzel et al., 2011)
- Reduced substance use (Simpson et al., 2007)
- Reduced PTSD symptoms (on all four clusters of the DSM-IV®; Rosenthal et al., 2011)

Mantras and Affirmations

In Focus Meditation, the objective is to simply focus on, and repeat, a word or phrase of your choosing. The idea here is to choose a word, phrase, or statement that will help you counter stress or divert the mind from repetitive negative thoughts (also called ruminations).

The word or phrase you select, which may be considered a mantra or, affirmation may be anything you wish, so long as it is positive, helpful, and/or meaningful to you. The most ideal mantra/affirmation will be inspirational, motivating, and soothing. Some people choose spiritual or religious mantras, although this is not a requirement. You can choose any word or phrase as your mantra/affirmation, but here are some examples to get you thinking about what might work for you:

- Calm

- Peace

- Breathe

- I am strong

- I am a survivor

- I can do this

- My future is bright

- I can do anything I set my mind to

- God is my refuge and strength

Take a moment of silence to think about what you would like to choose as your mantra/affirmation. You can always change it later if you prefer!

Focus Meditation

In Focus Meditation, the objective is to maintain focus on just one word, affirmation, or mantra, repeating it for the duration of the practice.

To practice Focus Meditation, follow these steps:

1. First choose a mantra/affirmation that you will repeat during this meditation.

2. Sit with your back straight and your hands on your lap. Close your eyes or find a point on the floor to focus on, and gently shift your focus to the breath, just noticing what it feels like to breathe in and out, noticing the quality of the breath.

3. Using a quiet whisper, state your mantra/affirmation to yourself. Repeat the mantra over and over, repeating it continuously for approximately one minute.

4. Take a break from the mantra/affirmation and focus back on the breath for another minute or so. As you near the end of the minute, continue focusing on the breath as you allow the mantra to slowly come back into your mind.

5. Shift your focus back to your mantra/affirmation, and begin to repeat it again. If another thought enters your awareness, congratulate yourself on this awareness, accept its presence, and then return the focus back to the mantra. Continue repeating the mantra/affirmation for approximately 30 seconds, building up to 3-5 minutes with practice over time.

6. Continue alternating focused breathing and focus meditation, completing two or three additional cycles of one minute of focused breathing and 3 minutes of focus meditation.

7. At the end of these cycles, return the focus to the breath, taking two long, slow deep breaths through the diaphragm before opening your eyes and coming back into the room.

Tool 7-7 | Visualization Meditation (Closed Concentration)

> ### Symptoms Addressed
>
> - Concentration
> - Emotion regulation
> - Memory
> - DSM-5 PTSD arousal and reactivity symptoms

Visualization Meditation is similar to Focus Meditation, in that the objective is to focus one's entire attention on just one stimulus. However, instead of focusing on a single word, affirmation, or mantra, in Visualization Meditation, attention is directed toward an imagined stimulus or object, and the focus remains on this stimulus.

Just as in Transcendental Meditation®, this exercise trains individuals to improve concentration abilities and prevent distracting thoughts from surfacing by restricting one's attention to a single visualized stimulus. Visualized stimuli could be a flower, a beating heart, the ocean, an image of a loved one, or a distinct landscape.

VISUALIZATION MEDITATION TIPS

- Because this technique incorporates intentional mental imagery, unwanted, intrusive images related to traumatic events may be suppressed, as intentional mental imagery can reduce the presence of unwanted, intrusive, trauma-related images. However, if an individual tends to dissociate or experiences trauma-related intrusive images, this meditation may be practiced with the eyes open, gently gazing downward to some static point.
- This exercise can be practiced for small periods of time (5-10 minutes), multiple times per day.
- If possible, encourage clients to begin forming a habit of redirecting their awareness back to the imagined stimulus when their minds wander from the Visualization Meditation.

KEY RESEARCH FINDINGS

- Greater pain relief (Zeidan et al., 2012)
- Improved body awareness (Holzel et al., 2011)
- Reduced substance use (Simpson et al., 2007)

Visualization Meditation

In Visualization Meditation, the objective is to maintain focus on just one object or image that you visualize in your mind.

To practice Visualization Meditation, follow these steps:

1. First choose an imagined object or stimulus that you will focus on with your eyes closed, during the entirety of this meditation. If you do not feel comfortable closing your eyes, choose a static object in the environment that you can direct your focus to during this practice.

2. Sit with your back straight and your hands on your lap. Begin to gently close your eyes, and then start to bring into your mind's eye an image of the stimulus or object you want to envision.

3. Maintain your focus on this object, visualizing it as best as you can. If you would like, using a quiet whisper, you can state the object you are visualizing, repeating it if this aids you in maintaining your focus on the visualized object. Keep your attention directed to this visualized object for approximately one minute.

4. Next, you may choose to take a break from the visualized object and shift your attention to the breath for a moment, just noticing what it feels like to breathe in and out. After approximately one minute, slowly begin to bring the visualized object back into your mind's eye.

5. Now, shift your focus back to the visualized object, once again focusing solely on this image in your mind. If another image or thought enters your awareness, congratulate yourself on this awareness, accept its presence, and then return the focus back to the visualized object. Continue focusing on this imagined object for approximately 3 minutes.

6. Continue alternating brief periods of focused breathing with Visualization Meditation, completing two or three additional cycles of one minute of focused breathing followed by 3 minutes of Visualization Meditation.

7. At the end of these cycles, return the focus to the breath, taking two long, slow deep breaths through the diaphragm before opening your eyes and coming back into the room.

<table>
<tr><td>Tool
7-8</td><td># Resource Meditation (Closed Concentration)</td></tr>
</table>

> ## *Symptoms Addressed*
>
> - Concentration
> - Emotion regulation
> - Memory
> - DSM-5 PTSD arousal and reactivity symptoms

Resource Meditation is like Focus Meditation, in that the objective is to focus one's entire attention on just one stimulus. In this practice, however, the object of concentration is a chosen area of the body that has been identified as a resource, as described in Chapter 5, Tool 5-7: Scanning for Strength. A resource can be anything that feels supportive, strong, or safe to an individual. In Scanning for Strength, the objective is to identify strength, or resources, in various areas of the body. If a client has already completed Scanning for Strength, they may already be aware of a place in the body where they experience strength and/or safety. In this practice, individuals connect with this resource, experience the strength or safety in that area, and remain focused on it for the duration of the meditation.

RESOURCE MEDITATION TIPS

- If an individual tends to dissociate or experiences intrusive traumatic images, this meditation may be practiced with the eyes open, gently gazing downward at some stimulus, ideally at the area of the body.
- This exercise can be practiced for small periods of time (5-10 minutes), multiple times per day.
- If possible, urge clients to begin forming the habit of redirecting their awareness back to the resource when their minds wander from it during Resource Meditation.

KEY RESEARCH FINDINGS

- Greater pain relief (Zeidan et al., 2012)
- Improved body awareness (Holzel et al., 2011)
- Reduced substance use (Simpson et al., 2007)

Resource Meditation

In Resource Meditation, the objective is to identify and then focus on just one area of the body that feels strong or safe

To practice Resource Meditation, follow these steps:

1. First, locate an area of the body that makes you feel safe, supported, or strong. This area of the body is referred to as a resource.

2. Once you have identified a "resourced" area of your body, begin to close your eyes, bringing your attention to that area of the body. If you do not feel comfortable closing your eyes, you may keep your eyes open and, if possible, gaze at the area of the body that is resourced. Alternatively, you may choose a static object in the environment that you can direct your focus to during this practice.

3. With your eyes closed, begin to feel into this resource, connecting with it mentally. If this area of the body is accessible from the outside of the body, you may also place your hand on this area (a shoulder, for example).

4. Now, feeling into the body, simply maintain your focus on this resource, noticing any sensations in that area and continuing to attend to it. Keep your attention directed to this area of the body for approximately one minute.

5. Next, you may choose to take a break from the resourced area of the body and shift your attention to the breath for a moment, just noticing what it feels like to breathe in and out. After approximately one minute, slowly begin to bring your focus back to the resourced area of the body.

6. With your attention now back on the resource, feel into this area of the body and keep your focus here. If another image or thought enters your awareness, congratulate yourself on this awareness, accept its presence, and then return the focus back to the visualized object. Continue focusing on this area of the body for approximately 3 minutes.

7. Continue alternating brief periods of focused breathing with Resource Meditation, completing two or three additional cycles of one minute of focused breathing followed by 3 minutes of Resource Meditation.

8. At the end of these cycles, return the focus to the breath, taking two long, slow deep breaths through the diaphragm before opening your eyes and coming back into the room.

Self-Compassion Meditation (Closed Concentration)

Symptoms Addressed

- Concentration
- Emotion regulation
- Memory
- DSM-5 PTSD arousal and reactivity symptoms

In Self-Compassion Meditation, individuals focus their attention on an area of the body that feels unsafe, painful, or uncomfortable. Many individuals suffering from post-trauma symptoms experience parts of the body as unsafe or distressing. The goal of this meditation is to bring attention and compassion to an area of the body the individual experiences as distressing. This increased connection with the body promotes non-avoidance of the body and the self, increases interoception (the ability to feel into internal states), and reduces self-criticism.

SELF-COMPASSION MEDITATION TIPS

- If an individual tends to dissociate or experiences intrusive traumatic images, this meditation may be practiced with the eyes open, gently gazing downward at some stimulus, ideally at the affected area of the body.
- This exercise can be practiced for small periods of time (5-10 minutes), multiple times per day.
- Ask clients, when possible, to try to begin forming a habit of redirecting their awareness back to the distressing area when their minds wander from it during Self-Compassion Meditation.

KEY RESEARCH FINDINGS

- Greater pain relief (Zeidan et al., 2012)
- Improved body awareness (Holzel et al., 2011)
- Reduced substance use (Simpson et al., 2007)
- Improved self-compassion (Weibel, 2008; Wong, 2011)

Self-Compassion Meditation

The goal of Self-Compassion Meditation is to become aware of an area of the body that is experienced as unsafe, painful, or upsetting, and then send compassion to that area while also learning how to relax it. When you send compassion to these areas of the body, it can help you feel more safe and relaxed, and can improve your relationship with your body.

To practice Self-Compassion Meditation, follow these steps:

1. *First, identify an area or region of the body that feels distressing, unsafe, painful, or otherwise upsetting. This will be the area to connect with during this practice.*

2. *Once you have identified this area, begin to close your eyes and take a few deep breaths through the diaphragm, noticing what it feels like to breathe in and out.*

3. *Still focusing on taking long, deep breaths in and out, now begin to shift your awareness to the area of discomfort in the body. Imagine that you are directing the breath to this area, imagining that you are breathing fresh, calming air through that area of the body. Stay here for a moment, breathing relaxation through the distressing area of the body, imagining air flowing through that area as you inhale, and back through the area in the opposite direction as you exhale. As you do this, imagine that you are calming and soothing this area as you breathe through it.*

4. *Continuing to breathe peace and relaxation through this region of the body, invite yourself to consider whether love or compassion may be sent to this area. Ask yourself, "Could I send compassion and love to this area of the body, despite my experience of it?"*

5. *Focusing on this distressed area, invite yourself to send feelings of compassion, love, or gratitude to this area of the body. For instance, while breathing through this area you might repeat, "You're going to be okay," or "I am thankful for your presence," or "You are a sacred part of me," or "You are safe right now." The statement you choose to repeat is not as important as the intention and feeling behind it. Choose any statement to repeat to this area that elicits feelings of love, gratitude, or compassion.*

6. *Maintain your focus here, attending to this area of the body, breathing relaxation through the area and repeatedly sending compassion or love to the region. If you experience an increase in distress as you focus on this area, remain compassionate about that experience, soothing your body, acknowledging the discomfort, and continuing to breathe into the area with love and relaxation. If the distress is too intense, give yourself permission to stop with a simple focus on your breath for a minute, and then gently refocus on the distressing area. Repeat this until you notice the distress decreasing.*

7. *Stay here with the body for a few more moments, and then return the focus to the breath, taking two long, slow deep breaths through the diaphragm before opening your eyes and coming back into the room.*

Alternating Meditations (Open/Closed)

> ## *Symptoms Addressed*
>
> - Concentration
> - Emotion regulation
> - Memory
> - DSM-5 PTSD arousal and reactivity symptoms

As discussed earlier in this chapter, open awareness and closed concentration exercises build different skills. Specifically, open awareness meditations train individuals to watch, but not restrict attention, simply being aware of where it drifts. Closed concentration meditations train individuals to sustain attention to one experience, thought, emotion, stimulus, or area of the body. When the mind wanders, the individual redirects their attention back to the object or experience of focus.

In Alternating Meditations, the objective is to combine both open awareness and closed concentration practices in one sitting. This approach to meditation is described by Chade-Meng Tan in the book, *Search Inside Yourself* (2012). Tan, an early Google engineer who brought Mindfulness to Google, asserts that alternating between different types of meditations is a great way to build both open awareness and closed concentration skill sets in a fast, efficient manner. To practice Alternating Meditations, individuals alternate between closed concentration and open awareness exercises, practicing each for short periods of time (five minutes or under).

ALTERNATING MEDITATIONS TIPS

- If an individual tends to dissociate or experiences intrusive traumatic images, this practice may be done with the eyes open, gently gazing downward at some stimulus, ideally at the affected area of the body (if one has been selected).
- It is recommended that open/closed meditations be alternated every 2-5 minutes.
- It is also recommended that individuals set a recurring alarm, timer, or bell that signals when to end one meditation and switch to another.

KEY RESEARCH FINDINGS

- Greater pain relief (Zeidan et al., 2012)
- Improved body awareness (Holzel et al., 2011)
- Reduced substance use (Simpson et al., 2007)
- Improved self-compassion (Weibel, 2008; Wong, 2011)

Alternating Meditations

In Alternating Meditations, the objective is to combine both open awareness and closed concentration practices in one sitting by alternating between these practices for short periods of time.

To practice Alternating Meditations, select one open awareness and one closed concentration meditation from this chapter. You will alternate between these two techniques, practicing each at least twice for 2-5 minutes each. Before beginning Alternating Meditations, it is recommended that you set a recurring timer or alarm that will sound every few minutes, signaling to you that it is time to switch meditations.

If you find that a specific meditation seems more suited to longer practices (more than five minutes), experiment with additional meditation combinations to discover which techniques work best for you during Alternating Meditation.

Compassion and Gratitude Meditation (Open/Closed)

Symptoms Addressed

- Concentration
- Emotion regulation
- Memory
- Dysregulated interoception
- Self-criticism
- DSM-5 PTSD arousal and reactivity symptoms

Compassion and Gratitude Meditation (also known as loving-kindness meditation when it contains the compassion element alone) is a meditation containing both open and closed elements that involves actively cultivating compassion and gratitude. This is accomplished by directing expressions of well wishes, compassion, and gratitude to the self (Stahl & Goldstein, 2010), other people, animals, and even nature (Wong, 2011).

This type of meditation usually contains repetitive statements related to compassion-cultivation, such as, "May you be at peace... may you be healthy..." There are many variations of compassion and gratitude meditations (including most forms of prayer), and it is recommended that clients feel free to adjust the language and emphasis of the practice as needed, to best accomplish the goal of cultivating compassion and gratitude.

COMPASSION AND GRATITUDE MEDITATION TIPS

- If an individual tends to dissociate or experiences intrusive traumatic images, this practice may be practiced with the eyes open, gently gazing downward at some stimulus.
- It is recommended that this meditation be practiced for short periods of time (5-10 minutes).
- When desired, individuals may alter the wording of this meditation to better fit with their values, beliefs, and/or religious practices.

KEY RESEARCH FINDINGS

- Greater pain relief (Zeidan et al., 2012)
- Improved body awareness (Holzel et al., 2011)
- Reduced substance use (Simpson et al., 2007)
- Improved self-compassion (Weibel, 2008; Wong, 2011)
- Reduced depression (Fredrickson, 2008)
- Reduced anger (Hofmann, Grossman, & Hinton, 2011)

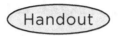

Compassion and Gratitude Meditation

In the Compassion and Gratitude Meditation, the objectives are to promote compassion toward the self and others, and to increase feelings of gratitude. To complete Compassion and Gratitude Meditation, follow the instructions below.

Sitting comfortably with your back straight, or lying down, begin to close your eyes and bring the focus to the breath. Notice what it feels like to breathe in and out, and take a few deep breaths just focusing on the sensation of breathing.

1. **Gratitude and Compassion Toward the Self:**

   Begin to expand your awareness past the breath to include the entire body. You can imagine your awareness as a large, bright yellow circle that expands from your abdomen, which houses the breath, to the entire body (including your head). With the image of your entire body in mind, state the following:

   "This is me.

   I am thankful for this body.

   I am thankful for this mind.

   I am thankful for this spirit.

   I am doing the best I can in life.

   May my body, mind, and spirit be healthy.

   May my body, mind, and spirit be safe.

   May my body, mind, and spirit be honored and loved.

   May I honor myself.

   May I love myself."

   Remain still with these intentions for a few moments. Repeat this step with 1-3 additional loved ones or friends.

2. **Gratitude and Compassion Toward Loved Others:**

   Next, expand the bright yellow circle of awareness beyond you to include a close loved one or friend. Imagining the expanded circle of awareness and this individual, state the following to this individual in your mind:

"That is you.

I am thankful for your body.

I am thankful for your mind.

I am thankful for your spirit.

I know that you are doing the best you can in life.

May your body, mind, and spirit be healthy.

May your body, mind, and spirit be safe.

May your body, mind, and spirit be honored and loved.

I honor you.

I love you."

Remain still with these intentions for a few moments. Repeat this step with 1-3 additional loved ones or friends.

3. **Gratitude and Compassion Toward Liked Others:**

Next, expand the bright yellow circle of awareness beyond your loved ones to include a liked acquaintance or friend. Imagining the expanded circle of awareness and this individual, state the following to this individual in your mind:

"That is you.

I am thankful for your body.

I am thankful for your mind.

I am thankful for your spirit.

I know that you are doing the best you can in life.

May your body, mind, and spirit be healthy.

May your body, mind, and spirit be safe.

May your body, mind, and spirit be honored and loved.

I honor you.

I like you."

Remain still with these intentions for a few moments. Repeat this step with 1-3 additional liked ones or friends.

4. **Gratitude and Compassion Toward Difficult Others:**

Now expand the bright yellow circle of awareness beyond your acquaintances and friends to include an individual who you find to be difficult. These types of individuals may be difficult to like, relate to, or interact with. Imagine the expanded circle of awareness around this difficult individual, and state the following to this individual in your mind:

"That is you.

I am thankful for your body.

I am thankful for your mind.

I am thankful for your spirit.

I know that you are doing the best you can in life.

May your body, mind, and spirit be healthy.

May your body, mind, and spirit be safe.

May your body, mind, and spirit be honored and loved.

May I understand you better.

May I feel compassion toward you.

I honor you."

Remain still with these intentions for a few moments. Repeat this step with 1-3 additional difficult individuals.

8

Cognitive Tools

Cognitive tools are largely top-down techniques that help clients use their minds to change their brains. Specifically, cognitive tools are effective when the goal is to strengthen the top, cortical areas of the brain, such as those in the prefrontal cortex. It is usually recommended that these types of techniques be emphasized in therapy after bottom-up tools are mastered. This is because the subcortical activation that characterizes post-trauma symptoms suppresses cortical areas that need to be accessible for cognitive techniques to be effective, and bottom-up techniques can de-activate that subcortical activation.

THE BRAIN ON COGNITIVE TOOLS

Cognitive tools change the brain in **three** key ways, all of which help clients reduce and better manage post-trauma symptoms.

1. **Thinking Brain (Center area of the Prefrontal Cortex):** Increased activation of specific center areas of the prefrontal cortex, referred to as the ventromedial prefrontal cortex (vmPFC). Activation of the vmPFC improves self-awareness, self-regulation, and emotion regulation. Specifically, strengthening this area helps individuals to better evaluate risk, reflect on past events (which is necessary for cognitive restructuring), and extinguish feelings of fear related to trauma triggers.

2. **Thinking Brain (Lateral areas of the Prefrontal Cortex):** Increased activation of lateral regions within the prefrontal cortex, referred to as the dorsolateral prefrontal cortex (dlPFC). Strengthening of the dlPFC is associated with improved attention, working memory, empathy, relating to others, posttraumatic growth. In the context of PTSD, dlPFC activation may improve concentration, reduce feelings of isolation, and increase one's ability to connect with and relate to others.

3. **Self-Regulation Center (Cingulate):** Increased activation of the self-regulation center of the brain, which is involved in thought and emotion regulation and decision-making.

EVIDENCE-BASED COGNITIVE THERAPIES FOR PTSD

This chapter presents brain-changing cognitive tools to incorporate into trauma treatment. It is worth mentioning, however, that while most evidence-based therapies for PTSD (or trauma treatment more broadly) do not have neuroscience-specific research supporting them, other types of research have found them to be very effective for some individuals. The cognitive tools presented here are not intended to be recommended *over* empirically-supported treatments for PTSD; rather, they are brain-informed tools that can be incorporated into trauma treatment along with many other methods.

Many evidence-based, empirically-supported treatments for PTSD already include cognitive elements. Examples of these include eye movement desensitization and reprocessing (EMDR), cognitive processing therapy (CPT), trauma-informed CBT (TF-CBT), stress inoculation training (SIT), prolonged exposure (PE), and other types of cognitive behavioral therapies (CBTs). While most of these therapies are trauma-focused, meaning that they help the client manage thoughts and memories related to the traumatic event itself, others (such as SIT and CBTs) emphasize skill development and thought management that is not trauma-specific, but can be effective for trauma.

Handout

Cognitive Tools

Cognitive tools are largely top-down techniques, meaning that with these techniques, you use your thoughts to change your brain. This is different from bottom-up techniques, in which you use the body to change the brain. Typically, top-down exercises are great for strengthening the high up, thinking areas of your brain. When these areas of the brain are activated, it becomes easier to think clearly, concentrate, regulate thoughts and emotion, and connect with others. It is usually recommended that top-down techniques be practiced after bottom-up tools are mastered.

Cognitive tools change the brain in **three** ways:

1. **Increased activation of the thinking center (ventromedial prefrontal cortex):**
   - Improves self-awareness
   - Improves self-regulation
   - Improves ability to extinguish fear

2. **Increased activation of the thinking center (dorsolateral prefrontal cortex):**
   - Improves concentration and attention
   - Improves social awareness and "social intelligence"
   - Improves empathy and connectedness to others

3. **Increased activation of the self-regulation center (cingulate):**
   - Improves emotion regulation and self-regulation
   - Improves decision-making

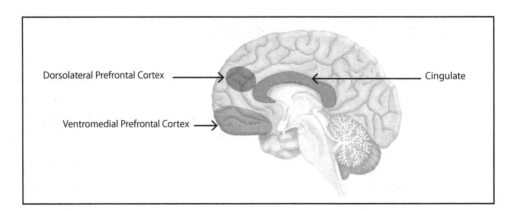

Trauma-Focused (TF) vs. Non-Trauma-Focused (NTF) Cognitive Tools

Cognitive tools fall into one of two categories: trauma-focused (TF) or non-trauma-focused (NTF). Trauma-focused tools are ones that work with trauma-related thoughts and memories, whereas non-trauma-focused tools emphasize ways to work with thoughts in a broader sense (whether the thoughts be trauma-related or not). NTF tools teach clients how to become aware of or manage thoughts, whereas TF tools help clients think about, manage, or process trauma-related memories or thoughts more specifically.

This workbook focuses on NTF tools specifically, as opposed to TF tools. The NTF techniques described here can be used for trauma-related thoughts and memories when desired, but this is not a requirement, and the instructions provided for these tools do not instruct clients to work with traumas. Many of the NTF tools in this workbook are examples of "cognitive reappraisal," which is a type of emotion regulation strategy commonly studied by neuroscientists. Cognitive reappraisal is defined as "changing the way one thinks about a stimulus in order to change its affective impact" (Buhle et al., 2014).

The question about whether a client needs, or would even benefit from, TF tools is somewhat controversial. This workbook assumes that trauma-focused work will not be needed for every client. While this workbook acknowledges evidence-based TF interventions, the emphasis will be on NTF tools more generally. Research has shown that NTF cognitive tools may activate key brain areas that help trauma survivors recover. For detailed instruction in TF tools, it is recommended clinicians obtain training in EMDR, TF-CBT, CPT, PE, or other evidence-informed protocols.

Trauma-Focused vs. Non-Trauma-Focused Cognitive Tools

The cognitive tools you learn in therapy may fall into one of two categories: trauma-focused (TF) or non-trauma-focused (NTF) techniques. Trauma-focused tools are ones in which you and your therapist work with trauma-related thoughts and memories, whereas non-trauma-focused tools emphasize ways for you to work with and manage thoughts in a broader sense.

For instance, NTF tools may teach you how to become aware of or manage distressing thoughts, whereas TF tools are meant to help you manage and process memories directly related to traumatic events. NTF tools can help you strengthen your brain, but without having to talk about the specific trauma.

For some people, the thought of having to stir up memories of traumatic events is understandably scary and anxiety-provoking. It may even feel re-traumatizing if it feels like you relive traumatic events when you recall them. However, it is important for you to understand that the goal of all therapy is not necessarily to revisit past trauma-related memories.

While this can be immensely helpful for some individuals in the context of a close and trusting therapeutic relationship, not all people will benefit from TF approaches. It is encouraged that you have an ongoing dialogue with your therapist regarding your preferences, needs, treatment planning, and treatment progress. This ongoing collaboration between you and your therapist will help clarify whether a TF approach may be beneficial and, if so, what type of TF intervention may be best.

Third Person Perspective

```
          Symptoms Addressed
    ───────────────────────────────────

  • Concentration
  • DSM-5 PTSD alterations in cognition and
    mood symptoms
  • Stress response
  • DSM-5 PTSD arousal and reactivity symptoms
```

The Third Person Perspective (TPP) exercise involves reappraising a recent event or argument that elicited negative emotions. The purpose of TPP is to have the client recall, think about, and process this event or conflict in a more balanced, productive manner that reduces negative emotions and improves one's ability to regulate emotion. TPP has been shown to improve relationship quality and reduce distress in married couples, and similar cognitive reappraisal exercises have been shown to strengthen brain areas involved in cognitive and emotion regulation.

THIRD PERSON PERSPECTIVE TIPS

- If possible, it is recommended that clients complete this exercise soon after the distressing event or conflict.

- Encourage clients to practice patience with themselves when they find it difficult to maintain a third-party perspective, since this can be quite challenging for most people.

- Even if a client cannot buy into a third person perspective, it is recommended that this cognitive exercise be practiced. It often takes consistent practice for a client's perspective to shift. Simply going through the process of cognitive reappraisal changes the brain; buy-in is not required for healthy brain change!

- Recommend that individuals practice this exercise frequently, as practice makes progress.

KEY RESEARCH FINDINGS

- Improved marital quality and reduced conflict distress (Finkel et al., 2013)

- Improved emotion regulation (Finkel et a., 2013)

- Fewer depression symptoms after experiencing stressful events (Troy et al., 2010)

(Adapted from methods described in Finkel, E. J., Slotter, E. B., Luchies, L. B., Walton, G. M., & Gross, J. J. (2013). A brief intervention to promote conflict reappraisal preserves marital quality over time. *Psychological Science, 24*(8).)

Third Person Perspective

To practice TPP, follow these steps:

1. Spend about 5 minutes writing down a summary of a recent distressing event or argument. In this summary, focus on the facts only, describing what was said and done, as opposed to focusing on your interpretations of or feelings about the incident.

2. Now think about this incident from the perspective of a neutral third party, a person who wants the best for all parties involved. Who might this third party be? Ideally, it will be someone you respect, perhaps someone very wise whom you know or have known in the past. Spend approximately 10 minutes writing down what this third party would say to you regarding this situation or argument. Some questions to consider include:

   a. How might this person think about the situation?

   b. What would this person say to you?

   c. What advice would this person give to you?

   d. How might he or she find the good that could come from this situation?

   e. How might this person reassure and support you, while also staying neutral?

3. After completing this exercise, consider the following:

   a. What obstacles did you face in trying to adopt a third-party perspective?

   b. Are there important relationships in your life that could benefit from your occasionally taking a third-party perspective?

   c. How might you be successful when trying to take a third-party perspective in the future?

   d. How might taking this perspective help you reduce the distress you feel during disagreements in your relationships?

4. Out-of-session assignment:

   a. On a daily basis for the next week, review the third person perspective that you write down, spending approximately 5 minutes with it each day.

   b. For the next week, do your best to practice third person perspective-taking when you find yourself in the middle of a conflict or experiencing negative emotions toward someone in your life.

Broadening Your Perspective

Symptoms Addressed

- Concentration
- DSM-5 PTSD alterations in cognition and mood symptoms
- Stress response
- DSM-5 PTSD arousal and reactivity symptoms

Broadening Your Perspective teaches clients to reappraise distressing events by incorporating additional information that helps to reduce the distress they feel when remembering these events. This information can include facts about the event (who was present, when it took place, etc.) as well as speculations or opinions. Speculations may include information such as the moods or life circumstances of someone involved in the distressing event, or other factors outside of the client that may have influenced how the event occurred or was interpreted.

The following pages present examples of how to complete this technique, and a blank worksheet for clients wanting to practice these exercises.

BROADENING YOUR PERSPECTIVE TIPS

- If possible, it is recommended that clients complete this exercise soon after the distressing event or conflict.
- Encourage clients to identify additional information that is true and that they can "buy into."
- It is recommended that individuals practice this exercise frequently, as practice makes progress, and practice is required to shift neural networks.

KEY RESEARCH FINDINGS

- Improved emotion regulation (Gross, 2010)
- Fewer depression symptoms after experiencing stressful events (Troy et al., 2010)
- Less anger and more positive emotions (Mauss et al., 2007)

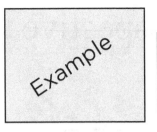

Example

Broadening Your Perspective

Have you ever felt distressed by your own thoughts about an event, but struggled to think differently about it? Broadening Your Perspective will help you do just that. This technique helps you think differently about negative events so that you may begin to feel differently (less distressed) as well. This is done by incorporating additional information that can help ease negative emotions about what happened to you. Here is an example of how you might complete this technique.

1. **Write down a few sentences about a distressing event that occurred recently with another individual. Be specific about the facts of the event, such as what happened, who was there, where it took place, and when it took place. Refrain from interpretations or speculations about the causes of the event right now.**

   I was standing in a long line at the grocery store last week, and this woman had four children who were running around arguing with one another, asking for candy, and bumping my cart. They had no respect for personal space and the mother did not do anything to control them. In fact, she just stood there looking like she was spacing off. Finally, after several minutes, the line moved, but this event ruined my mood for the rest of the evening.

2. **Next, write down a few sentences about *why* the event occurred, and how you interpret the cause and meaning of the event.**

   The event occurred because the mother was lazy and did not want to control her kids. She is inconsiderate and does not care about other people's comfort and personal space. This is why kids grow up to be rude adults! Parents are supposed to discipline their kids, not let them run wild while other people around them suffer.

3. **Identify the "main character(s)" of this event, besides yourself. Who was the main person, or main people, who you believe caused the event to happen? Just list them below.**

   The lady at the grocery store. It wasn't the kids' faults really; it was that lady, their mother.

4. **Now, go back to the first two steps and re-read what you wrote about the facts of the event, as well as your interpretations of the event. When you think about the event like this, and the main character(s) involved, what emotions do you feel? What emotions did you feel at the time the event was happening?**

   I feel mad now, and I felt mad as heck then! I also felt disrespected at the time.

5. **With the event still in your mind, imagine that you are the main character (or one of the main characters) of that event. Pretending for a moment that you are that person, begin to speculate why the main character may have acted the way they did. List at least five explanations for the main character's behavior *that do not reflect poorly on the main character or imply malicious intent* toward others. These are not facts about the situation; rather, they are speculations about the cause of another person's behavior that are either neutral or positive.**

   a. *She could have just learned a family member has cancer and was preoccupied with thoughts about that.*

   b. *Maybe a couple of the children were not hers, but were friends of her own children, and so maybe she did not feel she could discipline them.*

   c. *She could have been a single parent who was overwhelmed and did not know how to handle the situation better.*

   d. *Maybe she is trying to ignore the bad behavior as a way of getting it to stop. It could be that yelling at them makes the behavior worse, and her therapist told her to try to ignore bad behavior for a while instead.*

   e. *She could have just come from an appointment where she received very bad or sad news that she feels stunned by.*

6. **Imagine that the main character was in fact experiencing the things you just listed above. What emotions do you feel now, with this broadened perspective and additional information?**

   I now feel like there is still no excuse for her acting like that, but I feel less angry with her, and more compassion toward her, if it were true that something bad had just happened. If she was just trying to ignore the bad behavior, I do not feel as much compassion toward her, but if she had just received very bad news, I feel empathy and compassion for her.

Take Home Point: Our interpretations about *why* things happen strongly shape our emotional reactions to them. Events themselves do not "make" us feel bad or good; rather, it is how we think about them that creates suffering or contentment. This cognitive reappraisal exercise broadens our perspective and allows us to "step into others' shoes" to imagine how others' behaviors may make sense. This is not done in order to excuse the behavior, but to feel less distressed about it, so that it causes us less suffering! Keep in mind that while the cognitive reappraisal is based on speculation only, ALL interpretations are speculative anyway, and we rarely know the entire truth about any event or circumstance.

Broadening Your Perspective

Have you ever felt distressed by your own thoughts about an event, but struggled to think differently about it? Broadening Your Perspective will help you do just that. This technique helps you think differently about negative events so that you may begin to feel differently (less distressed) as well. This is done by incorporating additional information that can help ease negative emotions about what happened to you. If possible, complete this exercise soon after a distressing event or conflict, and practice this technique frequently.

1. **Write down a few sentences about a distressing event that occurred recently with another individual. Be specific about the facts of the event, such as what happened, who was there, where it took place, and when it took place. Refrain from interpretations or speculations about the causes of the event right now.**

2. **Next, write down a few sentences about *why* the event occurred, and how you interpret the cause and meaning of the event.**

3. **Identify the "main character(s)" of this event, besides yourself. Who was the main person, or main people, who you believe caused the event to happen? Just list them below.**

4. Now, go back to the first two steps and re-read what you wrote about the facts of the event, as well as your interpretations of the event. When you think about the event like this, and the main character(s) involved, what emotions do you feel? What emotions did you feel at the time the event was happening?

5. With the event still in your mind, imagine that you are the main character (or one of the main characters) of that event. Pretending for a moment that you are that person, begin to speculate why the main character may have acted the way they did. List at least five explanations for the main character's behavior *that do not reflect poorly on the main character or imply malicious intent* toward others. These are not facts about the situation; rather, they are speculations about the cause of another person's behavior that are either neutral or positive.

6. Imagine that the main character was in fact experiencing the things you just listed above. What emotions do you feel now, with this broadened perspective and additional information?

Take Home Point: Our interpretations about *why* things happen strongly shape our emotional reactions to them. Events themselves do not "make" us feel bad or good; rather, it is how we think about them that creates suffering or contentment. This cognitive reappraisal exercise broadens our perspective and allows us to "step into others' shoes" to imagine how others' behaviors may make sense. This is not done in order to excuse the behavior, but to feel less distressed about it, so that it causes us less suffering! Keep in mind that while the cognitive reappraisal is based on speculation only, ALL interpretations are speculative anyway, and we rarely know the entire truth about any event or circumstance.

Remembering Your Past Self

> ## Symptoms Addressed
>
> - Concentration
> - DSM-5 PTSD alterations in cognition and mood symptoms
> - Stress response
> - DSM-5 PTSD arousal and reactivity symptoms

One reason why let-downs, disappointments, and upsetting events can feel so intensely distressing is that individuals often believe that the outcomes of these things will be far-reaching and impactful. The individual feels upset *right now,* but also believes that the distress, or the outcomes of the event or situation, will last a very long time. This only serves to intensify the emotional reaction the individual experiences. Remembering Your Past Self is a helpful tool because it teaches clients to reappraise distressing events, fears, or disappointments by remembering past stressors and disappointments and assessing how they still impact the client's current life.

In general, most people are very poor at anticipating how present events will impact their emotional state in the future. The ability to predict how something will make us feel in the future is referred to "affective forecasting" (Wilson & Gilbert, 2003), and research has shown that humans are not good at this! Specifically, we tend to overestimate both how very good events will feel in the future (such as winning the lottery), and also how bad the bad stuff will feel in the future (such as not getting your dream job).

When individuals overestimate how bad something will feel in the future, it creates more suffering in the present. The purpose of this exercise is to recognize how difficult it can be to even remember day-to-day stressors from five years ago, as well as how rare it is for stressors to continue to impact one's life for years. This in turn can provide the client with a new realization, which is that current stressors are unlikely to create a lasting impact in their life.

REMEMBERING YOUR PAST SELF TIPS

- It is recommended that individuals practice this exercise whenever they experience strong anxiety or disappointment about distressing things that have happened or that may happen.
- This is a writing exercise, but it can also be practiced as a formal mindfulness exercise. To complete this as a mindfulness exercise, have the client close their eyes and bring into their mind's eye an image of their past self.

KEY RESEARCH FINDINGS

- Improved emotion regulation (Gross, 2010)
- Fewer depression symptoms after experiencing stressful events (Troy et al., 2010)
- Less anger and more positive emotions (Mauss et al., 2007)

Remembering Your Past Self Worksheet

One reason why let-downs, disappointments, and upsetting events can feel so upsetting is that we often believe that the outcomes will last a very long time. We feel upset right now, but also believe that the distress will continue indefinitely, which actually makes us feel worse!

Remembering Your Past Self encourages you to look back on past distressing events, fears, or disappointments and think how they still impact (or don't impact!) your current life. It is recommended that you practice this exercise when you experience strong anxiety or disappointment about things that have happened, or that you're worried might happen. Here is an example of how you might complete this technique.

1. **Write down a few sentences about a distressing or disappointing event that occurred recently. This could be an instance where you did not succeed or perform in the way you had hoped, and perhaps in response you feel down, disappointed, and worried about how it will impact you in the future. Just write down the facts of this situation, including what happened, where you were, when it happened, and who else was involved.**

   I applied for my dream job close to my home about a month ago, and over the past few weeks, I completed multiple rounds of interviews with upper management executives at the company. After making it through all the interview rounds, I did not receive an offer. I tried really hard to get this position and have been working for it for nearly a decade, and I failed.

2. **When you think about the event or situation, what emotions do you feel?**

   I feel disappointment, hopelessness, and fear about my career going forward.

3. **What does your mind tell you about how your future will be impacted by this event or situation?**

   This job was the key to me becoming the type of professional I've always wanted to be. I'm afraid I'll be trapped in my current job forever and will never progress to become anything important or meaningful. Even if I do find another opportunity like this last one, I'll probably not get that job either, and will just stay bored and stuck.

4. **Now, take a break from the present moment and try to connect with a memory of who you were in the past. Specifically, try to remember yourself five years ago during the current month. Where did you live at that time? Who were the important people in your life? What was your job, or school like? How did you spend your time? Connect with this past self for a moment. Be as specific as possible.**

Five years ago this month, I was living in Oklahoma City, OK and I had just started a fellowship. I was getting ready to get married in a few months and was enjoying time with my fiancé. I had two dogs and my hair was much longer, and I spent quite a bit of time with friends. I can't remember exactly, but since the month is October, I assume that at that time I was also preparing for Halloween.

5. **Next, still thinking about who you were, and what your life was like five years ago this month, try to remember what your day-to-day stressors were at that time, and the things you were worried or concerned about. What were your fears? Your main sources of stress?**

Five years ago during this month, I had just started a fellowship that I had to complete in order to formally enter my profession. I can't remember much about this particular month five years ago, but I think I was stressed about passing my licensing exam and was trying to complete a large project that was taking longer than I wanted it to. I do not remember the particulars of these, but I know that these were the main things going on in my life at that time. I do remember that I was terrified of not passing the licensing exam because if I failed, it would have meant re-taking it months later and that would have been miserable.

6. **You may have noticed that it was difficult to complete the last two steps. If you were able to identify stressors from five years ago, ask yourself the question, "Are those stressors still a part of my day-to-day life?" What happened with those stressors? Did they resolve? If so, how? Is the outcome of those stressors still impacting you?**

I finished the project I was stressed about. I can't remember when, but I did finish it. I took the licensing exam in December and passed it. I was nervous at the time I took it, but I did fine. If I hadn't passed it, I guess I would have gone through the pain of studying more for it and re-taking it, but I probably would have passed it sometime before now. The things I was stressed about back then don't matter at all now. In fact, I never think about them at all, as I am too busy worrying about other things now!

Take home point: You may notice that only the most intense of stressors still impact you five years later. Also, even those truly life-altering stressors will often feel different, and more manageable, than how they felt five years ago. The exception to this can be traumatic events which, because of how they are encoded in the brain, may feel as though they do not "age" much. Aside from traumatic events, most stressors, even intense stressors, resolve over time and do not impact one's life for years! Just as the stressors from five years ago have become less relevant, your current stressors will also likely become much less relevant in the future. Remember this perspective when you find yourself catastrophizing the future impact of your current-day stressors.

Remembering Your Past Self

One reason why let-downs, disappointments, and upsetting events can feel so upsetting is that we often believe that the outcomes will last a very long time. We feel upset right now, but also believe that the distress will continue indefinitely, which actually makes us feel worse!

Remembering Your Past Self encourages you to look back on past distressing events, fears, or disappointments and think how they still impact (or don't impact!) your current life. It is recommended that you practice this exercise when you experience strong anxiety or disappointment about things that have happened, or that you're worried might happen.

1. **Write down a few sentences about a distressing or disappointing event that occurred recently. This could be an instance where you did not succeed or perform in the way you had hoped, and perhaps in response you feel down, disappointed, and worried about how it will impact you in the future. Just write down the facts of this situation, including what happened, where you were, when it happened, and who else was involved.**

2. **When you think about the event or situation, what emotions do you feel?**

3. **What does your mind tell you about how your future will be impacted by this event or situation?**

4. Now, take a break from the present moment and try to connect with a memory of who you were in the past. Specifically, try to remember yourself five years ago during the current month. Where did you live at that time? Who were the important people in your life? What was your job, or school like? How did you spend your time? Connect with this past self for a moment. Be as specific as possible.

5. Next, still thinking about who you were, and what your life was like five years ago this month, try to remember what your day-to-day stressors were at that time, and the things you were worried or concerned about. What were your fears? Your main sources of stress?

6. You may have noticed that it was difficult to complete the last two steps. If you were able to identify stressors from five years ago, ask yourself the question, "Are those stressors still a part of my day-to-day life?" What happened with those stressors? Did they resolve? If so, how? Is the outcome of those stressors still impacting you?

Take home point: You may notice that only the most intense of stressors still impact you five years later. Also, even those truly life-altering stressors will often feel different, and more manageable, than how they felt five years.

The exception to this can be traumatic events which, because of how they are encoded in the brain, may feel as though they do not "age" much. Aside from traumatic events, most stressors, even intense stressors, resolve over time and do not impact one's life for years! Just as the stressors from five years ago have become less relevant, your current stressors will also likely become much less relevant in the future. Remember this perspective when you find yourself catastrophizing the future impact of your current-day stressors.

Channeling Your Future Self

Symptoms Addressed

- Concentration
- DSM-5 PTSD alterations in cognition and mood symptoms
- Stress response
- DSM-5 PTSD arousal and reactivity symptoms

Channeling Your Future Self teaches clients to reappraise distressing events, fears, or disappointments by imagining the long-term impact of those events from the perspective of a future self. As discussed in Tool 8-4, one reason why let-downs, disappointments, and upsetting events can feel so intensely distressing is that individuals often believe that the outcomes of these things will be far-reaching and impactful.

However, research has shown that individuals are poor at predicting how present events will affect their future emotional states (Wilson & Gilbert, 2003), and tend to overestimate the future impact of present negative events. The purpose of this exercise is to imagine what life will look like (and feel like!) in the future by connecting with the future self, who can provide a compassionate perspective about the current situation.

CHANNELING YOUR FUTURE SELF TIPS

- It is recommended that individuals practice this exercise whenever they experience strong anxiety or disappointment about distressing things that have happened or that may happen.
- This is a writing exercise, but it can also be practiced as a formal mindfulness exercise. To complete this as a mindfulness exercise, have client close their eyes and bring into their mind's eye an image of their future self.

KEY RESEARCH FINDINGS

- Improved emotion regulation (Gross, 2010)
- Fewer depression symptoms after experiencing stressful events (Troy et al., 2010)
- Less anger and more positive emotions (Mauss et al., 2007)

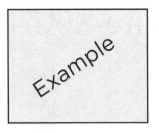

Channeling Your Future Self Worksheet

One reason that upsetting events can feel so terrible is that we often believe that the pain will last a very long time. We feel upset right now, but also believe that the distress will continue indefinitely, which actually makes us feel worse! Channeling Your Future Self helps you think differently about distressing events by imagining the long-term impact of those events from the perspective of your future self, who can provide a compassionate perspective about your current situation. It is recommended that you practice this exercise when you experience strong anxiety or disappointment about things that have happened, or that you're worried might happen. Here is an example of how you might complete this technique.

1. **Write down a few sentences about a distressing or disappointing event that occurred recently. This could be an instance where you did not succeed or perform in the way you had hoped, and perhaps in response you still feel down, disappointed, and worried about how it will impact you in the future. Just write down the facts of this situation in an objective way, including what happened, where you were, when it happened, and who else was involved.**

   I applied for my dream job close to my home about a month ago, and over the past few weeks I completed multiple rounds of interviews with upper management executives at the company. After making it through all the interview rounds, I did not receive an offer. I tried really hard to get this position and have been working for it for nearly a decade, and I failed.

2. **When you think about the event or situation, what emotions do you feel?**

   I feel disappointment, hopelessness, and fear about my career going forward.

3. **What does your mind tell you about how your future will be impacted by this event or situation?**

   This job was the key to me becoming the type of professional I've always wanted to be. I'm afraid I'll be trapped in my current job forever and will never progress to become anything important or meaningful. Even if I do find another opportunity like this last one, I'll probably not get that job either, and will just stay bored and stuck.

4. **Now, take a break from the present moment and try to imagine yourself, and your life, five years from now. Where will you live in five years? Who will be the most important people in your life? What will you look like? What will your job be? How will you spend your time? Try to imagine your future self, five years from now, as clearly as you can.**

Five years from now, I will still live here, in Kansas City, and my daughter will be five years older. Wow, it is hard to imagine that! The most important people in my life will be my husband, daughter, and family. I will still have my friends, and maybe there will be a few new friends I will make as well. I will be in the same profession, but am not sure the direction it will take me, as that will depend on the opportunities that come my way (and that I create) between now and then. I will look similar to how I look now, but I guess I will look slightly older. I imagine myself to be healthy and happy overall.

5. **As you continue to imagine your future self, five years from now, think about what your day-to-day stressors will be at that time. What do you think you will be concerned about then? What will be taking up mental space in your mind?**

   I guess I imagine that I might be stressed about managing my daughter's school schedule with my work schedule, since she will be in school by that time. I may also be stressed about expanding my business, and I might feel sad about getting so old. Maybe I'll have a mid-life crisis.

6. **Are your anticipated future stressors different from your current day stressors? When you look into the future, does it seem likely that you will still be concerned about the stressors you are currently experiencing? Is the stressor or disappointment you wrote about in Step 1 still substantially impacting you in five years?**

   I can't be sure, but I don't imagine that not getting that job will be something that will still bother me in five years. While I'll never be happy about that let-down, it is unlikely that it will cause me suffering forever. There will probably be so much that happens between now and then that this will be a distant memory.

Take home point: While present stressors and disappointments can feel intense in the moment, those emotions rarely last for months, much less years, into the future. People often underestimate their ability to bounce back from disappointments and move forward, but we know from psychological research that even very upsetting let-downs rarely have a long-term impact on one's happiness.

One way to remember that most bad things will not impact your life long-term is to imagine your future self, think about how your life will be different, and consider what your stressors will be at that time.

Channeling Your Future Self

One reason that upsetting events can feel so terrible is that we often believe that the pain will last a very long time. We feel upset right now, but also believe that the distress will continue indefinitely, which actually makes us feel worse!

Channeling Your Future Self helps you think differently about distressing events by imagining the long-term impact of those events from the perspective of your future self, who can provide a compassionate perspective about your current situation. It is recommended that you practice this exercise when you experience strong anxiety or disappointment about things that have happened, or that you're worried might happen.

1. **Write down a few sentences about a distressing or disappointing event that occurred recently. This could be an instance where you did not succeed or perform in the way you had hoped, and perhaps in response you feel down, disappointed, and worried about how it will impact you in the future. Just write down the facts of this situation, including what happened, where you were, when it happened, and who else was involved.**

2. **When you think about the event or situation, what emotions do you feel?**

3. **What does your mind tell you about how your future will be impacted by this event or situation?**

4. Now, take a break from the present moment and try to imagine yourself, and your life, five years from now. Where will you live in five years? Who will be the most important people in your life? What will you look like? What will your job be? How will you spend your time? Try to imagine your future self, five years from now, as clearly as you can.

5. As you continue to imagine your future self, five years from now, think about what your day-to-day stressors will be at that time. What do you think you will be concerned about then? What will be taking up mental space in your mind?

6. Are your anticipated future stressors different from your current day stressors? When you look into the future, does it seem likely that you will still be concerned about the stressors you are currently experiencing? Is the stressor or disappointment you wrote about in Step 1 still substantially impacting you in five years?

Take home point: While present stressors and disappointments can feel intense in the moment, those emotions rarely last for months, much less years, into the future. People often underestimate their ability to bounce back from disappointments and move forward, but we know from psychological research that even very upsetting let-downs rarely have a long-term impact on one's happiness.

Evaluating Self-Blame

Symptoms Addressed

- Concentration
- DSM-5 PTSD alterations in cognition and mood symptoms
- Stress response
- DSM-5 PTSD arousal and reactivity symptoms

One way to remember that most bad things will not impact your life long-term is to imagine your future self, think about how your life will be different, and consider what your stressors will be at that time.

The next two tools, Evaluating Self-Blame and Finding the Nugget of Truth, are cognitive reappraisal exercises that encourage clients to consider the function of self-blame and guilt, and how these emotions may be related to a person's sense of control. Clients get to reflect on the effectiveness of these emotions, as well as the costs they incur. Finally, in Finding the Nugget of Truth, clients explore ways to decrease self-blame and guilt.

EVALUATING SELF-BLAME TIPS

- It is not recommended that this exercise be used when a sense of moral injury is present. Moral injury refers to the emotional suffering that results when a client is the perpetrator of, or fails to prevent, traumatic events. This exercise is instead recommended when a client's sense of self-blame or guilt results from events that were largely (or at least partially) out of their control.

- It is recommended that individuals practice this exercise whenever they experience strong feelings of self-blame or guilt related to a past event.

- Clients should be encouraged to step through this technique on a regular basis, as it is somewhat complex and requires practice before becoming effective.

- This technique can be practiced with clients who experience intense guilt and self-blame related to traumatic events. However, with these clients, it is recommended that the exercise be mastered with self-blame and guilt related to non-traumatic events *first*, before attempting this practice with emotions related to traumatic events.

KEY RESEARCH FINDINGS

- Improved emotion regulation (Gross, 2010)
- Fewer depression symptoms after experiencing stressful events (Troy et al., 2010)
- Less anger and more positive emotions (Mauss et al., 2007)

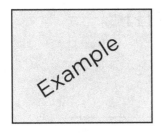

Evaluating Self-Blame Worksheet

This exercise asks you to consider why you might experience self-blame and guilt, and how these emotions may be related to your sense of control. Here is an example of how you might complete this technique.

1. **Write down a few sentences about a distressing event or situation that you frequently blame yourself for, or about which you experience guilt.**

   I blame myself for my boyfriend leaving me. We were very close and it took me a long time to trust him. When I finally put myself out there and let him in, he didn't like what he saw and pushed me away because I'm not good enough and I'm not lovable. I should try harder to be a better person and be more successful so that someone will love me.

2. **An adaptive function of self-blame and guilt is that they can motivate individuals to avoid making the same mistakes in the future. If an individual feels terrible for something they have done, they are unlikely to do it again! These emotions can be adaptive when they motivate individuals to make good decisions moving forward. When you consider your own self-blame, do you believe it is helpful at this time? How might it change your future behavior in healthy ways?**

   I feel like it is true that it is my fault that my boyfriend left me, but I don't have any idea what I can do in the future to be good enough for someone to love me. I don't know what I would need to become for him to take me back, or how to become that person for him., I don't really see how my self-blame is helping me improve myself for future relationships. I think it's more likely that it is making me want to close off and just not trust anyone ever again, which probably isn't so healthy.

3. **Keep in mind, however, that self-blame and guilt can have other not-so-helpful functions as well. For instance, sometimes individuals experience strong guilt or self-blame as a way to either hold onto, or avoid having, other emotional experiences. One example of this is when an individual experiences self-blame, and in doing so, is able to maintain a sense of control and avoid feelings of helplessness. Are guilt and self-blame working for you, or against you? Are some of the functions of your self-blame/guilt unhelpful to you?**

   In this example the individual strongly blames herself for what happened and believes that if she had made different decisions, she would not have been assaulted. Notice that in this line of thinking, causation is not attributed to the rapist, which seems peculiar until you can understand the function of this individual's self-blame.

From the survivor's perspective, she was in control of everything that happened that night, including another person's behavior. By blaming herself for what happened, she is able to maintain a strong sense of control. By believing that she was totally in control of what happened, she can avoid feeling helpless, out of control, and unsafe walking through the world. If, conversely, she attributed her rape to the individual who assaulted her, she may feel helpless, out control, and fearful that this type of event may occur again in the future. If she did not cause the event, then it makes her vulnerable to experiencing additional traumatic events in the future, which can be terrifying to imagine.

In other words, it is possible that this individual experiences self-blame as a way to feel in control and avoid feeling helpless. This is an example of a possible function of her self-blame and guilt.

There is nothing inherently wrong with this type of emotion regulation and mental gymnastics. In fact, it is intelligent and quite sophisticated. However, as stated before, interpretations of events that lead to the experience of self-blame and guilt can actually halt recovery and healing after stressful or traumatic events. While feeling out of control and helpless is also not preferable, keep in mind that ongoing self-blame, shame, and guilt often prevent healing.

A common scenario that illustrates this is with survivors of sexual violence who blame themselves for their assault. Here's how the thinking may go:

"If I hadn't been drinking that night, I wouldn't have been raped. It's my fault for going to the party alone, going to that guy's room, and for drinking all night beforehand. I deserved for that to happen to me because I was so stupid in my decision-making. If I hadn't been so irresponsible, I would have stayed safe and my life wouldn't be ruined."

4. **What impact do you believe your own self-blame might be having on your healing and recovery? At this time, is your self-blame helpful, as described in Step 2, or has it become unhelpful?**

   Again, I still feel like it is my fault that my boyfriend left, but the self-blame isn't really helping me right now, it is just making me feel worse and worse about myself.

Evaluating Self-Blame

This exercise asks you to consider why you might experience self-blame and guilt, and how these emotions may be related to your sense of control.

1. Write down a few sentences about a distressing event or situation that you frequently blame yourself for, or about which you experience guilt.

2. An adaptive function of self-blame and guilt is that they can motivate individuals to avoid making the same mistakes in the future. If an individual feels terrible for something they have done, they are unlikely to do it again! These emotions can be adaptive when they motivate individuals to make good decisions moving forward. When you consider your own self-blame, do you believe it is helpful at this time? How might it change your future behavior in healthy ways?

3. Keep in mind, however, that self-blame and guilt can have other not-so-helpful functions as well. For instance, sometimes individuals experience strong guilt or self-blame as a way to either hold onto, or avoid having, other emotional experiences. One example of this is when an individual experiences self-blame, and in doing so, tries to maintain a sense of control and avoid feelings of helplessness. However, this can lead to the individual becoming "stuck" in distressing, self-defeating thoughts and emotions, and can hinder natural healing. Are guilt and self-blame working for you, or against you? Are some of the functions of your self-blame/guilt unhelpful to you?

4. What impact do you believe your own self-blame might be having on your healing and recovery? At this time, is your self-blame helpful, as described in Step 2, or has it become unhelpful?

Finding the Nugget of Truth

> ## *Symptoms Addressed*
>
> - Concentration
> - DSM-5 PTSD alterations in cognition and mood symptoms
> - Stress response
> - DSM-5 PTSD arousal and reactivity symptoms

Finding the Nugget of Truth is the second part of a cognitive reappraisal exercise that encourages clients to consider the function of self-blame and guilt, and how these emotions may be related to a person's sense of control. That step, along with the effectiveness of these emotions, is described in the previous tool, Evaluating Self-Blame. In this tool, Finding the Nugget of Truth, ways to decrease self-blame and guilt are outlined.

FINDING THE NUGGET OF TRUTH TIPS

- It is not recommended that this exercise be used when a sense of moral injury is present. Rather, this exercise is recommended when a client's sense of self-blame or guilt results from events that were largely (or at least partially) out of their control.

- It is recommended that individuals practice this exercise whenever they experience strong feelings of self-blame or guilt related to a past event.

- Clients should be encouraged to step through this technique on a regular basis, as it is somewhat complex and requires practice before becoming effective.

- This technique can be practiced with clients who experience intense guilt and self-blame related to traumatic events. However, with these clients, it is recommended that the exercise be mastered with self-blame and guilt related to non-traumatic events *first*, before attempting this practice with emotions related to traumatic events.

KEY RESEARCH FINDINGS

- Improved emotion regulation (Gross, 2010)
- Fewer depression symptoms after experiencing stressful events (Troy et al., 2010)
- Less anger and more positive emotions (Mauss et al., 2007)

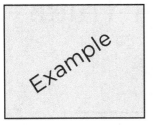

Example

Finding the Nugget of Truth Worksheet

Finding the Nugget of Truth is a technique that help you examine and work through feelings of self-blame. It is recommended that you practice this exercise whenever you experience strong feelings of self-blame or guilt related to a past event. Here is an example of how you might complete this technique.

1. **If you believe your self-blame might be negatively impacting your healing process, you may want to consider working with this emotion directly. To begin doing this, read the following statements and circle the ones that may apply to your situation. Even if you do not believe these statements, circle the ones that may contain "a nugget of truth" about your situation and feelings of self-blame.**

   - *I did the best I knew how to do in that [situation/relationship/context].*

   - *There is nothing specific that I can identify that would have likely changed the outcome of that situation.*

   - *The causes of that situation include other people's decisions and actions in addition to my own.*

   - *When I made the decisions I did in that situation, I did not anticipate the outcome I received, even if I "should have."*

   - *I did not want the outcome I received in that situation and did not intentionally try to create that outcome.*

   - *It is possible that this outcome could have happened to another person as well.*

   - *It is possible that this outcome could have occurred even if I had done some things differently (even if unlikely).*

   - *The self-blame I feel is not changing me for the better.*

   - *The self-blame I feel is causing me additional suffering for no identifiable good reason.*

   - *I may be blaming myself in order to punish myself.*

   - *I may be blaming myself in order to prevent bad things from happening to me in the future.*

   - *When I blame myself, I feel more in control of my life.*

2. **After you have identified and circled statements that resonate with you, examine each statement in detail and answer the following questions about each statement:**

The statement: "The causes of that situation include other people's decisions and actions in addition to my own" has a nugget of truth, maybe.

- **What is the "nugget of truth" in this statement, even if I don't totally believe it?** *There were technically two people in the relationship, not just one (me), and he was the person who actually ended the relationship.*

- **What is the evidence for this statement being partially true?** *Like I said, there were two people in the relationship, and he was the person who ended the relationship, so he did play a role in this situation. It was his decision, and his action, so even though I still think it's my fault, I can see that he played some part in it.*

- **Would anyone else in my life, or anyone else that I might talk to about this situation think that there is a nugget of truth in this statement? (It does not have to be the case that *everyone* would think there is truth to the statement; just consider whether *anyone* else would agree that there is truth in it.) If someone else would agree that this statement contains a nugget of truth, what would they say is true about it?** *One of my friends said she does not think the break- up is completely my fault. She also said that she thinks I tend to blame myself because I have low self-esteem, and mentioned that I tended to overlook the role he played in our arguments.*

- **Has anyone else ever said anything to me that indicates that this statement might contain some truth?** *My therapist has encouraged me to examine the dynamic between my ex-boyfriend and myself, as opposed to just blaming myself for everything.*

3. **It is recommended that you complete Steps 1 and 2 several times, as part of a regular cognitive practice.** Over time, you may notice that your feelings of self-blame very slowly decrease. This change will not be immediate, and some self-blame will likely remain. However, as self-blame decreases, even by a small amount, it is likely that more healing and healthy processing of the situation will take place. In this practice, the goal is to chip away at self-blame with hard work over time, not eradicate it quickly. To keep yourself motivated to continue shifting your self-blame, write a couple of sentences below describing why you want to work on this destructive emotion, and what you hope the outcome will be when you have practiced this exercise.

I want to work on my self-blame because I am afraid that if I don't, I may end up choosing dating partners who are not a good fit for me and unintentionally sabotage future relationships. I want to feel confident about myself and find someone who will accept and love me. I hope when I work on my self-blame that I will be able to let go of this relationship so that I can be free to find the right person.

Finding the Nugget of Truth

Finding the Nugget of Truth is a technique that help you examine and work through feelings of self-blame. It is recommended that you practice this exercise whenever you experience strong feelings of self-blame or guilt related to a past event.

1. **If you believe your self-blame might be negatively impacting your healing process, you may want to consider working with this emotion directly. To begin doing this, read the following statements and circle the ones that may apply to your situation. Even if you do not believe these statements, circle the ones that may contain "a nugget of truth" about your situation and feelings of self-blame.**

   - I did the best I knew how to do in that [situation/relationship/context].

   - There is nothing specific that I can identify that would have likely changed the outcome of that situation.

   - The causes of that situation include other people's decisions and actions in addition to my own.

   - When I made the decisions I did in that situation, I did not anticipate the outcome I received, even if I "should have."

   - I did not want the outcome I received in that situation and did not intentionally try to create that outcome.

   - It is possible that this outcome could have happened to another person as well.

   - It is possible that this outcome could have occurred even if I had done some things differently (even if unlikely).

   - The self-blame I feel is not changing me for the better.

   - The self-blame I feel is causing me additional suffering for no identifiable good reason.

   - I may be blaming myself in order to punish myself.

   - I may be blaming myself in order to prevent bad things from happening to me in the future.

   - When I blame myself, I feel more in control of my life.

2. **After you have identified and circled statements that resonate with you, examine each statement in detail and answer the following questions about each statement:**

- What is the "nugget of truth" in this statement, even if I don't totally believe it?

- What is the evidence for this statement being partially true?

- Would anyone else in my life, or anyone else that I might talk to about this situation think that there is some truth to this statement? (It does not have to be the case that everyone would think there is truth to the statement; just consider whether anyone else would agree that there is truth in it.)

- If someone else agreed that this statement contains truth, what would they say is true about it?

- Has anyone else ever said anything to me that indicates that this statement might contain some truth?

3. **It is recommended that you complete Steps 1 and 2 several times, as part of a regular cognitive practice.** Over time, you may notice that your feelings of self-blame very slowly decrease. This change will not be immediate, and some self-blame will likely remain. However, as self-blame decreases, even by a small amount, it is likely that more healing and healthy processing of the situation will take place.

In this practice, the goal is to chip away at self-blame with hard work over time, not eradicate it quickly. To keep yourself motivated to continue shifting your self-blame, write a couple of sentences below describing why you want to work on this destructive emotion, and what you hope the outcome will be when you have practiced this exercise.

The 4-3s

Symptoms Addressed
• Concentration
• DSM-5 PTSD alterations in cognition and mood symptoms
• Stress response
• DSM-5 PTSD arousal and reactivity symptoms

The 4-3s tool is a cognitive reappraisal and positive psychology exercise that helps clients identify possible positive outcomes to negative events and situations. The result of practicing a broader and more positive perspective to life events is that clients can better recognize what is currently going well in their lives, and acknowledge how they are contributing to those things that are going well for them.

THE 4-3S TIPS

- It is recommended that individuals practice this exercise on a daily basis, ideally right before bed, so that the client can reflect on the day as a whole and experience positive, hopeful emotions before bed.

- Clients may incorporate this practice into mindfulness practices, such as prayer or a loving-kindness meditation.

- This practice can be adapted for use in couple therapy, where each person in the couple dyad identifies the other person's positive contributions to the relationship.

- It is not recommended that clients complete the first two 3s of this exercise (identifying and cognitively reappraising not-so-ideal events) for recent, extremely stressful or traumatic events. Asking clients to engage in cognitive restructuring of traumatic events before they have processed the events and gained a sense of safety and stability can be re-traumatizing.

KEY RESEARCH FINDINGS

- Improved emotion regulation (Gross, 2010)
- Fewer depression symptoms after experiencing stressful events (Troy et al., 2010)
- Less anger and more positive emotions (Mauss et al., 2007)

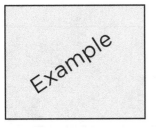

The 4-3s Worksheet

The 4-3s exercise helps you identify possible positive outcomes to negative events and situations, and recognize what is currently going well in your life and why. This tool can be used with any negative event; however, do not complete the first two 3s of this exercise (identifying and cognitively reappraising not-so-ideal events) for extremely stressful or traumatic events that have happened recently. Here is an example of how you might complete this technique.

1. **What are three not-so-ideal or not-so-great things that happened in your life today? State each of these not-so-great things below:**

    1. *I received rude service at a restaurant.*

    2. *When I arrived at my favorite store they were closed.*

    3. *I never got a response today on an important email.*

2. **Now, for each of these not-so-ideal things, identify three possible neutral or positive aspects or outcomes of these things.**

    Neutral or positive aspects or outcomes of not-so-ideal thing #1:

    1. *I still got to eat my favorite dish.*

    2. *The waitress' rude attitude does not have any real impact on my life.*

    3. *Her behavior has reminded me of the importance of treating others well, and so I'm likely to be mindful of this when I interact with others now.*

    Neutral or positive aspects or outcomes of not-so-ideal thing #2:

    1. *I was able to get home faster than I would have, so I spent a bit more time with my children.*

    2. *I have made a mental note of their new closing time so that this does not happen again.*

    3. *Even though I was disappointed I could not shop there today, at least I did not make any impulsive purchases, which is tempting when I am there!*

    Neutral or positive aspects or outcomes of not-so-ideal thing #3:

    1. *Perhaps I will hear back tomorrow.*

2. *Not hearing anything back today does not mean that the person's response to me is negative in any way.*

3. *I have heard this person can be a bit slow to respond to email. If this continues to be the case, I can call them or stop by their office soon instead of using email to communicate.*

3. Next, list three positive things that happened in your life today:

1. *I made progress on a project at work.*

2. *I had a good evening relaxing with my spouse.*

3. *It was a beautiful day out, so I took my dog for an enjoyable walk.*

4. Finally, name three ways that you contributed to each of the positive things that happened to you today. What role did you play in these good things happening?

What I did to contribute to positive thing #1:

1. *I set my intention to focus hard on the project and I closed out my email so I would not be distracted.*

2. *When I noticed feeling stuck on different parts of the project, I took a deep breath and pushed through the discomfort.*

3. *I arrived at work on time so that I could start on the project right away.*

What I did to contribute to positive thing #2:

1. *I made an attempt to let go of work-related stress and focus on my spouse.*

2. *I suggested we watch a funny movie together tonight.*

3. *I refrained from being critical when my spouse did not finish the dishes.*

What I did to contribute to positive thing #3:

1. *I made time to take the dog out and prioritized taking a walk over other things.*

2. *I focused on what nature looked and felt like as we walked, and did my best to stay in the present moment.*

3. *I was affectionate toward my dog before and after the walk, which likely allowed me to enjoy it more.*

The 4-3s

The 4-3s exercise helps you identify possible positive outcomes to negative events and situations, and recognize what is currently going well in your life and why. This tool can be used with any negative event; however, do not complete the first two 3s of this exercise (identifying and cognitively reappraising not-so-ideal events) for extremely stressful or traumatic events that have happened recently.

1. What are three not-so-ideal or not-so-great things that happened in your life today? State each of these not-so-great things below:

   1.

   2.

   3.

2. Now, for each of these not-so-ideal things, identify three possible neutral or positive aspects or outcomes of these things.

   Neutral or positive aspects or outcomes of not-so-ideal thing #1:

   1.

   2.

   3.

   Neutral or positive aspects or outcomes of not-so-ideal thing #2:

   1.

   2.

   3.

   Neutral or positive aspects or outcomes of not-so-ideal thing #3:

   1.

   2.

   3.

3. Next, list three positive things that happened in your life today:

   1.

   2.

   3.

4. Finally, name three ways that you contributed to each of the positive things that happened to you today. What role did you play in these good things happening?

   What I did to contribute to positive thing #1:

   1.

   2.

   3.

   What I did to contribute to positive thing #2:

   1.

   2.

   3.

   What I did to contribute to positive thing #3:

   1.

   2.

   3.

Approaching Fear Despite Fear

> ## *Symptoms Addressed*
>
> - Concentration
> - DSM-5 PTSD alterations in cognition and mood symptoms
> - Stress response
> - DSM-5 PTSD arousal and reactivity symptoms

Approaching Fear Despite Fear is a cognitive reappraisal exercise that helps clients change the way they think about important but feared situations to build the ability to face them and engage with them. Many traumatized clients develop fears that hold them back from living the life they want, and they may feel paralyzed and unable to overcome those fears. While evidence-based strategies, such as exposure techniques, are very effective, it can also be helpful for clients to learn how to reinterpret feared situations to make them easier to overcome.

APPROACHING FEAR DESPITE FEAR TIPS

- It is recommended that individuals practice this exercise with several different feared situations, starting with mildly/moderately feared situations and working up to more intensely feared situations. For instance, clients may start with anxiety-provoking situations that elicit distress between 30-40 on the distress thermometer (see Tool 3-1).

- Clients should be encouraged to practice this technique only for anxiety-provoking situations that are meaningful to them or important to overcome, since completing this exercise requires ongoing motivation to reappraise feared situations.

- It is recommended that this technique be practiced in conjunction with behavioral anxiety management approaches, such as exposure techniques.

KEY RESEARCH FINDINGS

- Improved emotion regulation (Gross, 2010)
- Fewer depression symptoms after experiencing stressful events (Troy et al., 2010)
- Less anger and more positive emotions (Mauss et al., 2007)

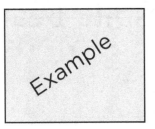Example

Approaching Fear Despite Fear Worksheet

Oftentimes, survivors of trauma develop fears that hold them back from living the lives they want, and facing these fears can be extremely difficult. Your therapist may help you manage these fears with behavioral strategies, but cognitive methods such as this one may also be useful. The following examples will help you begin to reappraise feared situations so that you can approach them despite fearing them!

1. **Write down a few sentences describing something that you fear doing, but that is also very important to you. This should be something that elicits a score between approximately 30-40 on the distress thermometer. For some individuals, this might be attendance at their child's soccer game, practicing assertiveness skills and boundary-setting, or applying for a new job.**

   I fear submitting my artwork to an upcoming art show. I enjoy producing the art, but am terrified that people will think I'm a fraud. I'd just forget about it, but it's important to me because my art is meaningful and I think it might be helpful to people who have gone through things similar to those I have experienced. I figure if I can help even one person with my art, I will have succeeded.

2. **Now, write a few sentences about what you fear about this task, thing, or situation. What does your mind tell you about it that increases your fear? When you think of approaching this situation, what are the thoughts/fears that hold you back?**

   I am terrified that people will think I'm a "wannabe" artist and a fraud. I sometimes look at the work and think, "It's not that good; it looks like an amateur did this, who am I fooling?" The closer I get to submitting samples of my work, the louder that voice in my head becomes, and I feel very scared that it will not be accepted and that people will judge me.

3. **When you imagine these feared outcomes of the feared situation, where do you feel it in your body? What are the sensations that accompany the fear?**

   I feel like my stomach flips and my breathing becomes shallow.

4. **Next, write down at least three reasons that this feared situation/thing is important to you, despite the fear it produces in you.**

   First, it is possible that my art could help other people because it could make them feel like they are not alone. Second, it would be good to express myself and it could feel freeing. Finally, it would make me feel like a real artist if I were to appear in an art show. It would symbolize progress.

5. **For a moment, imagine that you have done that feared thing and succeeded. When you imagine success, how do you feel emotionally?**

   I feel great, like I am on top of the world! I feel happy, like I have finally made it as an artist.

6. **Keep imagining what it will be like when you face your fear and succeed. What will you gain from this? List at least three ways that accomplishing this will change your life for the better (even if in very small ways).**

   I will have greater confidence in my abilities. I will also feel like a successful artist, and I will have courage to apply to more art shows in the future.

7. **When you imagine the feeling of success, how does it feel in the body? How are the physical sensations of self-confidence and success different from the sensations of fear?**

   In my body, I feel like my heart is racing a bit, but not in a bad way. I feel both excited and content all at once, and I feel a bit warm inside. I can feel myself smiling. This is different from how fear feels, because with fear I feel like I can't breathe very well and I feel sick to my stomach. I'm also not smiling when I feel afraid.

Strategy 1: Induce positive physical sensations to approach feared situations: Consider for a moment the impact that fear-related physical sensations may have on your thoughts. It is often the case that when our bodies experience fear-related sensations, we produce thoughts that are consistent with that fear, even if those thoughts do not reflect truth or reality. If you can work first with your physical sensations, replacing fear-related sensations with those associated with success and happiness, the resulting thoughts can begin to change as well.

One way to elicit the physical sensations of success, happiness, and empowerment is to imagine what it would feel like to succeed, and what the positive outcomes of this would be, as you did in steps 3 and 4. Whereas sensations related to fear may make you want to withdraw, sensations related to positive feelings often produce a desire to approach. Before approaching a feared situation, it can be helpful to take a few moments to imagine the feelings and outcomes of success, and to intentionally connect with those physical sensations, since those positive sensations will help you approach, rather than avoid, the feared situation.

Strategy 2: Reappraise the worst-case scenario and the consequences of failure: Two things that keep individuals from approaching their fears are: 1) their thoughts about what constitutes failure, and what failure means (including the consequences of failure), and, 2) catastrophic thoughts about the worst-case outcomes of approaching their fears. To approach fear despite fear, one helpful strategy is to begin working on shifting these two types of thoughts. The following points and questions may help you begin to change the way you think about fears and failure:

- Can I redefine failure and success such that even small steps toward the feared situation count as success? Any approach toward fear can be considered practice, or training, and can be considered success.

- Keep in mind that success may be re-defined not as reaching your end goal right away, but rather as "failing great." Author Kim Liao was rejected 43 times by various literary magazines and publishers one year, but instead of feeling defeated, she set a new goal: Obtain 100 rejections each year (http://lithub.com/why-you-should-aim-for-100-rejections-a-year/). According to Liao, a friend of hers, a very successful author, gave her the following advice: "Collect rejections. Set rejection goals. I know someone who shoots for 100 rejections in a year, because if you work that hard to get so many rejections, you're sure to get a few acceptances, too." This can be a fantastic way to reframe rejection; Each rejection gets you closer to your ultimate goal, and is considered a "win" of sorts!

- View fear-facing as brain training, since that is what it is! When you feel afraid, the fear center of your brain activates. While this makes you want to avoid and pull away, when you do this, it actually reinforces and strengthens your anxiety.

- If, however, you move toward a feared situation when the fear center of your brain activates, you change the brain for the better! Three things can happen. First, you begin to strengthen areas of your brain associated with emotion regulation. Second, you slowly de-activate the fear center of the brain, which makes the feared situation feel less dangerous. Third, you re-encode the feared situation as less dangerous in the memory center of the brain, making it so that it will be slightly less scary to do that feared thing again in the future.

Approaching Fear Despite Fear

Oftentimes, survivors of trauma develop fears that hold them back from living the lives they want, and facing these fears can be extremely difficult. Your therapist may help you manage these fears with behavioral strategies, but cognitive methods such as this one may also be useful. The following instructions and strategies will help you begin to reappraise feared situations so that you can approach them despite fearing them!

1. **Write down a few sentences describing something that you fear doing, but that is also very important to you. This should be something that elicits a score between approximately 30-40 on the distress thermometer. For some individuals, this might be attendance at their child's soccer game, practicing assertiveness skills and boundary setting, or applying for a new job.**

2. **Now, write a few sentences about what you fear about this task, thing, or situation. What does your mind tell you about it that increases your fear? When you think of approaching this situation, what are the thoughts/fears that hold you back?**

3. **When you imagine these feared outcomes of the feared situation, where do you feel it in your body? What are the sensations that accompany the fear?**

4. **Next, write down at least three reasons that this feared situation/thing is important to you, despite the fear it produces in you.**

5. **For a moment, imagine that you have done that feared thing and succeeded. When you imagine success, how do you feel emotionally?**

6. **Keep imagining what it will be like when you face your fear and succeed. What will you gain from this? List at least three ways that accomplishing this will change your life for the better (even if in very small ways).**

7. When you imagine the feeling of success, how does it feel in the body? How are the physical sensations of self-confidence and success different from the sensations of fear?

Strategy 1: Induce positive physical sensations to approach feared situations: Consider for a moment the impact that fear-related physical sensations may have on your thoughts. It is often the case that when our bodies experience fear-related sensations, we produce thoughts that are consistent with that fear, even if those thoughts do not reflect truth or reality.

If you can work first with your physical sensations, replacing fear-related sensations with those associated with success and happiness, the resulting thoughts can begin to change as well. One way to elicit the physical sensations of success, happiness, and empowerment is to imagine what it would feel like to succeed, and what the positive outcomes of this would be, as you did in steps 3 and 4.

Whereas sensations related to fear may make you want to withdraw, sensations related to positive feelings often produce a desire to approach. Before approaching a feared situation, it can be helpful to take a few moments to imagine the feelings and outcomes of success, and to intentionally connect with those physical sensations, since those positive sensations will help you approach, rather than avoid, the feared situation.

Strategy 2: Reappraise the worst-case scenario and the consequences of failure: Two things that keep individuals from approaching their fears are: 1) their thoughts about what constitutes failure, and what failure means (including the consequences of failure), and, 2) catastrophic thoughts about the worst-case outcomes of approaching their fears. To approach fear despite fear, one helpful strategy is to begin working on shifting these two types of thoughts. The following points and questions may help you begin to change the way you think about fears and failure:

- Can I redefine failure and success such that even small steps toward the feared situation count as success? Any approach toward fear can be considered practice, or training, and can be considered success.

- Keep in mind that success may be re-defined not as reaching your end goal right away, but rather as "failing great."

- View fear-facing as brain training, since that is what it is! When you feel afraid, the fear center of your brain activates. While this makes you want to avoid and pull away, when you do this it actually reinforces and strengthens your anxiety. If, however, you move toward a feared situation when the fear center of your brain activates, you change the brain for the better! Three things can happen.

  First, you begin to strengthen areas of your brain associated with emotion regulation. Second, you slowly de-activate the fear center of the brain, which makes the feared situation feel less dangerous. Third, you re-encode the feared situation as less dangerous in the memory center of the brain, making it so that it will be slightly less scary to do that feared thing again in the future.

Focusing Away, Focusing Near

```
┌──────────────────────────────────────────────────┐
│              Symptoms Addressed                    │
│   ──────────────────────────────────────────      │
│                                                    │
│    • Concentration                                 │
│    • DSM-5 PTSD avoidance symptoms                 │
│    • Stress response                               │
│    • DSM-5 PTSD arousal and reactivity symptoms    │
│                                                    │
└──────────────────────────────────────────────────┘
```

Focusing Away, Focusing Near is a two-part cognitive technique. The Focusing Away (Part I) component is adapted from methods described in a neuroimaging study published in 2014 (Denkova, Dolcos, & Dolcos), which found that individuals who completed this technique showed increased prefrontal cortex (thinking brain) activation and reduced amygdala (fear brain) activation.

In this technique, individuals are instructed to focus *away from* emotional aspects of negative memories, and instead focus only on the facts, or the contextual details of the memories. This allows individuals to work with these memories from an emotional distance and begin to habituate to them.

In the second part of this technique, Focusing Near (Part II), clients begin to slowly engage with the emotional content of the negative event/memory. This is not a sink or swim approach to negative memories; rather, clients are eased into remembering, experiencing, and working with the emotional aspects of the memories in a titrated manner.

Note that for trauma clients, in particular, Focusing Away is helpful but insufficient on its own, as stopping here would encourage avoidance, which would likely exacerbate symptoms. In Focusing Near, clients slowly engage with, and habituate to, negative memories. Because this two-part technique is more advanced than the other cognitive techniques presented in this chapter, detailed instructions are provided for both clients and therapists.

Clinicians are encouraged to lead the client through both parts of this technique. The Clinician Handouts (below) correspond to the Client Handouts, and should be used in tandem. While clients will practice habituation at home as they progress through this technique (see step 8 of Part I, and step 11 on Part II), each step outlined on the handouts should be completed with the help of the clinician, to ensure the client does not become overwhelmed or show signs of dissociation.

FOCUSING AWAY, FOCUSING NEAR TIPS

- It is recommended that clinicians ask for a distress score or temperature reading at the beginning of, several times during, and after both Focusing Away and Focusing Near exercises. An emphasis on evaluating distress is critical so that a client does not become distressed to the point of reaching their boiling point.

- While completing Focusing Away, encourage the emphasis to remain on the contextual details of the memory, and encourage clients to refrain from focusing on emotional aspects of this memory.

- After becoming skilled at practicing this technique with mildly and moderately negative events, clients may opt, with the help of the clinician, to begin practicing this exercise with more intensely negative (or traumatic) memories.

- Practice an arousal-reducing exercise (such as diaphragmatic breathing or a body-based exercise) after completing Focusing Away or Focusing Near exercises, as these techniques can be stressful for clients.

KEY RESEARCH FINDINGS

- Increased activation of the prefrontal cortex (Denkova, Dolcos, & Dolcos, 2014)

- Decreased activation of the amygdala (Denkova, Dolcos, & Dolcos, 2014)

- Decreased negative emotions related to the negative memory processed in this technique (Denkova, Dolcos, & Dolcos, 2014)

Part I, Focusing Away

To practice Focusing Away with clients, follow these steps:

1. Instruct the client that you will be working with them to learn how to process, and reduce the distress related to, negative memories.

2. Before starting, have the client identify a bottom-up, relaxing technique that they can practice with you if they begin to feel overwhelmed by this exercise.

3. Ask the client to begin by bringing to mind a *mildly negative memory*. (It is strongly recommended that clinicians introduce this technique to clients using a mildly negative memory. If appropriate, clients can then repeat this tool with more intensely negative, or even traumatic memories. Keep in mind that, in order to change the brain in positive ways, clients do not necessarily have to work with traumatic memories while completing this exercise.)

4. Once the client has accessed a mildly negative memory, provide them with paper and a pen, and tell them to write down "just the facts" of this memory, including who was there, when it happened, where it happened, and what exactly happened. In other words, ask them to write down, in paragraph form, the "whos, whats, wheres, and whens" of the situation. As they begin to draft a narrative of this mildly negative memory, also encourage the client to focus *away* from any emotional aspects of the memory, including what their feelings were at the time or how they feel about it now. This seems counterintuitive, as therapists usually help clients enter emotionality, not avoid it. However, this technique helps clients process emotional memories by first focusing *away* from any emotions related to the event, focusing instead on the "cold hard facts" of the memory.

5. After they have drafted the narrative of this memory, do a temperature reading using the distress thermometer described in Tool 3-1. Specifically, ensure that the client is not at their boiling point, the point at which they feel too overwhelmed to engage with the memory. After you ask the client for their temperature, also ask them, "Is that level of distress acceptable to you right now?" If they reply yes, then move to the next step. If not, they will need to take a break and reduce their distress using a bottom-up technique.

6. Now, ask the client to read the memory out loud. After they complete this, once again take a temperature reading, ask them whether the distress level is acceptable, and discuss how this exercise went for them.

7. If, at any point, the client's temperature is at or past their boiling or freezing point, have them disengage from the memory and practice a bottom-up, stress-reducing exercise to "lower their temperature."

8. Finally, have the client take home this written memory and engage with it for approximately 10 minutes per day, reading it repeatedly. Encourage the client *not* to complete this assignment right before bed. This repeated exposure to the memory facilitates habituation and processing of the contextual details of this memory. After the client has habituated to the memory for 1-2 weeks, progress to Part II: Focusing Near, to begin processing the emotional aspects of the memory.

Clinician
Handout

Part II, Focusing Near

To practice Focusing Near, follow these steps:

1. To begin, first check in with the client regarding their current distress level associated with the written memory. Their distress level should be lower than it was when they began habituating to the memory. If the distress has not reduced, or it has risen, this may be due to the client not engaging with the memory (due to avoidance), or due to the client remembering additional details about the event that are distressing. If this occurs, clinicians should discuss the cause of the lingering distress, and clients may need to spend additional time habituating to the written memory before moving onto Part II.

2. If the client's distress has lowered and is still acceptable, begin Part II by having the client review the written memory, silently, and circling any word or phrase that may contain emotional content. These are words or phrases that, when the client connects with them, elicit emotions. Some words may bring up feelings of happiness or joy, such as thinking about a beloved pet's name, while others (such as alley, car, policeman, rain, etc.) may produce negative emotions.

   At this point in the technique, clients are not encouraged to identify the emotions or discuss them; rather, they simply identify where emotional content may be located in the written memory. If the client is having difficulty accessing their own emotions, they may circle words, phrases, or sections that they believe *another person* might have an emotional reaction to.

3. After the client has circled all of the words/phrases that contain emotional content for them, ask them to pause and check in with a temperature reading to ensure their distress level is acceptable.

4. Next, starting at the beginning of the written memory, have the client state the first word or phrase that is circled. When they state this word, ask them the question, "What emotion goes with this word?" and instruct them to write down that emotion next to the circle, or off to the side of it/above it. If the client begins to describe thoughts related to the emotion, redirect them back to simply identifying the emotion that goes with that word. The goal here is to contain emotions, gradually easing into them in a titrated manner. Complete this exercise with every circled word or phrase.

5. At this point, the client will have a memory with several circles and emotion words. Now, on a fresh sheet of paper, ask the client to re-write the memory, verbatim, but adding in the emotion words. One idea is to have the client simply add on to the end

of a circled word/phrase, "… and I felt [insert emotion here]." For instance, if the circled word was "lake" and the emotion is "fear," the new sentence may now read, "I approached the lake and I felt fear." This new version of the written memory will be exactly the same as the first draft, except that these emotion words will have been added.

6. Once again, pause and ask the client to check in with a temperature reading and ensure their distress level is acceptable.

7. Assuming the client's distress level is manageable and acceptable, instruct them to take home this new narrative and spend about 10 minutes with it per day, reading it repeatedly as they did at the end of Phase I, Focusing Away. Have the client complete this step for 1-2 weeks.

8. The next, and longest, step is to review and discuss with the client each place in the narrative where emotion was identified (each place where the circles had been on the first draft). Specifically, the clinician should ask the client to provide more information about each of these emotional words/phrases. This is referred to as "unpacking" the emotion. Questions that help the client explore, process, and unpack the emotional aspects of the memory include:

   • What were you thinking at this point?

   • What were you seeing/smelling/hearing at that time?

   • You felt [insert emotion here] then, what do you feel now, as you look back?

   • What else does this piece of the memory remind you of?

   Repeat these steps with each emotional spot in the memory (circled word/phrase).

9. Take a few moments after each emotional spot has been unpacked and allow the client to write down the answers to these (and any other) questions on a separate sheet of paper. Remember to check in with the client about their distress level and its acceptability on a regular basis.

10. The extended narratives of the emotional aspects of the memory can then be integrated into the main written narrative by re-writing the entire memory with the new extended pieces added. The client may need to habituate to each new extended emotional spot in the memory separately. It may take several weeks to unpack every emotional spot.

11. After each emotional spot has been unpacked, the client can habituate to the new, extended narrative of the mildly negative memory by engaging with it daily at home (as in Part I). When the client is able to do this, they may consider whether they would be willing to repeat this process with more intensely negative memories.

Part I, Focusing Away

1. First, identify a bottom-up, relaxing technique that you can practice if you begin to approach your boiling point during this exercise. Which technique would you like to commit to using if you become overwhelmed?

2. Next, bring to mind a *mildly negative memory* and describe it briefly to your therapist. This should be a mildly negative memory, not an intensely negative or traumatic memory.

3. Now, spend a few moments writing down "just the facts" of this memory, including who was there, when it happened, where it happened, and what exactly happened. As you do this, focus *away* from emotional aspects to the memory, including what your feelings were at the time or how you feel about it now. Here are some elements you may include as you write about this memory:

    a. Where and when the event occurred.

    b. Who was present during the event, and what they said and/or did.

    c. What the scenery around you looked like.

    d. Any smells associated with the event.

    e. Any sounds associated with the event.

    f. What exactly happened, including the sequence of events.

    g. How the event began and ended.

    If you find it difficult to focus away from the emotional aspects of the memory, be patient with yourself, as this is a challenging task for most people. When you find your mind wandering to these emotional aspects, gently redirect your attention to the contextual (factual) aspects of the memory.

4. Now, pause and check in with your own distress level. Your therapist will help you do this. On the distress thermometer scale of 1-100, how distressed do you feel now that you have written about this memory? Does this distress level feel acceptable to you right now? If not, take a break from this exercise and practice the bottom-up technique you identified earlier. If so, continue to the next step.

5. The next step is to read the memory out loud to your therapist. After this, once again check in with yourself about your distress level, and ensure it feels manageable and acceptable to you.

6. Finally, your therapist may ask you to take home this written memory and engage with it for approximately 10 minutes per day, reading it repeatedly. If you do this, make sure that you are not engaging with it before bed, as it could impact your sleep! Your therapist will only recommend this step if your distress level is low.

Part II, Focusing Near

1. Begin Part II by reviewing the written memory, silently, and circling any word or phrase that may contain emotional content. These are words or phrases that, when you read them, produce emotions in you.

2. Check in and take your distress temperature. What is your distress level? Is it tolerable? If so, continue to the next step.

3. Next, starting at the beginning of the written memory, bring your attention to the first circle and ask yourself, "What emotion goes with this word?" Write down that emotion next to the circle, or off to the side of it/above it. Complete this exercise with every circled word or phrase.

4. Now, on a fresh sheet of paper, re-write the memory, verbatim, but now adding the emotional words. This can be done by simply adding on to the end of a circled word/phrase, "… and I felt [insert emotion here]." For instance, if the circled word was "lake" and the emotion is "fear," the new sentence may now read, "I approached the lake and I felt fear." This new version of the written memory will be exactly the same as the first draft, except that these emotion words will have been added.

5. Once again, pause and check in with a temperature reading and ensure your distress level is acceptable.

6. At this point, your therapist may instruct you to take home this new narrative and spend about 10 minutes with it per day, reading it repeatedly as you did at the end of Phase I, Focusing Away.

7. The last and longest step of this phase will be to begin discussing, processing, and writing more information about each emotional spot in your memory. Your therapist will guide you through this process, which is referred to "unpacking the memory." Questions that your therapist may ask you can include:

   - What were you thinking at this point?

   - What were you seeing/smelling/hearing at that time?

   - You felt [insert emotion here] then, what do you feel now, as you look back?

   - What else does this piece of the memory remind you of?

   This step will be repeated with each emotional spot in the memory (circled word/phrase).

8. After each emotional spot is discussed and "unpacked," your therapist will ask you to take a few moments to write down the answers to the above (and any other) questions on a separate sheet of paper before integrating them into the larger written narrative of the memory. Eventually, the goal is to unpack all of the emotional spots of the memory, create an expanded written narrative of the memory, and then process it.

References

For your convenience, purchasers can download and print worksheets and handouts from www.pesi.com/TTT

Barrett, S. (2013). *Secrets of your cells: Discovering your body's inner intelligence.* Sounds True.

Berceli, D. (2005). *Trauma releasing exercises: A revolutionary new method for stress/trauma recovery.* Charleston, S.C: Create Space Publishers.

Bernardi, L., Sleight, P., Bandinelli, G., Cencetti, S., Fattorini, L., Wdowczyc-Szulc, J., & Lagi, A. (2001). Effect of rosary prayer and yoga mantras on autonomic cardiovascular rhythms: Comparative study. *BMJ: British Medical Journal, 323(7327)*, 1446.

Block, R. A., Arnott, D. P., Quigley, B., & Lynch, W. C. (1989). Unilateral nostril breathing influences lateralized cognitive performance. *Brain and Cognition, 9(2)*, 181-190.

Bowden, A., Lorenc, A., & Robinson, N. (2012). Autogenic training as a behavioural approach to insomnia: A prospective cohort study. *Primary Health Care Research & Development, 13(2)*, 175-185.

Bremner, J. D. (1999). Does stress damage the brain? *Biological Psychiatry, 45(7)*, 797-805.

Buhle, J. T., Silvers, J. A., Wager, T. D., Lopez, R., Onyemekwu, C., Kober, H., Weber, J., & Ochsner, K. N. (2014). Cognitive reappraisal of emotion: A meta-analysis of human neuroimaging studies. *Cerebral Cortex, 24(11)*, 2981-2990.

Carmody, J., & Baer, R. A. (2008). Relationships between mindfulness practice and levels of mindfulness, medical and psychological symptoms and well-being in a mindfulness-based stress reduction program. *Journal of Behavioral Medicine, 31(1)*, 23-33.

Chen, W. C., Chu, H., Lu, R. B., Chou, Y. H., Chen, C. H., Chang, Y. C., O'Brien, A. P. & Chou, K. R. (2009). Efficacy of progressive muscle relaxation training in reducing anxiety in patients with acute schizophrenia. *Journal of Clinical Nursing, 18(15)*, 2187-2196.

Colzato, L. S., Szapora, A., & Hommel, B. (2012). Meditate to create: The impact of focused-attention and open-monitoring training on convergent and divergent thinking. *Frontiers in Psychology, 3,* 116.

Couser, J. I., Martinez, F. J., & Celli, B. R. (1992). Respiratory response and ventilatory muscle recruitment during arm elevation in normal subjects. *Chest, 101(2)*, 336-340.

Craft, L. L., & Perna, F. M. (2004). The benefits of exercise for the clinically depressed. *Primary Care Companion to the Journal of Clinical Psychiatry, 6(3)*, 104.

Cropley, M., Ussher, M., & Charitou, E. (2007). Acute effects of a guided relaxation routine (body scan) on tobacco withdrawal symptoms and cravings in abstinent smokers. *Addiction, 102(6)*, 989-993.

Damasio, A. (2003). Feelings of emotion and the self. *Annals of the New York Academy of Sciences, 1001(1)*, 253-261.

Davidson, R. J., Kabat-Zinn, J., Schumacher, J., Rosenkranz, M., Muller, D., Santorelli, S. F., Urbanowski, F., Harrington, A., Bonus, K. & Sheridan, J. F. (2003). Alterations in brain and immune function produced by mindfulness meditation. *Psychosomatic Medicine, 65(4)*, 564-570.

Denkova, E., Dolcos, S., & Dolcos, F. (2014). Neural correlates of 'distracting' from emotion during autobiographical recollection. *Social Cognitive and Affective Neuroscience, 10(2)*, 219-230.

Dhiman, C., & Bedi, H. S. (2010). Effect of autogenic training and mental imagery on the trait anxiety of the hockey players. *British Journal of Sports Medicine, 44*(Suppl 1), 61-82.

Dolbier, C. L., & Rush, T. E. (2012). Efficacy of abbreviated progressive muscle relaxation in a high-stress college sample. *International Journal of Stress Management, 19(1)*, 48.

Emerson, D., & Hopper, E. (2011). *Overcoming trauma through yoga: Reclaiming your body.* North Atlantic Books.

Erickson, K. I., Voss, M. W., Prakash, R. S., Basak, C., Szabo, A., Chaddock, L., et al. (2011). Exercise training increases size of hippocampus and improves memory. *Proceedings of the National Academy of Sciences, 108(7)*, 3017-3022.

Etkin, A., & Wager, T. D. (2007). Functional neuroimaging of anxiety: A meta-analysis of emotional processing in PTSD, social anxiety disorder, and specific phobia. *American Journal of Psychiatry, 164(10)*, 1476-1488.

Finkel, E. J., Slotter, E. B., Luchies, L. B., Walton, G. M., & Gross, J. J. (2013). A brief intervention to promote conflict reappraisal preserves marital quality over time. *Psychological Science, 24(8)*, 1595-1601.

Fredrickson, B. L. (2008). Promoting positive affect. *The Science of Subjective Well-Being*, 449-468.

Fried, R. (1993). The role of respiration in stress and stress control: Toward a theory of stress as a hypoxic phenomenon. In P. M. Lehrer & R. I. Woolfolk (Eds.), *Principles and Practice of Stress Management*, (pp. 301-331). New York: Guilford Press.

Gard, T., Taquet, M., Dixit, R., Hölzel, B. K., Dickerson, B. C., & Lazar, S. W. (2015). Greater widespread functional connectivity of the caudate in older adults who practice kripalu yoga and vipassana meditation than in controls. *Frontiers in Human Neuroscience, 9*, 137.

Gard, T., Hölzel, B. K., Sack, A. T., Hempel, H., Lazar, S. W., Vaitl, D., & Ott, U. (2012, Nov). Pain attenuation through mindfulness is associated with decreased cognitive control and increased sensory processing in the brain. *Cerebral Cortex, 22(11)*, 2692-702. doi: 10.1093/cercor/bhr352. Epub 2011 Dec 15.

Germain, A., James, J., Insana, S., Herringa, R. J., Mammen, O., Price, J., & Nofzinger, E. (2013). A window into the invisible wound of war: Functional neuroimaging of REM sleep in returning combat veterans with PTSD. *Psychiatry Research: Neuroimaging, 211(2)*, 176-179.

Goyal, M., Singh, S., Sibinga, E. M., Gould, N. F., Rowland-Seymour, A., Sharma, R., et al. (2014). Meditation programs for psychological stress and well-being: A systematic review and meta-analysis. *JAMA Internal Medicine, 174(3)*, 357-368.

Green, S. M. (2011). *I am not stressed! How about you? A look at the impact of progressive muscle relaxation on the autonomic nervous system.* Howard University.

Gu, X., & FitzGerald, T. H. (2014). Interoceptive inference: Homeostasis and decision-making. *Trends Cogn Sci, 18(6)*, 269-70.

Hagman, C., Janson, C., & Emtner, M. (2011). Breathing retraining - A five-year follow-up of patients with dysfunctional breathing. *Respiratory Medicine, 105(8)*, 1153-1159.

Hariprasad, V. R., Varambally, S., Shivakumar, V., Kalmady, S. V., Venkatasubramanian, G., & Gangadhar, B. N. (2013). Yoga increases the volume of the hippocampus in elderly subjects. *Indian Journal of Psychiatry, 55*(Suppl 3), S394.

Hasegawa, M., & Kern, E. B. (1977, January). The human nasal cycle. *In Mayo Clinic Proceedings* (Vol. 52, No. 1, pp. 28-34).

Herbert, B. M., & Pollatos, O. (2012). The body in the mind: On the relationship between interoception and embodiment. *Topics in Cognitive Science, 4(4)*, 692-704.

Hofmann, S. G., Grossman, P., & Hinton, D. E. (2011). Loving-kindness and compassion meditation: Potential for psychological interventions. *Clinical Psychology Review, 31(7)*, 1126-1132.

Hölzel, B. K., Lazar, S. W., Gard, T., Schuman-Olivier, Z., Vago, D. R., & Ott, U. (2011). How does mindfulness meditation work? Proposing mechanisms of action from a conceptual and neural perspective. *Perspectives on Psychological Science, 6(6)*, 537-559.

Hopper, J. W., Frewen, P. A., Van der Kolk, B. A., & Lanius, R. A. (2007). Neural correlates of reexperiencing, avoidance, and dissociation in PTSD: Symptom dimensions and emotion dysregulation in responses to script driven trauma imagery. *Journal of Traumatic Stress, 20(5)*, 713-725.

Huang, M. X., Yurgil, K. A., Robb, A., Angeles, A., Diwakar, M., Risbrough, V. B., ... & Huang, C. W. (2014). Voxel-wise resting-state MEG source magnitude imaging study reveals neurocircuitry abnormality in active-duty service members and veterans with PTSD. *Neuroimage: Clinical, 5*, 408-419.

Hughes, K. C., & Shin, L. M. (2011). Functional neuroimaging studies of post-traumatic stress disorder. *Expert Review of Neurotherapeutics, 11(2)*, 275-285.

Kabat-Zinn, J. (1990). *Full catastrophe living: Using the wisdom of your body and mind to face stress, pain, and illness.* New York: Delacorte Press.

Kasai, K., Yamasue, H., Gilbertson, M. W., Shenton, M. E., Rauch, S. L., & Pitman, R. K. (2008 Mar 15). Evidence for acquired pregenual anterior cingulate gray matter loss from a twin study of combat-related posttraumatic stress disorder. *Biological Psychiatry, 63(6)*, 550-556.

Kemps, E., Tiggemann, M., & Christianson, R. (2008). Concurrent visuo-spatial processing reduces food cravings in prescribed weight-loss dieters. *Journal of Behavior Therapy and Experimental Psychiatry, 39(2)*, 177-186.

Kerr, C. E., Jones, S. R., Wan, Q., Pritchett, D. L., Wasserman, R. H., Wexler, A., ... & Littenberg, R. (2011). Effects of mindfulness meditation training on anticipatory alpha modulation in primary somatosensory cortex. *Brain Research Bulletin, 85(3-4)*, 96-103.

Khouri, H. & Haglund, K. (2016). *Trauma-Informed Yoga: Concepts, Tools, & Skills.*

Kitayama, N., Quinn, S., & Bremner, J. D. (2006). Smaller volume of anterior cingulate cortex in abuse-related posttraumatic stress disorder. *Journal of Affective Disorders, 90(2)*, 171-174.

Krause-Utz, A., Veer, I. M., Rombouts, S. A., Bohus, M., Schmahl, C., & Elzinga, B. M. (2014 Oct). Amygdala and anterior cingulate resting-state functional connectivity in borderline personality disorder patients with a history of interpersonal trauma. *Psychological Medicine, 44(13)*, 2889-2901.

LeDoux, J. E. (2000). Emotion circuits in the brain. *Annual Review of Neuroscience, 23(1)*, 155-184.

Lee, M. S., Kim, B. G., Huh, H. J., Ryu, H., Lee, H. S., & Chung, H. T. (2000). Effect of Qi training on blood pressure, heart rate and respiration rate. *Clinical Physiology and Functional Imaging, 20(3)*, 173-176.

Levine, P. A. (1997). Waking the tiger: *Healing trauma: The innate capacity to transform overwhelming experiences.* North Atlantic Books.

Liberzon, I., & Garfinkel, S. N. (2009). Functional neuroimaging in post-traumatic stress disorder. *In Post-Traumatic Stress Disorder* (pp. 297-317). Humana Press.

Liberzon, I., & Sripada, C. S. (2007). The functional neuroanatomy of PTSD: a critical review. *Progress in Brain Research*, 167, 151-169.

Lolak, S., Connors, G. L., Sheridan, M. J., & Wise, T. N. (2008). Effects of progressive muscle relaxation training on anxiety and depression in patients enrolled in an outpatient pulmonary rehabilitation program. *Psychotherapy and Psychosomatics, 77(2)*, 119-125.

Malinowski, P. (2013). Neural mechanisms of attentional control in mindfulness meditation. *Frontiers in Neuroscience, 7*, 8.

Matsuo, K., Taneichi, K., Matsumoto, A., Ohtani, T., Yamasue, H., Sakano, Y., ... & Asukai, N. (2003). Hypoactivation of the prefrontal cortex during verbal fluency test in PTSD: A near-infrared spectroscopy study. *Psychiatry Research: Neuroimaging, 124(1)*, 1-10.

Mauss, I. B., Bunge, S. A., & Gross, J. J. (2007). Automatic emotion regulation. *Social and Personality Psychology Compass, 1(1)*, 146-167.

Miu, A. C., Heilman, R. M., & Miclea, M. (2009). Reduced heart rate variability and vagal tone in anxiety: Trait versus state, and the effects of autogenic training. *Autonomic Neuroscience: Basic and Clinical, 145(1)*, 99-103.

Nakagawa, S., Sugiura, M., Sekiguchi, A., Kotozaki, Y., Miyauchi, C. M., Hanawa, S., ... & Kawashima, R. (2016). Effects of post-traumatic growth on the dorsolateral prefrontal cortex after a disaster. *Scientific Reports, 6*, 34364.

Protopopescu, X., Pan, H., Tuescher, O., Cloitre, M., Goldstein, M., Engelien, W., ... & Silbersweig, D. (2005). Differential time courses and specificity of amygdala activity in posttraumatic stress disorder subjects and normal control subjects. *Biological Psychiatry, 57(5)*, 464-473.

Rauch, S. L., Whalen, P. J., Shin, L. M., McInerney, S. C., Macklin, M. L., Lasko, N. B., ... & Pitman, R. K. (2000). Exaggerated amygdala response to masked facial stimuli in posttraumatic stress disorder: A functional MRI study. *Biological Psychiatry, 47(9)*, 769-776.

Rosas-Ballina, M., Olofsson, P. S., Ochani, M., Valdés-Ferrer, S. I., Levine, Y. A., Reardon, C., ... & Mak, T. W. (2011). Acetylcholine-synthesizing T cells relay neural signals in a vagus nerve circuit. *Science, 334*(6052), 98-101.

Rosenthal, J. Z., Grosswald, S., Ross, R., & Rosenthal, N. (2011). Effects of transcendental meditation in veterans of Operation Enduring Freedom and Operation Iraqi Freedom with posttraumatic stress disorder: A pilot study. *Military Medicine, 176(6)*, 626-630.

Routledge, F. S., Campbell, T. S., McFetridge-Durdle, J. A., & Bacon, S. L. (2010). Improvements in heart rate variability with exercise therapy. *Canadian Journal of Cardiology, 26(6)*, 303-312.

Rowe, M. M. (1999). Teaching health-care providers coping: Results of a two-year study. *Journal of Behavioral Medicine, 22(5)*, 511-527.

Russell, M. (2014). Diaphragmatic breathing and its effect on inhibitory control. University of Kentucky.

Sanjiv, K., & Raje, A. (2014). Effect of progressive muscular relaxation exercises versus transcutaneous electrical nerve stimulation on tension headache: A comparative study. *Hong Kong Physiotherapy Journal, 32(2)*, 86-91.

Schmahl, C. G., Vermetten, E., Elzinga, B. M., & Bremner, J. D. (2003). Magnetic resonance imaging of hippocampal and amygdala volume in women with childhood abuse and borderline personality disorder. *Psychiatry Research: Neuroimaging, 122(3)*, 193-198.

Schmalzl, L., Powers, C., & Henje Blom, E. (2015 May 8). Neurophysiological and neurocognitive mechanisms underlying the effects of yoga-based practices: towards a comprehensive theoretical framework. *Frontiers in Human Neuroscience, 9*, 235.

Seth, A. K. (2013). Interoceptive inference, emotion, and the embodied self. *Trends in Cognitive Sciences, 17(11)*, 565-573.

Seth, A. K., Suzuki, K., & Critchley, H. D. (2011). An interoceptive predictive coding model of conscious presence. *Frontiers in Psychology, 2*, 395.

Shavanani, A. B., Madanmohan, & Udupa, K. (2003, Jul). Acute effect of Mukh bhastrika (a yogic bellows type breathing) on reaction time. *Indian Journal of Physiology and Pharmacology, 47*, 297-300.

Shin, L. M., Rauch, S. L., & Pitman, R. K. (2006). Amygdala, medial prefrontal cortex, and hippocampal function in PTSD. *Annals of the New York Academy of Sciences, 1071*(1), 67-79.

Shin, L. M., Wright, C. I., Cannistraro, P. A., Wedig, M. M., McMullin, K., Martis, B., ... & Rauch, S. L. (2005, Mar). A functional magnetic resonance imaging study of amygdala and medial prefrontal cortex responses to overtly presented fearful faces in posttraumatic stress disorder. *Archives of General Psychiatry, 62(3)*, 273-281.

Shinozaki, M., Kanazawa, M., Kano, M., Endo, Y., Nakaya, N., Hongo, M., & Fukudo, S. (2010). Effect of autogenic training on general improvement in patients with irritable bowel syndrome: A randomized controlled trial. *Applied Psychophysiology and Biofeedback, 35(3)*, 189-198.

Simmons, A., Strigo, I. A., Matthews, S. C., Paulus, M. P., & Stein, M. B. (2009). Initial evidence of a failure to activate right anterior insula during affective set-shifting in PTSD. *Psychosomatic Medicine, 71(4)*, 373.

Simpson, T. L., Kaysen, D., Bowen, S., MacPherson, L. M., Chawla, N., Blume, A., ... & Larimer, M. (2007, Jun). PTSD symptoms, substance use, and vipassana meditation among incarcerated individuals. *Journal of Traumatic Stress, 20(3)*, 239-249.

Sleiman, S. F., Henry, J., Al-Haddad, R., El Hayek, L., Haidar, E. A., Stringer, T., ... & Chao, M. V. (2016, Jun 2). Exercise promotes the expression of brain derived neurotrophic factor (BDNF) through the action of the ketone body -hydroxybutyrate. doi: 10.7554/eLife.15092.

Stahl, B., & Goldstein, E. (2010). *A mindfulness-based stress reduction workbook*. New Harbinger Publications.

Stan ák Jr, A., & Kuna, M. (1994). EEG changes during forced alternate nostril breathing. *International Journal of Psychophysiology, 18(1)*, 75-79.

Stetter, F., & Kupper, S. (2002). Autogenic training: A meta-analysis of clinical outcome studies. *Applied Psychophysiology and Biofeedback, 27(1)*, 45-98.

Streeter, C. C., Gerbarg, P. L., Saper, R. B., Ciraulo, D. A., & Brown, R. P. (2012). Effects of yoga on the autonomic nervous system, gamma-aminobutyric-acid, and allostasis in epilepsy, depression, and post-traumatic stress disorder. *Medical Hypotheses, 78(5)*, 571-579.

Streeter, C. C., Whitfield, T. H., Owen, L., Rein, T., Karri, S. K., Yakhkind, A., ... & Jensen, J. E. (2010). Effects of yoga versus walking on mood, anxiety, and brain GABA levels: A randomized controlled MRS study. *The Journal of Alternative and Complementary Medicine, 16(11)*, 1145-1152.

Tan, C. M. (2012). *Search inside yourself: Increase productivity, creativity and happiness [ePub edition].* HarperCollins UK.

Taylor, A. G., Goehler, L. E., Galper, D. I., Innes, K. E., & Bourguignon, C. (2010). Top-down and bottom-up mechanisms in mind-body medicine: Development of an integrative framework for psychophysiological research. *EXPLORE: The Journal of Science and Healing, 6(1)*, 29-41.

Teasdale, J. D., Segal, Z. V., Williams, J. M., Ridgeway, V. A., Soulsby, J. M., & Lau, M. A. (2000, Aug). Prevention of relapse/recurrence in major depression by mindfulness-based cognitive therapy. *Journal of Consulting and Clinical Psychology, 68(4)*, 615-23.

Telles, S., Singh, N., & Puthige, R. (2013). Changes in P300 following alternate nostril yoga breathing and breath awareness. *BioPsychoSocial Medicine, 7(1)*, 11.

Thomason, M. E., Marusak, H. A., Tocco, M. A., Vila, A. M., McGarragle, O., & Rosenberg, D. R. (2015). Altered amygdala connectivity in urban youth exposed to trauma. *Social Cognitive and Affective Neuroscience, 10(11)*, 1460-1468.

Troy, A. S., Wilhelm, F. H., Shallcross, A. J., & Mauss, I. B. (2010). Seeing the silver lining: Cognitive reappraisal ability moderates the relationship between stress and depressive symptoms. *Emotion, 10(6)*, 783.

Turakitwanakan, W., Mekseepralard, C., & Busarakumtragul, P. (2013, Jan). Effects of mindfulness meditation on serum cortisol of medical students. *Journal of the Medical Association of Thailand, 96*, Suppl 1, S90-5.

Upadhyay Dhungel, K., Malhotra, V., Sarkar, D., & Prajapati, R. (2008, Mar). Effect of alternate nostril breathing exercise on cardiorespiratory functions. *Nepal Medical College Journal, 10(1)*, 25-7.

Ussher, M., Spatz, A., Copland, C., Nicolaou, A., Cargill, A., Amini-Tabrizi, N., & McCracken, L. M. (2014). Immediate effects of a brief mindfulness-based body scan on patients with chronic pain. *Journal of Behavioral Medicine, 37(1)*, 127-134.

van der Kolk, B. A., McFarlane, A. C., & Weisaeth, L. (Eds.). (1996). *Traumatic stress: The effects of overwhelming experience on mind, body, and society.* The Guilford Press: New York.

van der Kolk, B. (2014). *The body keeps the score.* New York: Viking.

Veerabhadrappa, S. G., Herur, A., Patil, S., Ankad, R. B., Chinagudi, S., Baljoshi, V. S., & Khanapure, S. (2011). Effect of yogic bellows on cardiovascular autonomic reactivity. *Journal of Cardiovascular Disease Research, 2(4)*, 223-227.

Villemure, C., eko, M., Cotton, V. A., & Bushnell, M. C. (2013). Insular cortex mediates increased pain tolerance in yoga practitioners. *Cerebral Cortex, 24(10)*, 2732-2740.

Wehrenberg, M. (2008). *The 10 best-ever anxiety management techniques: Understanding how your brain makes you anxious and what you can do to change it.* WW Norton & Company.

Wei, G. X., Xu, T., Fan, F. M., Dong, H. M., Jiang, L. L., Li, H. J., ... & Zuo, X. N. (2013, Apr 9). Can Taichi reshape the brain? A brain morphometry study. *PLoS One, 8(4)*, e61038.

Weibel, D. T. (2007). *A loving-kindness intervention: Boosting compassion for self and others* (Doctoral dissertation, Ohio University).

Wald, J., & Taylor, S. (2008). Responses to interoceptive exposure in people with posttraumatic stress disorder (PTSD): A preliminary analysis of induced anxiety reactions and trauma memories and their relationship to anxiety sensitivity and PTSD symptom severity. *Cognitive Behaviour Therapy, 37(2)*, 90-100.